Praise for
Threading My Prayer Rug

One of *Booklist*'s Top Ten Religion and Spirituality Books of 2016

One of *Booklist*'s Top Ten Diverse Nonfiction Books of 2017

Honorable Mention in the 2017 San Francisco Book Festival Awards, Spiritual Category

"Take this journey on Sabeeha's prayer rug, and you will be enchanted as she vividly and beautifully transports you through rich and elaborate threads of a lifetime lived with love, intelligence, and compassion—an inspiration to all."
—Ranya Tabari Idliby, coauthor of *The Faith Club* and author of *Burqas, Baseball and Apple Pie*

"Funny and frank, acute, and compassionate, this story of an immigrant 'fish out of water' who falls in love with her adopted American home is for all of us, and for all times—but current events also make it the story for this time. As Americans consider who they were, are, and want to be in the future, they could have no better guide than Sabeeha Rehman. I can't imagine our country, or my bookshelf, without her."
—Susan Choi, author of *A Person of Interest* and *My Education*

"With anti-Islamic sentiments on the rise in this country, *Threading My Prayer Rug* is a refreshing look at what it is really like to be a Muslim in the US today. With humor, charm, and great insight, Sabeeha Rehman recounts how one can be both a devout Muslim and an American wife, mom, grandmother and community activist."
—Jan Goodwin, award-winning author, journalist, and Senior Fellow at Brandeis University's Schuster Institute of Investigative Journalism

"Coming to America is seldom associated with discovering one's faith—let alone Islam. Rich in exotic detail, Sabeeha's true-life story is funny, sweet, beautiful, warm, and deeply touching to any reader, who will note how much the heart and soul of a Muslim mother is like that of any other."

—Imam Feisal Abdul Rauf, founder of Cordoba House,
author of *What's Right With Islam* and *Moving the Mountain*

"*Threading My Prayer Rug* is a warm, wise, and wonderful book. Ms. Rehman writes in a wry and often humorous style that is understanding of human foibles yet gently pushes readers of all backgrounds to become fuller and more engaged human beings. As an Orthodox rabbi working to strengthen cooperation between Jews and Muslims, I was moved by her involvement in Muslim-Jewish coalition-building efforts."

—Rabbi Marc Schneier, president of
the Foundation for Ethnic Understanding and
coauthor with Imam Shamsi Ali of *Sons of Abraham*

"Sabeeha Rehman's prose resonates with intimacy, wisdom, and wit. She achieves a richly textured narrative that introduces readers to the rituals and enduring values of her Muslim faith as she, her husband Khalid and their sons Saqib and Asim integrate into the American melting pot. At the conclusion of her classic text, Ms. Rehman affirms, 'Together we will change the discourse, quell violence with knowledge, and banish phobias to the fringe as we work together in unity of the spirit.' This reader was moved to respond, 'Ameen . . . Amen.'"

—Sidney Offit, former president of the Authors Guild Foundation
and Authors League Fund and author of *Memoir of a Bookie's Son*

"A charming and engrossing book, *Threading My Prayer Rug* provides a window to a culture and people we do not know enough about. . . . Readable, easy to relate to, and inspiring!"

—Sumbul Ali-Karamali, author of *The Muslim Next Door:
the Qur'an, the Media, and that Veil Thing*

"*Threading My Prayer Rug* is a beautifully written memoir of a cosmopolitan and faithful Pakistani-American Muslim woman. It's recommended for all who want to have a sense of how the tapestry of American Islam is shaped by the contributions of a variety of Muslims, including those from South Asia."

—Omid Safi, Director, Duke Islamic Studies Center

"Rehman's personal journey is her own, but speaks broadly to all immigrant journeys in contemporary America. With so much discussion about immigrants from Muslim in the national conversation, it's good to have a story with this unique perspective."

—*Booklist*, starred review

"Rehman's spirited debut memoir illuminates the challenges of living an authentically Muslim life in America. . . . With sparkling anecdotes about everything from the 'Christmas-ization of Eid' to engineering her son's marriage, Rehman lends a light heart and an open mind to the process of becoming a multicultural 'hybrid.'"

—*Publishers Weekly*

"A heartfelt memoir plumbs the multilayered experience of being Muslim in America. With a steady infusion of verve and personality, Rehman immerses readers in the traditions of a Middle Eastern culture. . . . Rehman's memoir offers a deeper understanding and appreciation for Muslim lifestyles while imparting a message of unity and international fellowship. A culturally rich and rewarding personal chronicle of ethnic faith and intermingled tradition."

—*Kirkus*

"An entertaining and honest story of one woman's journey to fuse the cultures of her past and present to create her own experience . . . Her story is permeated with hilarious personal experiences and asides as she adapts to the country she will soon call home. Rehman lends a strong and compelling voice to moderate Muslims, and her discussion of her faith and the areas she believes need modernization illustrate the different opinions within the Muslim community."

—*Library Journal*

"The country needs this counterbalancing personal story to correct the pervasive misunderstanding of what Islam is truly about and the contributions to our American democracy that most American Muslims make every day of their lives. Exceptionally well written and consistently compelling read from beginning to end. . . . Somebody donate a copy of *Threading My Prayer Rug* to every Republican member of Congress, every Republican member of a state legislature, and every Republican governor who advocates for preventing Muslims from settling in their state."

—*Midwest Book Review*

"A warm, amusing and, for a Jewish reader, a surprisingly familiar story."

—*Jewish Week*

"That one masterstroke of penmanship and objective thought is the ultimate grand finale to a lifelong effort of understanding not only other faiths, but also her own."

—*Dawn* newspaper (Pakistan)

Threading
MY
PRAYER
RUG

threading
MY
PRAYER
RUG

One Woman's Journey
from Pakistani Muslim
to American Muslim

SABEEHA REHMAN

With a New Preface by the Author

Arcade Publishing • New York

First Paperback Edition

Arcade Publishing books may be purchased in bulk at special discounts for sales promotion, corporate gifts, fund-raising, or educational purposes. Special editions can also be created to specifications. For details, contact the Special Sales Department, Arcade Publishing, 307 West 36th Street, 11th Floor, New York, NY 10018 or arcade@skyhorsepublishing.com.

Arcade Publishing® is a registered trademark of Skyhorse Publishing, Inc.®, a Delaware corporation.

Visit our website at www.arcadepub.com.
Visit the author's website at sabeeharehman.com.

10 9 8 7 6 5 4 3 2

Library of Congress Cataloging-in-Publication Data

Names: Rehman, Sabeeha, author.
Title: Threading my prayer rug: one woman's journey from Pakistani Muslim to
    American Muslim / Sabeeha Rehman.
Description: New York, NY: Arcade Publishing, 2016.
Identifiers: LCCN 2016007676 (print) | LCCN 2016009024 (ebook) | ISBN
    978-1-62872-663-3 (hardback) | ISBN 978-1-62872-862-0 (paperback | ISBN
    978-1-62872-879-8 (ebook)
Subjects: LCSH: Rehman, Sabeeha. | Pakistani American women—Biography. |
    Pakistani Americans—Biography. | Muslims—United States—Biography. |
    Muslim women—United States—Biography. | BISAC: RELIGION / Islam /
    General. | BIOGRAPHY & AUTOBIOGRAPHY / Cultural Heritage. |
BIOGRAPHY &
    AUTOBIOGRAPHY / Women. | BIOGRAPHY & AUTOBIOGRAPHY /
Religious.
Classification: LCC E184.P28 R44 2016 (print) | LCC E184.P28 (ebook) | DDC
    305.8914/122073—dc23
LC record available at http://lccn.loc.gov/2016007676

Cover design by Laura Klynstra
Cover photo: Shutterstock
Author photograph by Kristin Boncher

Printed in the United States of America

In memory
of
my loving parents
Farrukh Akbar and Lieutenant Colonel Kazim Akbar

CONTENTS

PREFACE TO THE PAPERBACK EDITION

People often ask me why I wrote this book. The short answer is, "Because my husband wanted me to." Honestly, he had been urging me to write it for more than twenty years, and I kept putting it off. But when my eight-year-old grandson with autism was detained at the airport because his name matched that of a terrorist, I got serious. I wrote *Threading My Prayer Rug* because I don't want my children and my grandchildren to be afraid to say, "I am a Muslim." I wrote it because I want the reader to know that the heart and soul of a Muslim mother is like that of any other; and I want the reader to say, "Muslims are people just like us."

My husband and I had been active in interfaith dialogue since the late 1980s. This outreach took on more urgency after 9/11, but it was specifically the vitriolic reaction to the proposed Islamic cultural center in downtown Manhattan that jolted me into the realization that we had so much work to do to make ourselves known. "You have to write your book. Interfaith dialogue in New York City will take us only so far. We have to go beyond our comfort zones. You have to tell your story," my husband urged. "You have to take your message from this coast to the west, and to the mountains in the north, the desert in the south, and the heartland."

The book was released on a hot summer day in July in the midst of a heated election year, with anti-Muslim rhetoric at a fever pitch. To their credit, people thirsty to know more about "the Muslim" packed into the Corner Bookstore in New York City on the afternoon of my book launch. As the line to get in snaked around the corner, the management had to shut the doors and a staff member positioned himself outside, in order to assure the crowd they would be allowed in for the reception once the reading was over and the chairs had been removed to make room.

When someone makes the time to read my memoir, searches for my contact information, and takes the time to write, telling me that he is giving copies of the book to friends and family as Christmas presents and urging them to pass it on, I am overwhelmed with gratitude. When a reader tells me that now she wants to get to know her Muslim neighbor or invite the parents of her children's Muslim friends, I say, *"Alhamdulillah!"* (Praise be to God). When I get an email from a perfect stranger telling me that he is thinking of me in these troubled times and is in solidarity with us, I know that he and many like him have our backs. A woman wrote me that she is a Christian and is working on a project to help community members understand the Muslim faith, and she is using this book as her guide. Another said that he has his talking points and knows what to say when he hears people ask the uninformed question, "Why haven't American Muslims disavowed extremism?" And so many tell me that they are recommending it to their book clubs, to which I respond by offering to Skype with them. The most delightful session I had was with the students of a writing class at the American University in Cairo, where Kathleen Saville, an American teacher and author, assigned the Egyptian girls to read a chapter of the book and then asked me to talk to the class over Skype.

A Muslim dad of Pakistani descent told me that he is encouraging his seventeen-year-old daughter to read it because it will help her understand where her "brown/Asian/desi" parents came from—not as in literally the place but as in why they do and say things that they do. Immigrants, children of immigrants, Muslim, Christian, Jewish, Hindu, say to me, "This is my story. . . . This is my grandmother's story. . . . Your lives could easily be almost any couple's lives." When I heard a reader say that this book does so much to show the human and humane side of Islam, I felt I had scratched the surface. When he said, "You pulled back the curtain on cultural practices and spiritual practices," I felt that I had finally made a dent. But the comment that touched me deeply was when a reader wrote, "Your friends and family have become my friends and family." Friendship—the best of all gifts.

All this is what I was hoping for. What I did not expect was that I would find myself in the role of premarital counselor, as in an interfaith marriage. I am happy to report that the beautiful couple is now happily married.

What I also did not expect was that the book would become my launching pad for responding to the anti-Muslim attacks in the aftermath of the elections. By the time the ballots were cast, I had developed a network of friends and readers. They reached out to me, offering e-comfort; and I reached out to them, asking them to give me a platform.

Disturbed by the surge in attacks against Muslims, my husband and I had made a decision. Our goal: Raise awareness about Islam and about Muslims in America. Our objective: Give lectures on Muslims in America. Our strategy: "Invite us and we will come." We sent an email out to our network across America, a network we had built during our stay at the Chautauqua Institution, where we had given daily lectures on "Being Muslim in America" to a standing room–only audience. Many had bought my book and had stayed connected with me. I reached out to my sisters in the Sisterhood of Salaam Shalom. Well, within days after hitting the Send button, invitations started coming in and our calendars filled up. We have been traveling to towns we had to look up on Google Maps, staying in the homes of people we had never met, relishing the warmth of their hospitality, speaking to audiences of one hundred plus, doing book readings in local bookstores, and making new friends. At Sunday services in a church, my husband was asked to give the *Adhan*, the Muslim call to prayer, with translation. Later, an attendee said, "I finally know what the call to prayer means."

And it all started with a book.

During the Q and A session of a book reading I was doing in a church, a gentleman raised his hand. "How can we help Muslims?"

"Make a Muslim friend. Invite me into your living room. Let's move beyond meeting in houses of worship and large meeting halls. Let's chat, one-on-one over a meal, and get to know one another. I will invite you into my home. Let friendships develop and watch the magic work."

The pastor's wife was in the audience. No sooner had the discussion ended, then she walked over to me. "I am so inspired by what you said."

"What did I say?" Of course, by then I had forgotten half of what I had said.

"Make a Muslim friend. I think it's a great idea. I am going to talk to the congregants."

Sure enough, a few weeks later I got an email from her. They loved the idea, and she had lined up eleven families ready to host Muslim families in their homes for dinner. She gave me a list of dates and had scheduled a planning meeting. I had to scramble—to find Muslim families to take part. Together, we mapped out the ground rules, did the matching of families to families, and spent some memorable evenings sharing our stories over the dinner table. In turn, the Muslim families reciprocated and hosted Christian families in their homes. By the time this goes to press, more than fifty families of Christians and Muslims will have become friends, allies, and ambassadors. You may come across some of them sitting together on a bench in Central Park, watching their children scrambling up the rocks.

And it all started with a book.

The doors kept opening, one after the other. At my book launch last July, a woman in the audience handed me her brochure and later invited me to do a book reading for her group. At that Q and A, someone asked, "How can we engage with Muslims?" and I related briefly the interfaith dialogue I was involved in. A few weeks later, the organizer contacted me. They wanted to hold an interfaith dialogue—a one-time event only—and asked if I could convene a group of Muslim women. The planning that went into it, you would have thought we were holding international peace talks. A facilitator was brought on board, formats were developed, breakout sessions were planned, color-coded group numbers were assigned, and when I walked into the venue, there were flip charts in every room. Well, within the first fifteen minutes of the meeting, the discussion got so engaging, so invigorating, so spontaneous that the facilitator sent me a quiet message: "NO NEED FOR BREAK-OUT GROUPS—IT'S FLOWING VERY WELL, LET IT FLOW." By the time the meeting came to a close, we had decided that one meeting was not enough. The Daughters of Abraham in Dialogue was launched and we meet every month to just talk. Of course, we plan the topic of the dialogue, but we just talk.

And it all started with a book.

One morning when I opened my inbox, there was an email from a rabbi. He had heard about my book, had heard me speak, and asked if I could convene a group of young Muslims—as in age thirty and below—for a Sabbath dinner in his home with a group of Jewish youth. As the youngsters huddled over on the sofas, exchanging contact information, we could see where this was headed. There were going to be more of these, as in a Muslim family hosting the next gathering on Holocaust Remembrance Day, or as in the rabbi asking me to speak at a candle-light vigil at Columbus Circle on the Fast of Esther.

And it all started with a book.

While I contemplate the theme for my next book, I stay connected with my network through my blog. I blog on topics related to the themes of my memoir, i.e., being Muslim in America, on current events that impact American Muslims, and whatever else is on my mind that, in my humble opinion, is worth sharing. The piece that generated the most interest was one I wrote after the desecration of the Jewish cemeteries in the United States titled, "Today I Am a Jew." Another favorite was "My Downton Abbey in Pakistan." You can visit my blog page on my website: sabeeharehman.com.

On this journey, I have also become keenly aware of how much I don't know and appreciate that before I expect my fellow Americans to embrace diversity; I first have to open my arms, my heart, and my mind—or stretch them. I will hang out with people who disagree with me, read autobiographies of people who shock me, and become a member of groups where I feel totally out of place. I may just learn something as I make myself uncomfortable. That would make for an exciting new book.

Threading
MY
PRAYER
RUG

PROLOGUE

Not a Mosque, and Not at Ground Zero

New York, 2010

Am I safe in here? Do they know I'm a Muslim? Can they tell by the look on my face that I'm one of them? Don't look them in the eye.

I lowered my gaze and walked into the crowd, making my way through the meeting hall, up the aisle, through the rows of people waving posters saying, "No Mosque at Ground Zero." I found my way to the back, out of sight of the protestors, and took a seat.

I am surrounded by hate.

I had been volunteering in the office of Imam Feisal Abdul Rauf and his wife, Daisy Khan. When one day the imam had described his vision of a Muslim community center in downtown Manhattan, I couldn't fathom that I was in the moment of "history in the unmaking."

A space for faith, fun and fitness, R&R, and interfaith gatherings! A place of our own—to meet and greet, to learn and share, to feast and celebrate, to swim and gym, with room for all faiths. Cool!

I was there when the Finance Committee of the Community Board reviewed the project. Sitting along the wall, I had watched Imam Feisal present the concept of the equivalent of a YMCA and 92nd Street Y. I was elated when the committee, giving their approval, asked, "How soon can you start?" I had noticed members of the press scribbling notes. I had stepped out onto Chambers Street, the majestic Municipal Building towering beyond; the evening was still bright, the spring air brushing my cheek, as I made my way to the number 6 subway train.

"There is bound to be an outcry," said my husband, who had attended the meeting with me. The STOP sign stopped me and I glanced up at him.

"Why would anyone object? Look at how supportive the committee was." My husband and I had yearned for a community center for our children; it didn't happen while they were growing up, but it was going to happen now.

I had gone home on a high; and the next morning my hopes were dashed. Having arrived early at the office, I picked up the phone on the first ring.

"This is WABC. We would like to interview the imam about his plans to build a mosque at Ground Zero."

A what? At where? Where did that phrase come from? It's not a mosque we are building, and it's not at Ground Zero.

The phone rang again. "This is WCBS . . ."

I called the imam on his cell phone. "Are you on your way to the office? The major media networks are lined up to interview you. Just so you know, they are calling your proposed Islamic cultural center downtown 'the mosque at Ground Zero.'"

That day, as I put on the hat of media scheduler, reporters of leading networks bumped into each other as they entered and exited. Watching them interview Imam Feisal, I knew that my husband had been right. A Sufi imam, dignified in demeanor, gentle in his expression, building bridges between Muslims and non-Muslims, and honored and acclaimed for his interfaith work, was now the focus of outrage— accused of insulting the memory of 9/11 victims and the most tragic violence against our country.

Why didn't I see it coming? I was so close on the inside. I just answered my question.

It's not a mosque, it is a community center, the imam explained to the interviewers over and over again.

It is not at ground zero, the imam said once more, and explained, once again, that this was to be a space open to all New Yorkers, a platform for multi-faith dialogue, a center guided by the universal values of all religions, a place of healing.

The Real Battle Is between Extremists and Moderates on Both Sides

I took note of Imam Feisal's mantra, "The battle is not between Islam and the West; the real battle is between the extremists and moderates on both sides."

It didn't matter. The phrase "mosque at ground zero" was too inflammatory to let go. It had too much potential to be put to rest as a mere community center. The opportunity was irresistible.

How did a unanimous approval last night turn into a poisonous inflammatory label this morning?

Months earlier, when the imam and Daisy Khan had run this by the civic, faith, and community leaders, the 9/11 families and 9/11 Memorial team, the mayor, and political leaders, no one had objected. After the imam had announced the project at an interfaith *iftar* in a church, the *New York Times* had run a front-page story on the project in December 2009. There had been no outcry then.

Why now?

It was the power of words: Mosque at Ground Zero.

Calls were made to community leaders and 9/11 families, trying to ease their anxiety.

Once they understand what this center stands for, any misgivings they may have should subside.

I Am Surrounded by Hate

Of course, that didn't happen. When I walked into the Community Board hearing, the place was packed with people holding placards with anti-Islam slogans that do not deserve mention. Taking my seat, I looked down across the room, spotting my husband and son in the speaker lineup. As the speakers took the mic, the room shuddered and shook with the sounds of hatred.

If they just listen—9/11 is not about Muslims vs. Ground Zero. Muslims also perished in 9/11. We are not trespassers—Ground Zero is sacred to us too; it is our tragedy too. If they just listen.

Testimonies against the project were amplified by cries of "Terrorists," "Down with Sharia," "Don't insult the memory of 9/11"; testimonies supporting the project were drowned out by booing and hissing. I forgot to breathe. It seemed that the walls holding the roof would give way.

Don't they see that we are not those people? Are we destined to carry the burden of their actions? This is not the America I know. Does America have two sides?

On the cold, hard bench, I felt warm tears on my cheek when a 9/11 family pleaded for tolerance; I said a prayer when clergymen from all faiths urged interfaith harmony; and I felt a surge of gratitude when politicians appealed for a place and a space for Muslims. I trembled when I heard voices calling, *"We don't want you here."* Islamophobia had reared its head, and I was witnessing humanity at its best, and at its worst.

Are they going to yell at me?

I cried when my son Asim spoke to the audience of his shock at seeing the smoke gushing out of the tower as he looked out from the window of his office building, of his flight up the streets, with the wall of soot chasing him, of his reaction when he turned to look back and could no longer see the tower, of the shouts of "Go back to where you came from" when he and the faithful walked out of the mosque on a Friday two days later. I recalled how hard I had prayed for his safety when I couldn't reach him by phone, how terrified I was.

Put yourself in their shoes. How would I feel if the Arizona memorial in Pearl Harbor took the shape of a Shinto shrine? It's not the same, but that is how it has been spun. They have been misfed, misled, and now it's too late to un-spin it.

Enraged by a speaker supporting the project, they stood up and, waving posters, started to shout the speaker down.

Should I duck?

The chairwoman issued a warning: those out of order will be escorted out. I saw the guards take their place behind the table where the board members were seated.

Exhale.

The community board voted; the project was approved. I watched the protestors leave. It wasn't defeat I saw on their faces; it was determination.

What is going to happen now?

I walked down into the pit, where my husband and son were standing with the imam. *I can't say, "Congratulations, project was approved." What is there to celebrate?*

I was spent. We all had the "What now?" look on our faces.

I fought a surge of bitter taste. Too often we are asked, "Why aren't the moderate Muslims speaking out?" The community center was to be a forum where American Muslims would stand side-by-side with men and women of peace, promoting religious tolerance. The extremists had drowned out the voices of the moderates.

Leaving the Scene

Hate mail and hate calls paralyzed the office. Daisy Khan and Imam Feisal needed me, and I abandoned them. My father, who was suffering from leukemia, had taken a turn for the worse. I walked off the set and took the first flight out to Pakistan. Planning to stay for two weeks, I ended up staying for three months.

I was in Pakistan, nursing my dying father, when the uproar around the community center project, now dubbed Park51, reached hysterical heights. Swept away in doctor visits, arranging for blood donors, transporting blood bags for transfusion, monitoring medications, hospitalizations, visitors, I was barely in touch with the news. Then my mother took a fall, fractured her hipbone, and was immobilized. Park51 fell off my screen.

My brother in Pakistan brought me back to this world. "Have you heard the news about what's happening in New York? Some Muslims have decided to build a mosque at Ground Zero. Why would they do something like that?"

Even Pakistanis have fallen for the rhetoric.

Picture the look on his face when I told him that his sister was one of those "some Muslims."

Friends from my college days came to visit. Park51 must have hit an even higher high, because they brought it up. "Unnecessary provocation," one of them said. There I go again, explaining the intent of the project.

My uncle advised me, "It would be wise if you built it someplace else."

Death Threats

After burying my father, I returned home to New York. The storm of Park51 had blown over, and I walked into the office to face the debris: ashes, soot, mud, and smoldering black smoke. The place was a fortress, buttressed by security. I walked into a new world trying to reconcile hate mail with warm and tender letters of support; trying to fathom how far one should go in standing by principle without taking the world down at the same time; how hard does one push in paving the way without causing a stampede; how does one amplify the voices of moderation without having those voices drowned out by the thunder of the extremists; and how do we carve a space for ourselves without stepping on the sentiments of our shared pain? Imam Feisal was not around—he had been advised to take the death threats seriously.

"You knew when to leave, and you knew when to come back," Imam Feisal said to me when he returned. I chuckled.

Go Where?

Were we naïve to have believed that there would be no outrage over a Muslim center four blocks from Ground Zero? What now? Should we back off, avoid the fallout, and move the center some place less controversial? Should we? A friend came to offer her condolences on my father's passing. Commenting on Park51, she said, "If you agree to move the project to another location, you will be setting a precedent: "Push, and we shall move." And move where?

"Ten blocks North?

"No, that's not far enough. Go to the upper tip of Manhattan.

"Not Manhattan. Go to the outer boroughs.

"Not New York City. Go Upstate.

"Not in my state.

"Perhaps not in the US?"

Dream, but don't get real.

The Fallout

The circuit breaker tripped right after the November elections. The crisis was over. Just like that. But it's not over. We got burnt, and Muslim communities across the nation felt the heat. Park51 never got built as originally envisioned. A planned mosque in Staten Island never rose. Approvals for a mosque in Tennessee came under fire. Mosques were vandalized, hate crimes increased, there was a Qur'an burning by a pastor in Florida. . . .

And whereas the dream of a Muslim community center was not realized in bricks and mortar, we did build a community without walls, gathering in spaces offered to us by churches, synagogues, and community centers, and offering faith-based and interfaith programs of learning, arts, culture, music, with room for people of all faiths and leanings. Come in . . . and welcome to America.

America, the nation that went through a soul-searching moment when anti-Muslim placards clashed with the red, white, and blue voices of compassion and tolerance, and when President Barack Obama and Mayor Michael Bloomberg stood up for what this nation stands for. We saw moderates of all faiths being galvanized to push back the forces of Islamophobia. Our comrades became our ambassadors, and we made friends.

I made my peace with the Islamophobes, acknowledging that we had not done enough to amplify the voices of moderation. Their vitriolic voices made me realize how much more work we had to do, and how much further we had to go to dispel the misconceptions about Muslims and to make ourselves known.

Will history report how so many were disenfranchised because of the acts of a few? Or will America change its course and make space for its Muslim citizens, so we can claim that we truly did overcome? Time and time again, our nation has exhibited resiliency in springing back, in pushing through the dark clouds and allowing sunshine to prevail, in letting the best in us outshine the worst. America, the nation

I choose to make my home, *will* part the sea. In my home, I will feel at home.

And to think that when I first came to the United States as a Pakistani bride, I had no intention of making America my home. I had arrived with the belief that America was no place to raise a child Muslim. I had plans for my yet-to-be born children. I was coming for two years, and when my husband completed his medical residency, we were going back to Pakistan. That was forty-four years ago.

PART ONE

An Arranged Marriage in Pakistan

1.

It's Arranged

November 1971
Rawalpindi, Pakistan

"You are getting married," Mummy announced.

I was at the CB College for Women, in between my post-graduate English literature classes, hanging out with my friends. Mummy had tracked me down.

"Your fiancé has arrived from New York," she informed me. "He has to return to America in two weeks. So you are taking off. Let's go. I have to take you to the tailor's to have your wedding outfit stitched."

I had gotten engaged a few weeks ago. A wedding date had not been talked about—but it had seemed like it was in the distant future. Or so I thought. But now he had come to Pakistan—all the way from New York—so I had to get married.

And that was that!

He is here!

"Coming to class tomorrow?" My friends Ruby, Tasneem, and Nighat giggled, poking me in the back as I walked away with Mummy in silence. They were teasing. We all knew that I was not coming back to class, not tomorrow, not ever.

I am getting married!

I am going to America!

I am getting married!

"How come he arrived so suddenly, without any notice?" I asked in Urdu as we sat in her 1970 Toyota.

"Your in-laws-to-be sent him a telegram asking him to come for his wedding whenever he has vacation time. He happened to be on vacation this month, so he took the first flight out."

People were right when they said he was an obedient son.

"When does he have to return?" I asked.

"In less than three weeks."

"When is my wedding?"

"Has to be within a week. Your visa has to be obtained right after the wedding, and procedures take time."

Made sense.

I cranked down the window and let the cool November breeze in, messing up my curly hair.

"We will be calling your in-laws-to-be this evening to set a wedding date." Mummy said.

"Have you or Daddy talked to him on the phone?" I asked. My future in-laws lived in Multan, three hundred miles southwest of Rawalpindi, which is where I presumed my fiancé was. We lived in Rawalpindi, a city in northern Punjab, nine miles south of the capital city of Islamabad and home to the military headquarters of the Pakistan armed forces.

"No. But he is flying in tomorrow to meet us." Mummy was excited, but I didn't miss the melancholic tone in her voice. Her daughter was leaving the nest and going away to America. Far, far away.

Mummy drove the car through the bazaars of Rawalpindi, weaving her way through the motorcycles, rickshaws, bicyclists, and an occasional donkey cart laden with bricks. A man pushing a cart loaded with oranges tried to cross the street. Cars honked, a man on a Vespa scooter braked hard, and the woman sitting behind him with a child in hand knocked into him, but held on. As I held my breath, my thoughts got ahead of me. *My future husband is coming tomorrow. What will it be like to see my fiancé for the first time? Will he attempt to talk to me? Will he be shy, or has living in America made him forward? Will I be too nervous to talk to him?*

Mummy parked in the center of a row of shops, including the tailor's shop. The sign in English and Urdu said, VOGUE HOUSE. A tall woman with a graceful carriage, Mummy always dressed exquisitely. She had olive skin, oval dark eyes, arched eyebrows, and a slender nose. Her jet-black hair was parted in the middle and pulled back into a braid that hung down to her hips. She had a youthful look. People always remarked, "You two look like sisters." She radiated beauty, charm, and gaiety. Her wit won over people at first contact, and women flocked to her side just to be in her company.

"Master Sahib." In her high-pitched voice, Mummy addressed the head tailor, who stood behind the glass counter, with sparkling outfits hanging along the walls. "You promised me that when my daughter was to be married, you would stitch her *gharara* within a week. Remember? Well, she is getting married in a week."

Master Sahib's face turned pale. "A week?"

"A week." Mummy was giving him no wiggle room. "Please take her measurements. Here is the fabric." Placing the bag on the counter, she pulled out the fabric that she had saved, oh, some ten years ago. She would often open the large metal trunk and show me the fabrics that she had been carefully putting away for my trousseau. "And this one is for your wedding." She would raise the red crepe de chine, which Daddy had brought from America in 1958 when he was attending a training course in Maryland, sponsored by the Pakistan Army. We picked out a gold embroidery design for the *gharara* and the *dupatta*—a spray of flowers the size of snowflakes, and a fan of fine strands dotted with the tiniest of leaves. For the *dupatta* trim, I picked a solid golden *gota* and *kiran* trimming. I stepped behind the screen, where Master Sahib pulled out a measuring tape and took my measurements.

I wish there was a better way. Granted he is older than my father, but holding a tape around my waist, bust, and hips. . . . Let's quickly get this over with.

"We will be back for the fitting in five days," Mummy told the tailor.

In a daze, Master Sahib just nodded. A promise was a promise. He is going to have to explain to his other customers why he cannot meet their deadlines. I made my way out, walking around the artisans, sitting cross-legged on the floor, heads bent, embroidering gold leaves on the fabric stretched across a loom—for a bride, I presumed.

Oh please, let him be taller than me in high heels.

Then it was off to the jewelers. Mummy picked out a diamond ring for my fiancé and asked them to have it fitted for size. He had mailed his measurements soon after the engagement. As I sipped the hot cardamom-flavored tea the jeweler had served, I trailed away in my thoughts.

So I am getting married. I wonder what he is like. I am sure I will like him. Everyone says he is such a nice person. But I cannot think about this now. I have a wedding to plan; there is work to be done, and so little time.

The hawker outside the shop pushed colorful, beaded, handcrafted purses at me. Mummy honked to hurry me, and I waved him aside and got in the car. The traffic policeman, in a khaki uniform and standing on a round platform in the intersection, extended his hand and held up his palm. Mummy stopped as my thoughts kept moving. The policeman blew his whistle, waved his hands, and Mummy put the car in gear and pushed the accelerator. The hotel was the next stop.

So swept away was I by the demands of the moment that for a while, I almost lost sight that it was *I* getting married—to someone I had never met—leaving my family to go off to a faraway wherever and start a new life with someone totally new to me, an actual stranger. I was too busy. Too busy to get nervous, too busy to think about the what-ifs.

President Yahya Khan's photo in military uniform hung on the hotel wall, and for a moment my thoughts transported me to East Pakistan, where a civil war raged. I quickened my pace to catch up with Mummy. The hall had to be reserved for the wedding reception.

I will deal with marriage after I get married. Right now, I have to focus on getting married. It will be fine. It always works out. You just have to make it work. I will be fine. But Mummy won't be fine. Her little girl is going away, and who knows when she will see her again? How will she deal with the void? Will she regret that she didn't accept the marriage proposal from the in-country family? I hope she is OK.

The car entered the cantonment, the military station within the city. The streets widened, and playgrounds opened the vista. Mummy pulled the car up outside the gate of our walled bungalow and honked the horn, and Aurangzeb, our help, emerged instantly to open the gate. In her high-pitched voice, Mummy was briefing the help on wedding preparations, and I walked up the stairs to my room, composing my to-do list.

The Proposal

It had started with a phone call. That summer, my parents and I were sitting in our sunroom overlooking the valley, when the phone rang. Mummy answered the phone. It was Aba Jee, my maternal grandfather, calling long distance from Multan. She listened for a while, and then I heard her say, "What is the boy's profession?"

Ah! A marriage proposal.

That was always the standard question parents asked about prospective husbands for their daughters.

My father, a lieutenant colonel sitting in his perfect military posture, winked at me. With his light skin, curly, light brown hair, and clipped British accent, he was often mistaken for a Brit when he lived in England in the 1950s. People said that I had my father's looks.

"*Aacha*," I see, said Mummy.

"*Jee*," OK, she said.

A few more OKs, and then she hung up and turned toward us.

"That was Aba Jee," she said. "He says that Bhai Rehman came to visit him and has asked for Bia's hand in marriage for his son. (My family and friends called me Bia.) The boy is a doctor in America and is doing his residency in New York. Aba Jee says that he has known the family for a long time, has known the boy since he was a child, and believes that he is just the right match for Bia. He is urging that we agree to the proposal."

"It sounds good, but we haven't met the boy," Daddy said. "Nor *can* we meet him, considering he is in New York."

They both looked at me inquiringly, but really for validation.

I gave them a noncommittal look. What did I know? I didn't know the boy either, so what can I say?

And it was left at that.

My first marriage proposal came four years prior, when I had just turned sixteen. My parents turned it down on the grounds that I was too young. Over the next few years, I continued to receive proposals—or rather, my parents received the proposals for me—all of which they turned down, either for the same reason or because they deemed the match unsuitable. Most proposals were from families we did not know; they had heard about me through word of mouth. As was the custom, mothers of eligible young men would put the word out. Can you recommend a suitable girl for my son? She should belong to a good family, pretty, preferably tall in height, well educated, and light-skinned. Aunties would spread the word and become self-appointed matchmakers. A ripe forum for matchmaking was weddings. Eligible girls would turn out in their finery, looking their best, and mothers on the lookout would scan the room for a girl who fit the bill. On the spot, discreet inquiries were made. Who is that girl in the green *shalwar kameez*? Is she spoken for? Who are her parents? Introduce me to them. Pleasantries were exchanged and both mothers sized each other up. If you made the first cut, the mother of the boy would then follow up with a visit to the girl's home. I was once picked up in a movie theater. I was with my uncle and some friends, and sitting on my right were two ladies who had been looking for a match for their brother. During intermission, they struck up a conversation and got all my bio data out of me—my name, my father's name, which college—and managed to identify a common acquaintance, my college professor. They showed up at the College of Home Economics in Lahore, where I was enrolled in the undergraduate program, and as luck would have it, spotted me outside the cafeteria. I did not recognize them. They asked if I could tell them where to find this professor. I still did not make the connection and dutifully escorted them. I can visualize how the conversation with the professor went.

What can you tell us about Sabeeha?

Does she have a good reputation? (I.e. she doesn't have any boyfriends, does she?)

What is her temperament like? (I.e. is she obedient and accommodating?)

The next day they came to the students' hostel to thank me and brought me a box of fruit. When they learned that I was preparing for a debate, they turned up again with reference material.

"Sabeeha, this is a marriage proposal in the works," my friends teased. When I went home for the holidays, my mother told me, "They were here last week and have asked for your hand." They were in a rush, wanted a wedding right away; my parents wanted me to complete my education—baccalaureate—so they turned down the proposal.

Proposals continued over the next two years. A friend of my mother would call her. "My friend is looking for a girl for her son and is interested in coming to see your daughter. May I bring them?" Mummy would ask her standard questions:

What is the boy's profession?

What is the family background?

If they scored high on those two points, a visit was granted. Mummy would instruct Aurangzeb to polish the brass table in the center of the red Persian carpet in the drawing room, place fresh flowers there, and replace Mummy's embroidered satin cushion covers with fresh ones to accent the off-white velour sofas. On the mantle were family photos, discreetly allowing a sneak preview. Razia, our cook, would prepare samosas and kebabs. The boy's family would come to visit. If the boy accompanied them, I was not to come forward. Those were the rules. I did however have the edge—an unfair edge. Daddy would place me in the room facing the verandah (porch), and when the family arrived, I got to peak from behind the curtains. He would welcome them in the verandah before leading them inside, giving me a few added moments to see the boy. At the right moment, Mummy would bring the ladies in the adjoining room, and I would come in and serve tea, and thus, the ladies in the boy's family would get to see me. If, on the other hand, the boy was not with them, I would join the family in the drawing room for tea but withdraw soon after. It was understood that, if things progressed to a point where my parents would seriously consider the proposal, I would get to see the boy in person. So far, that milestone had not been crossed with any of the proposals.

My grandfather called again—Auntie Hameeda, the mother of "the boy" was coming from Multan to visit us. The purpose of the visit was apparent—she was coming to propose in person, having laid the groundwork through the elder of the family, my grandfather. As is the custom, she would be staying with us. As was the custom, we would not ask her how long she would be staying; and when she left, we would ask her to come again, and next time, stay longer.

"Tell me again. How are we related to Auntie Hameeda and Uncle Rehman?" I asked Mummy.

She tried to explain the complex relationship, a consequence of intermarriages within the family. But it was the story of Uncle Rehman, the father of the boy, that caught my interest. Uncle Rehman was ten years old when a massive earthquake devastated the city of Quetta in 1935. His parents perished. He and his brother survived and were put on a train with other orphans and sent to the city of Multan, where wealthy benefactors took them in. My mother's uncle and aunt brought the Rehman brothers home. When the two brothers came of age, the family elders married them to two sisters—distant cousins of my mother.

So Auntie Hameeda is Mummy's distant cousin, and Uncle Rehman is an adopted cousin of sorts.

Uncle Rehman's family settled in Multan and frequently visited his adopted mother, whom we called Khala Jee, and my maternal grandparents, particularly on holidays, when Uncle Rehman made it a point to have his son go and pay his respects to the family elders. My path and the Rehman family's had never crossed.

Auntie Hameeda came to visit. She was an unassuming lady with gentle manners and a quiet disposition, and I felt at ease with her around, despite the sensitive nature of her visit. Auntie stayed in Daadee Amma's—my paternal grandmother's—room. Short-statured, light-skinned, with a round face and light brown hair tied back, she had a throaty voice and a joyous disposition. Her room was on the ground floor, making it easy for her to get in and out without having to negotiate the stairs. My paternal grandfather had passed away when Daddy was eight. The sunroom on the second floor with an unobstructed view of the valley, bathed in light, was our family room, with Mummy's sewing machine against the window, a divan with *gao takya* cushions for Mummy's repose, and a tea trolley in the corner, adorned with her handmade linen. Next morning, after Daddy left for the office, Auntie

Hameeda and Mummy sat down to talk in the sunroom. I rolled out the tea trolley, served them tea, and then discreetly withdrew into my room, giving them the privacy to discuss my future. I, "the girl," was to be conspicuously absent, was to behave as if I didn't know what was going on, and whereas it was understood that I knew, decorum required me to act otherwise and be demure. I noticed that Auntie had a big envelope in her hand.

It must contain photographs of "the boy."

An hour later, Mummy came into my bedroom, carrying a stack of photographs. "This is Khalid," she said, handing me the photographs, and sat down next to me on the bed.

So his name is Khalid.

Khalid. Hmmm!

I like the name Khalid. Wonder if that is fortuitous! Now let's not get carried away.

"Look at the smile in his eyes," Mummy noted.

"Yes. It's a nice photo." I spread the photos on my bed and started examining them, trying to read everything I could from a few images. The 8"x10" close-up was in black and white, a fancy car in the background. I looked closely. He had curly hair like mine, sideburns, gleaming straight teeth, and in those big eyes a hint of a smile. In a color photo, he stood at a distance, hands inside the coat pockets of his mustard-brown corduroy jacket, with the Washington Memorial towering in the background; in another under the cherry blossom trees in full bloom, same corduroy jacket, with a stunning backdrop of the tidal basin.

He is handsome.

"Can you tell how tall he is?" I asked.

"I wonder," she said.

"Can you tell if he is light-skinned?"

"I wonder." She squinted over the colored photo.

We pondered over the photos, scrutinizing every detail, reading too much into pictures that didn't tell a thousand words. If only these silent images could speak volumes. Perhaps they did.

I am sure he doesn't drink. They are a conservative family. I hope he doesn't smoke.

Auntie Hameeda had gone downstairs and was wooing Daadee Amma. If you can get the elders of the family on your side, you stand a good chance of getting to "yes." It worked. By the end of the day she had become her ally and was making a case for Khalid.

"I really like Hameeda," she said to my parents. "You should say yes to her." She knew the three golden rules in making a match: family, family, family. If the mother who raised this child was agreeable to you, she must have raised the boy right.

That afternoon, after siesta, aunts, uncles, and cousins descended on our house for high tea and to pay their respects to Auntie Hameeda— but really, to evaluate my latest marriage proposal. Auntie Hameeda was discreetly interviewed about Khalid by way of conversation, and as she proceeded to answer, a hush would fall over the room as everyone tuned in. They huddled in the drawing room. While Aurangzeb rolled in the trolley serving tea, the afternoon sun changed to crimson, and as the lights came on, they were still huddling over the photographs, handing the photos back and forth, posing questions to poor Auntie Hameeda as delicately as possible. I stayed upstairs in the sunroom, the sounds of laughter and exclamations, whiffs of conversations leaving me to wonder, "Now what that was all about?" Every now and then one of my cousins would race up the stairs to give me a report, and then go scrambling down.

That evening, Aba Jee called from Multan.

"Are you going to say yes?" he pressed Mummy and Daddy, impatiently.

"I have never met the boy," Daddy protested, stopping short of saying that even his daughter had never met the boy.

"But *I* have met the boy." Implying that is all that matters. No worries if "girl" hadn't met boy, or the girl's parents hadn't met boy. Grandpa knows best.

Then Khala Jee, Khalid's adoptive grandmother, called. "I practically raised that boy. He is just the right match for Bia."

This is a lot of pressure for Mummy and Daddy.

They found a way to buy time.

"Ask him to write to us," Mummy proposed to Auntie Hameeda.

Auntie was quiet for a moment. Then nodded in assent.

"I will write to Khalid and urge him to write, but my son is so shy, I don't know how he is going to write that letter," Auntie Hameeda confided in Daadee Amma later that night when they were alone.

I groaned! *Too shy to write a letter!*

By the way, my parents and Daadee Amma reported all this to me in near-real time. After every exchange (negotiation), they would come to my room and give me a report, ending with a "So what do you think?"

"Apa Hameeda is asking for a photograph of yours. Can you find one?" Mummy came into my room the morning Auntie Hameeda was leaving. Auntie Hameeda was older than Mummy, hence the *Apa*, as in elder sister.

Oh, my God! Of course they would like a photograph. After all, Khalid has rights too. Right? Now it's my turn to be scrutinized. Why didn't I think of it and have one ready? Do I have a pretty picture? I pulled out a passport-size photo—I wish I had smiled for this picture. I look so serious here—it will scare him away. Oh dear! Look hard, you unprepared young lady. OK. Here we go. This will do. A good balance of pretty and sensible, attire that reflects good taste but is not too loud.

I showed Mummy and Daddy the photos: the serious passport size, and the lovely 8"x10" black-and-white. "Which one should we give?" I asked.

"Both."

I stayed in my room until Mummy had given both photos to Auntie, before I came out to say good-bye. Remember, I am not supposed to know what is going on and certainly should not be seen as "pushing" myself. The entire family—except me, of course—piled into the car to take Auntie to the train station.

That evening the extended family convened again and had the likes of a roundtable meeting. The agenda: to accept or not to accept the marriage proposal.

He is a doctor. Plus.

New York is too far away. Minus.

The grandparents know the family very well. Plus.

They say he has a very good temperament. Is very responsible. Is very caring. Plus.

But we haven't seen him. Minus.

What if he decides to settle in America and not return to Pakistan? Huge minus.

No one has seen him since he went to America over two years ago. Has America changed him? Plus? Minus?

And where was I in all these discussions? Right in the middle—listening, but also listening to my inner voice. Khalid's proposal felt right. How irrational is that! I just had the feeling that this proposal was right for me. But I said nothing. I had not learned to trust my instincts, and I respected my parent's apprehension.

How can they marry their daughter off to someone they have never met? I have to trust their judgment. They know better than I as to what is good for me. They raised me and know me better than I know myself. And besides, what do I know about Khalid?

In keeping with Islamic values and Pakistani culture, I had never dated, nor had I ever had a boyfriend. I didn't even know any boys. How could I have? I was barely twelve when I was told in no uncertain terms that I was a big girl now and was no longer allowed to play with boys. I went to an all-girls high school, an all-girls college, and an all-girls graduate college. How was I to know any boys even if I had dared to cross that boundary? Just being seen speaking with a member of the opposite sex would have been scandalous for an unmarried girl. I didn't even speak with my male cousins. So how could I tell one proposal from the other? I left the responsibility to my parents. This is how my friends had gotten married, and this is how it would be for me.

Due Diligence

Mummy embarked on the equivalent of a background check. She made inquiries with family members who knew Khalid.

What can you tell me about him?

What is his personality like?

Tell me more. Tell me more.

Just put yourself in my mother's shoes and make a list of all the questions you would have about a prospective husband for your first-born. She asked all those, and more.

The result: glowing references; six-star reviews.

So where do we go from here?

"We should go to Multan and pay them a visit in their house—meet the whole family," Mummy suggested.

"Who should go?" I asked.

"All of us, of course."

Of course.

Multan, Pakistan

My parents, my sister Neena who was home on college break, my ten-year-old brother Salman, the uncles, the aunties, and the cousins all packed into their cars and headed off for a ten-hour drive to Multan, me included. Why should I be left behind?! I was, after all, the potential bride-to-be. All fifteen of us stayed at my grandparents' in their five-bedroom, sprawling, walled bungalow in Multan Cantonment. Khala Jee, Mummy's aunt and Khalid's adoptive grandmother, was there too.

Little did I realize at the time that our coming to Multan was a huge deal for Khalid's family. The signal was that we were seriously considering this proposal—which we were. As protocol would have it, Khalid's entire family first came to visit us, and then invited us to visit them. We sat on the lawn bordered by lemon trees, tea was served, and I finally got to meet Uncle Rehman and all seven of Khalid's younger siblings. Seven! *Masha'Allah.* Seven names to remember, fourteen when you factor in the given names and the nicknames, in descending order, starting with Khalid, the eldest. Uncle Rehman was a man of handsome features, slight build, dark skin, thinning hair, and a loud voice. In the presence of the parents, the siblings sat quiet, their heads moving to look at whichever elder was doing the talking.

They seem to be nice people. Simple, a bit on the conservative side, but nice.

I, of course, sitting in the midst, said nothing. Protocol called for me to be demure.

"Please come to our house for tea," Uncle Rehman formally invited us.

My parents accepted their invitation. It was quietly understood that I would not accompany them. A young girl visits the boy's house only after she is wed to him. Going any time sooner would be considered too forward. I should mention that by this time, Khalid had received my photographs.

I wonder what his reaction was when he saw my photo? What was his first impression?

I was home alone when they returned. They gathered around me, each raising their voice above the other.

"Khalid has an eye for photography. We saw the photos he sent." Uncle, who had indulged in photography, beamed. "He took this photograph of a plane taking off over the Jefferson Memorial, and he caught the jet stream in the photo. It's stunning!" Uncle, who had lived in Washington in 1956 on an army-training course, knew the terrain.

"He has beautiful handwriting. They showed us the letters he sent." Daddy had an appreciation for penmanship.

"He is also an artist. We saw this beautiful drawing done in charcoal." My cousin Anjum, a budding artist, proceeded to describe it.

"He stood first in Punjab University in medical school. We saw his gold medal." Mummy was impressed.

"The family is so together," Neena observed.

"Apa Hameeda said that he sings very well," Auntie commented.

He sings! Oh, my God, he sings! Oh, how perfect is that!

I had a passion for singing. Music was my soul food. I sang my way through high school and college, winning first prize—always—in singing competitions. But I was not allowed to sing professionally. Girls from respectable families didn't do that.

He sings!

Lobbying

Khalid's sister Rehana came to visit the next day, sat with me in the bedroom, and began the first in a series of all-day lobbying sessions. Rehana, barely twenty-two, her long hair knotted into a thick braid at the back, bringing out the round contours of her soft face, had the love-liest smile. Her dark eyes danced against her light skin. I sat quietly while she worked on her knitting. Every few minutes, she would pause, hold the outer edge of the knitting needle against her lower lip, look pensively into nowhere, a smile spreading gradually across her face, and reminisce.

"Bhai Jan has such a nice disposition"—referring to Khalid, who was two years older than her, as "dear brother," "His wife will be the luckiest woman in the world! He has such a gentle temperament. . . . He has a tremendous sense of responsibility. . . . He has such good taste. . . . He is such a fine person. . . . He is so caring and considerate. . . . He never gets angry. . . . He is so thoughtful . . . so patient. . . . Every girl in medical school had her eyes on him." She would go on and on, and each time she mentioned Bhai Jan, the love and admiration for her brother shone through her shy smile. After each compliment to her brother, she would relate an anecdote, driving home the point.

Does he stand gracefully like Daddy? Is he light-skinned?

Rehana came to visit the next day, and the day after that, and every day until I left. The two of us would sit in the bedroom, on the bed. She would talk, and I would listen in silence. I never asked her any questions about Khalid. That would have indicated that I was "interested," and that was out of bounds. Besides, inquiry was the domain of the elders. So I just listened. I have to admit, lobbying works. Through her I got to know my future husband—although I saw him through the eyes of an adoring little sister; months later I would describe him in precisely the same terms to my parents—except, of course, for the girls-in-medical-school bit—although I don't doubt it. Soon after, she and I would become very close and remain so until her passing.

The Letter

Daddy had to go back to Rawalpindi two days later to return to work. I was still in Multan when Daddy called me long distance.

"I just received a letter from Khalid." I could not miss the excite-ment in his voice.

That was fast. Maybe Rehana was right after all.

"It's a beautiful letter—appropriate, respectful. He has covered all the questions we had, and he seems to be artistic and has an appreciation for beauty. He describes the color of the leaves in the fall. It reminded me of the song 'The Autumn Leaves.'"

And Auntie Hameeda thought Khalid would be too shy to write.

I chuckled.

"What else does he say?"

"He says that he has two more years of medical residency, and then he will return to Pakistan."

"Good." I had no intentions of settling in the States.

"You can see the letter when you come. But I see this as the beginning of a relationship. I will write back to him, and we will see how things develop."

I wonder what his voice is like. Is he loud? Soft spoken?

No sooner had we gotten back to Rawalpindi, when Auntie Hameeda called. She was coming to visit, again.

But first, the letter.

I read Khalid's letter over and over again. And again. And so did Mummy, and Neena, and my aunts, and uncles, and cousins. Every sentence was scrutinized. And when all was said and done, the verdict was issued:

It was a nice letter.

Engaged
Rawalpindi, Pakistan

This time Auntie Hameeda arrived with Rehana. Now that Khalid had written the letter, would my parents be willing to accept the proposal?

Pressure!

Mummy and Daddy were "undecided."

Once again, the extended family convened. The same checklist was reviewed. We played upstairs downstairs. Upstairs, I kept Auntie Hameeda and Rehana company; downstairs, the elders gathered in Daadee Amma's room. The votes were pretty much lined up, and the "yeas" were outvoting the "undecided." Uncles, aunties, and grandparents were pushing for a "yes." Mummy and Daddy were pushing back:

"But we haven't seen him."

"What if he decides to settle permanently in the States?"

I would occasionally switch places with my cousins to come down to the meeting. Later, Daddy spoke to me in private.

"I think Apa Hameeda is here because she expects an answer. What should we tell them?" he asked.

"It's OK with me. You can say yes," I said with confidence.

"Are you sure?" Daddy was gentle and direct.

"I am."

I was.

Perhaps I am being irrational; but I am finally trusting my instincts, and this proposal feels right.

Next morning I went off to college. I returned to find the whole family gathered in the drawing room again. Rehana was beaming a little more than usual. I went straight to my room to put my books away. Daddy followed me.

"We just said yes," he told me.

"You did?" *Oh, my God. It's done.*

"But I asked you and you said it was OK with you." Daddy misunderstood the tone in my voice.

"Yes, yes, it is OK with me."

And so it was done. I was engaged.

In the end, I had cast the deciding vote.

Auntie asked for my measurements and ring size.

Oooh! This is getting real.

I had never worn a ring. Mummy used to say that the first ring I wear will be my engagement ring. I had liked the sound of that and had complied. Mummy used a tape band to measure my finger, and I handed over one of my *shalwar kameez* outfits to them. Now I was minus one outfit. Auntie Hameeda and Rehana said nothing to me about the fact that I was now engaged. All that would be rolled out ceremoniously when an engagement ceremony took place. They departed for Multan the next morning.

I designed and ordered the engagement announcement card. I had gift boxes with *ladoo* sweets ordered and had Aurangzeb deliver them to family and friends. When he had difficulty locating the home of one of my cousins, I went with him.

"You brought your *ladoos* yourself?" Engaged girls are supposed to be shy about such matters; celebrating is left to the elders.

Cousin's mother-in-law peered at the announcement card, reading, "son of Mr. and Mrs. Abdul Rehman," and asked me, "Who is this Abdul Rehman, very familiar name?" I suppressed a giggle. Abdul Rehman in Pakistan is as ubiquitous as John Smith is in the USA. It was like asking, "Who is this John Smith, very familiar name?" I answered her question, adding the earthquake story of Khalid's father. She was hard of hearing; I am soft-spoken; and the gossip that got back to my mother was that my parents were marrying me off to an old man, someone who was orphaned in the earthquake in 1935.

My friends at college shrieked when I walked into class, a box of *ladoos* in my hand, touting the announcement card. I had brought photos of Khalid, and they all leaped up, grabbing the photos from each other's hands, squealing and screaming.

"Let me see. Let me see."

"He is so handsome!"

"Look at those sideburns!"

"Do you think he talks with an American accent?"

I certainly hope not.

"Look, he also has curly hair. Your children are going to have the tightest curls."

I blushed.

Consensus: they approved.

"When is the wedding?"

"No idea. We haven't talked about a date. I guess whenever he can get time off."

At that time, only one of my classmates, Qaseem, was engaged. The rest of us were all waiting to get engaged and married. We had each gotten our bachelor's degree, and the next step was to get married to a suitable boy. So what did we girls do while we were ladies-in-waiting? No, we did not take up a job. This was 1971, and girls of marriageable age had to be in a state of readiness to tie the knot as soon as Prince Charming came along. Taking up a job would put a girl on the career track, and that would chip away at her marriageability. So those who were pushy enough like me were able to convince our parents that we get enrolled in a master's degree program in English literature in our hometown CB College. We wouldn't be going away to college, and therefore, whenever the marriage proposal came, we would be around to "be seen" by the boy's family, and if a proposal were accepted, we would just drop out of college and get married.

"What's going on?" our English poetry professor asked as she walked in, wearing a sari with her hair in a tight bun.

"Bia is engaged!" A loud chorus.

"I hope you won't drop out and get married before completing your master's program."

"Oh no, of course not." I didn't think I would be getting married any time soon.

A month later, I broke that promise. Or rather, it was broken for me.

But first, there was the engagement ceremony.

The Ceremony

Auntie Hameeda and Rehana were back in two weeks, with the engagement outfit, an orange *gharara* with gold embroidery, and a gold necklace with matching earrings. I was to don the outfit, the jewelry, and have an engagement ceremony without the ring and without the fiancé —not an unusual circumstance when the boy is overseas. I felt hesitant. The whole ceremony bit seemed incomplete without the boy. But the conformist in me complied, and it made everybody happy. It was the first engagement in both families, and they wanted to formalize it with a ceremony.

"We wanted to get the ring, but Khalid said that he wants to pick it out, and will bring it when he comes for the wedding," Auntie Hameeda said.

He wants to pick the ring himself.

I thought about it over and over again, and I think I smiled.

The family gathered in Mummy's walled garden, still blooming in October. I wore the orange *gharara,* was escorted out, seated, with my eyes lowered, looking demure and feeling totally awkward at this lonesome engagement. I missed my fiancé.

Can one get attached to someone in a photo? Was it the idea that Khalid was now my fiancé that made me smile and blush?

That evening, as Mummy and Auntie Hameeda chatted while Rehana and I sat by, Auntie asked, "When would you like to have the wedding?"

Before Mummy could muster a response, Rehana jumped in.

"Bhai Jan says," she said, referring to Khalid, "that he can either come this November or next year in November."

This was October.

"This November is fine." Mummy was decisive as always.

I didn't pass out. Nor did my heart miss a beat. I don't believe my jaw dropped either. I had been mentally prepared to get married ever since I passed the milestone of getting my bachelor's degree. As far as I was concerned, I was ready.

"But November is so close. We haven't made any preparations," Auntie Hameeda protested.

"Our preparations are complete. We can have the wedding next month."

By this Mummy meant that the trousseau was ready. Mummy had been saving gorgeous fabrics for my trousseau, clothes that would be stitched at the time of the wedding, and had bought all the jewelry, which was tucked away in the bank's locker.

"But *our* preparations are not done," Auntie tried to reason.

"Look. She is going away to America. In New York she won't have the opportunity to wear all that finery that you and I give her. In fact, the airlines won't allow her to carry more than a suitcase. So don't worry about getting her new outfits. There isn't much for you to prepare."

Auntie Hameeda was quiet. She was not quite ready for this.

And the conversation was left at that.

Had anybody thought of asking me? Daddy did. He spoke to me later that evening.

"This will mean that you won't be able to complete your masters," he said.

"That's OK," I said.

I loved English literature, and it would have been nice to have a master's degree, but in my mind, marriage came first. With my bachelor's degree in hand, my education was complete. The next step was marriage, and nothing in between. Marriage proposals for a girl peak around age seventeen to twenty. Once a girl was over twenty-one, her marriage prospects start declining. Not that I was counting, but I was turning twenty in a month.

Auntie Hameeda presumably spoke with Uncle Rehman, because the next day he called Daddy and said that they had sent a telegram to Khalid asking him to come next month for the wedding.

Four days later, Khalid landed in Pakistan.

You Have Mail

But first, there was the fuss over "the card." Soon after the engagement, Daddy had brought me home from college, and as I walked up to my room, I noticed Mummy say something to Daddy and he started running excitedly toward the drawing room. I quickly made a U-turn and ran down the stairs after them. They were huddled over a greeting card.

"It's a card from Khalid!" Daddy exclaimed.

"Can I see it?" It was a reasonable request. After all, he was my fiancé.

"Let me first read it."

I glanced at the envelope on the mantle.

"It's addressed to me! Why did you open it?" I turned and faced Mummy.

"I was so excited I couldn't resist."

It was a beautiful card. Even today, I smile when I think about the card and how it made me feel. I still remember the script:

Roses are brighter red
Skies are deeper blue

My life is more beautiful
Just after knowing you

Signed: "Love, Khalid."
My first moment of romance!
"See how boldly he wrote, 'Love, Khalid'?" Daddy said with a chuckle.
I took the card up to my room and put it by my bedside. A few hours later it was gone.
What on earth!
"I took it," said Mummy, "I wanted to show it to your aunt and uncle."
Excuse me! Can I have some privacy in my one-sided love life?
Of course, I didn't say that.
That afternoon Mummy's best friend came visiting, and, naturally, the card was up for display. By the evening, family members in town had paid a visit to see the card. My grandparents in Multan were notified, who in turn told Khalid's parents, leaving Auntie Hameeda mortified at her shy son's audacity.
Khalid would later tell me that he had no idea that the card would create such a stir.

He Said
And how was Khalid dealing with all this, by himself, at the other end of the world? After all, it was his marriage too.
It was only after we were married that I got to hear his side of the story. You may wonder how a young man in his twenties, living in America for several years, would readily agree to marry a girl his parents had picked for him. In Pakistan, there was very little opportunity for unmarried men and women to get to know one another, so one relied on the parents' choice. But in America, where one is exposed to the elements, outlook and mindset can change.
His mother had written to him early on about me. Well, not exactly early on, but soon *after* they had proposed.
"She is just the right girl for you," and then had gone on to describe my family credentials: whose granddaughter I was, whose daughter I

was, my father's profession, which college I had graduated from, my sweet temperament, my quiet disposition, how well I will adapt in America—how did she figure that out?—and of course my name—Bia—short for Sabeeha. Did any of this appeal to Khalid? Two things did: I had been a student at the College of Home Economics, and "Bia" had a nice ring to it. He wrote back and gave his consent. A few weeks later, a parcel arrived in the mail: my photographs.

That sealed it. He says he loved what he saw. Remember, I was only nineteen when this photograph was taken. A young woman is at her loveliest at this age, fresh as a flower with a touch of innocence. And if it is a black-and-white photo, one looks even lovelier. The icing on the cake was my short hair—how lucky could he get! He carried the picture around showing it to his friends. That photo sits on his desk today, and often when he looks at it, I find him smiling. To this day, Khalid likes to see me in my curly short hair, and it has to be a side parting, just like the photo.

When his parents asked him to write to my parents, stressing its importance, the dutiful son sat down to compose his thoughts. He had no idea that his letter was going to receive the scrutiny it got, or mean so much to us. He just did what he was asked to do. When he got the news that my parents had accepted the proposal, the first thing that entered his mind was to send me a card. He did not realize how Americanized he had become when, without any hesitation, he wrote, "Love, Khalid."

Then came the shock! A telegram from his father asking him to come to Pakistan to get married right away. This he was not ready for. He was not about to hop on a plane to get married at moment's notice. Besides, he had already spent one week of his four-week vacation. He wrote to his parents that he was not coming. This is not how weddings are planned. It was his wedding and he wanted to plan it well, he cannot just get up and come. What's the rush?

The day after he mailed the letter he had second thoughts. Maybe he had acted in haste.

"Can you all please come over? I need your advice." He called his friends, all of whom were Pakistani resident physicians.

They gathered in his studio apartment and listened to his arguments.

I don't have a proper apartment.

I haven't bought the ring.

I need new clothes.

I have already spent a week of my vacation.

I am not ready for this.

His support group listened to the cons; offered the pros. The verdict: Khalid should go. Rationale: In the larger scheme of things, these concerns are of little consequence and they can be worked out. Once engaged, why delay marriage? Trust your parents' decision; three weeks of vacation isn't so bad for a wedding; get your shopping done and go.

So it was decided, and so it was done.

Khalid took his friend Izhar and went shopping the next morning at Macy's in Herald Square. An engagement ring for me, a couple of suits for himself, and a camera. Then it was off to the Pakistan International Airlines office to get tickets for both of us. He sent a telegram to his parents and got onto the plane.

He Is Coming

Back in Rawalpindi, the phone lines started ringing the minute he landed.

"Khalid is here." That was his parents.

"He is very handsome, and he speaks with an American accent." That was my aunt reporting.

"We have to set a date for the wedding." That was my grandfather.

"Khalid is coming tomorrow to visit you." That was Uncle Rehman calling Daddy.

Khalid is coming!

I will get to see him before the wedding.

What will it be like?

How will I feel when I first see him?

Will I talk to him? Probably not.

Will he talk to me? Maybe.

I smiled.

A flutter of excitement filled the house. Uncles and aunts, cousins and all gathered to plan Khalid's arrival.

"Where will he stay?" someone asked.

"At our house, of course." Uncle, the consummate host, promptly offered his house.

"At our house," said Daddy decisively.

"No! He cannot stay here," I chimed in indignation.

"What do you mean, he cannot stay here?"

"It's not appropriate for the groom-to-be to be under the same roof as the bride-to-be." I was finally getting nervous.

"Listen to me, my dear old-fashioned daughter. This is our only chance to bond with him. This is no time to get traditional."

"I guess so. But it is going to be very awkward for me."

"If you insist, we will keep you in seclusion." Now Daddy was being funny. "But I want this time with my future son-in-law."

Should I try to get to know him—at least a little—or wait until after we are married?

How was all this playing out at Khalid's end?

When Khalid announced that he wanted to go to Rawalpindi to meet my family, Auntie Hameeda was flustered. She was busy with the wedding preparations and told him that she could not go with him.

"I will go by myself," the so-called shy son responded.

"Go by yourself! It's not proper. I have to escort you and introduce you to the family."

"I'll go," Rehana readily offered.

"Look. You all are busy with the wedding preparations and you need to be here. I can go by myself and I will be fine. Trust me."

"But you haven't met the family. How will you recognize them at the airport?"

"I'll find them."

Auntie Hameeda was beginning to see that her shy son wasn't so shy anymore.

At First Sight
"Who is going to the airport?"

Everyone. Everyone, except me. I stayed home alone at Uncle and Auntie's house in Lalazar. They had insisted that they be the first to host Khalid for dinner.

The plane must have landed just about now. Has he emerged from the plane? Will they recognize one another? How will they greet one another? How will Mummy and Daddy react when they first see him?

They must have left the airport by now.

Now they must be heading home.

Any minute now.

They came with a bang: horns blaring, headlights flashing, sounds and sights of a happy homecoming, signaling to me that they were not just happy, they were very happy. I held my breath.

From the landing upstairs, I heard the front door open, the pounding footsteps of a mob running up the stairs, and uncles, aunts, cousins, and siblings, all gushing with excitement, surrounded me.

"He is so handsome," my cousin Anjum squealed.

"He is tall."

"He is so Americanized."

"He has such a groovy personality."

"He is ... he is ..."

Voices upon voices, getting louder, pitch rising.

"I am telling her first," Uncle said, exerting his authority. "Quiet everyone. Your turn will come." He turned to me: "Bia, your fiancé is handsome, he is an inch taller than me, a shade darker than me, he speaks beautifully, he is graceful, he is friendly, he is confident, and he is cheerful."

Then everyone was chiming in, my cousins actually jumping and squealing, drowning each other's voices, giddy.

"Did you recognize him easily? Is he like his photos?" I asked.

"I spotted him right away. I dashed over to him and said, '*Khalid!*'" Uncle was acting like a teenager. "He is even better looking than his photos."

Then just as soon, they were all gone, downstairs to Khalid, where Mummy and Daddy were keeping him company. I was left to my own devices, or rather, with my thoughts.

It is going to be all right. Somewhere in my subconscious, I must have been worried: What if? *They look so happy—they all like him. If he had passed the first line of defense, it is going to be all right.*

I smiled, and then I felt my heart thump. *Oh dear, what's next?*

There was laughter coming up from below. As I sat in the lounge on the landing, I listened hard, trying to filter out the new voice from the chattering voices. I brought my palms to my hot face and waited for something to happen. I could feel my heart pound.

Daddy walked up the stairs.

I looked up.

He was smiling. He held out his hand, "Come. Let's go down."

"No. I am not going." *I cannot handle this.*

"It's OK, come on."

"I am not going," I shook my head over and over, a bit too hard.

I cannot deal with this first-encounter business.

I didn't trust how I was going to react.

What am I going to say? "Hello, you must be my future husband. Pleased to meet you."

Daddy must have read my thoughts. He very gently put his arms around my shoulder, and eased me out of the seat.

Please, God. Just let me get through this. Let me not make a scene.

With Daddy by my side, I walked into the drawing room not knowing what to expect or how I would react.

The drawing room was empty.

So much for a grand entrance!

They had all moved into the dining room. Daddy led me there. Everyone was seated at the table.

Oh God, no. That's him with his back to me. Speak of an awkward entrance! Now what?

"This is Bia," Daddy announced, with his arm around my shoulder.

Khalid leapt out of the seat, swung around to face me, and almost knocked the seat down. As he looked up, a little startled, our eyes locked for an instant.

Those eyes! The same face, but alive.

"*Assalaam Alaikum*," I greeted him with the blessing of peace, with my best smile, and dashed over to the empty seat at the farthest end of the table.

If there ever was a time when Khalid was struck speechless, this was it. But in all fairness, I had the edge. He didn't know that I was going to be presented, as he would later tease me. We took our seats, as family members looked on, savoring the moment at my expense.

I was seated at the head of the table, Uncle across from me, and Khalid next to Uncle. From my vantage, I had a direct view of Khalid, but he would have to lean forward and turn his head to see me, and everyone would notice—not that there was anything wrong with that. Again, I had the edge, and I blew it big time.

I dug my head in my plate and started eating. I wouldn't look up and didn't speak. The elders chatted away with Khalid, and the young cousins just ogled the two of us.

These kids! I know exactly what you are up to. "Is he looking at her? Is she looking at him? Are they looking at each other?" Kids, just cut it out and stop staring. I am not offering you any entertainment.

Khalid was chatty, and his American accent felt foreign. He looked different from his photos: more handsome, well built, with a grace and easy carriage—a lot that the photographs did not convey. He wore a brown tweed blazer, a tie, but I don't recall the color of his shirt, nor are there any photos of the occasion to remind me. Occasionally, I would steal a glance at him. I was hoping he wouldn't catch me doing that. I felt my hands shake, and I steadied my left hand in my lap.

Uncle and Auntie had laid out a feast. The aroma of chicken *pullao,* the crunchy whole spices of the *chapli kebabs*, and mouth-watering, velvety mutton korma with whole almonds floating in the curry did nothing for me. I would have eaten anything as long as I could bury my head in it.

I got through dinner, and by morning I had gotten past my nervousness. Perhaps it was a combination of Khalid's easy demeanor and my distraction with the wedding plans. After a while, I stopped being conscious of his presence and went about my business. I had a wedding to plan. Not very romantic, but I was calm and relaxed and for that I was grateful. We would all pack up into the car, Khalid in the front seat, I in the back, as we went from the tailor to the card shop, from the jewelers to the hotel and back to the tailor. I picked out a red wedding card with a gold outline of a bride sitting by her palanquin, with her hands clasped around her knees. I decided that I wanted the inscription to be in Urdu. We walked in and out of the shops together, sat at the same table for our meals, hung around in the same sunroom, and we talked with everyone except one another.

There will be time for that when we are married.

Khalid brought so much joy into our home in those two days. Everyone—and I mean, everyone—fell in love with him. He was at ease, funny, chatty, witty, charming, and with it. He brought a collection of music he had recorded on the spool tape and played the songs for Daddy, introducing him to Englebert Humperdinck and Neil Diamond. Daddy was taken; this young man who grew up in the conservative city of Multan had developed an ear for Western music. When Khalid offered the tape to Daddy to keep, Daddy was beyond appreciative. Khalid helped Mummy pick out colors and designs for my outfit, and Mummy was charmed. He kidded around with Neena, Salman, and my young cousins, humored them, and they just clustered around, monopolizing him. Uncle was enamored by his wit. Khalid had slid right in. The sounds of laughter rang from every room. Everyone was smiling, spirits soared, and my grandparents, all three of them, just beamed with delight and relief. I took it in from the sidelines, feeling that all was well with my world. This Americanized fiancé of mine respected the boundaries of culture, as he made no attempt to talk to me—until one impetuous moment when he crossed the line.

The Ring

"Khalid wants to give you the engagement ring on your twentieth birthday," Mummy told me.

My moment of romance!

She showed me the ring. A set of two, a wedding band and a solitaire, a round diamond held above the band in platinum prongs, like two fingers holding the stone. I held it, turned it around, admiring the one-of-a-kind design.

"Is his engagement ring ready?" I asked.

"We picked it up today." Mummy and I had selected Khalid's ring just a few days ago.

"Let me see." I looked at the heavy ring with a brilliant round diamond encased in four square platinum studs.

Now I can have a second engagement, this time with the fiancé.

For my birthday/engagement, all of my college friends descended with a bang. This was their chance to meet Khalid and have him to themselves before the surge of the wedding. I wore a midnight blue *shalwar kameez* over which I had embroidered swirls in silver thread. It was the same outfit in the black-and-white photograph we had sent Khalid.

I wonder if he recognized it.

Khalid wore a purple shirt and tie with the same brown tweed blazer. The whole family was there—of course—and my friends came dressed in colorful *shalwar kameez* and engulfed Khalid in a wave. He was spoken for, so the boundaries of segregation didn't apply. They joked, tried to get him nervous, and wouldn't let up. Each time he spoke with an American accent they would mimic him. He humored them, and the more he humored them, the more liberties they took. The birthday girl was forgotten. Khalid was the center of attraction, and the girls were having a ball. I watched as he laughed with them, the laughter of my friends conveying their approval.

They like him. And he isn't rattled. This small-town boy can hold his own.

"Let's do the engagement!" Tallat, my friend, tallest in height and loudest in pitch, had taken over the party. I was thrust onto a settee, and Khalid was placed beside me. This was the first time I sat beside him—close. Someone draped a *dupatta* over my head. Khalid took the ring from his pocket and slipped it on my finger. His fingers grazed mine, for a second. It was the first time we touched.

Nothing happened. No fireworks, no spine tingling. Mummy handed me Khalid's ring. I held the ring, turned toward Khalid, he held out his hand, and I started to slip the ring on. But Tallat got a hold of my fingers and slid the ring on for me.

Excuse me! I can handle giving my fiancé his ring.

My only moment slipped out of my fingers.

Thank you, Tallat.

The room had drowned in the shrieking of my friends: *Mubarak!* God must have felt bad for me, because what happened next doesn't happen. Khalid reached out, put his arm around my shoulder, and pulled me toward him in a kind-of-sideways hug.

It brought the house down.

Shrieks and more shrieks. Tallat, Ruby, and Khalida all screamed and squealed. Overcome, he had crossed the line, and they loved it. Even the elders suppressed a smile. *Did he just give me a hug in public?!*

In my shock, I couldn't even savor the moment. Later Daadee Amma would tell anyone and everyone who came to congratulate Mummy and Daddy, "He placed the ring on her finger, and then he gave her a hug, like this." She would act it out, her smile urging listeners to give their approval of her prospective grandson-in-law's demonstration of affection in public. "Isn't that nice," they would say, glancing at my beet-red face.

"Let's have some music," announced Tallat, the self-proclaimed master of ceremonies. Khalida took her place on the center of the red floral Persian carpet, tucked the *dholak* against her knees, and beat the two-sided hand drum with her hands, rhythmically against the leather skin. All my other friends clustered around in a circle, clapping in unison and, in a chorus led by Ruby and Tallat, singing Urdu wedding songs, swaying with the melody. The elders retreated to the sofas lined up against the wall, relishing the sounds of music and laughter. My friends were center-stage and sang until they were hoarse, laughing and teasing Khalid, and I felt my cheeks warm up.

Did he really hug me!

"Now Khalid has to sing," Ruby proclaimed.

Oh dear! Poor Khalid. He has done well so far, but I don't think he is ready for this.

"Khalid is going to sing. Khalid is going to sing," they chanted. "Bia sings so well. Let's see if you can get a note out," they goaded him.

"Sure. I'll sing."

Is he serious? Why does he want to give them more fodder? These girls will chew him up.

Khalid started singing "*Aashian jal gaya*," a popular contemporary Urdu *ghazal* sung by Habib Wali Mohammad.

Not bad. Darn good, in fact. Good taste in ghazals.

He sang away with a smile, perched on the chair, and the girls clustered around him on the floor, looking up, making faces at him, trying to get him nervous; in the end they gave up and joined him in chorus, swaying to the tune.

"Now you have to sing an American song." These girls were not letting up. And Khalid wasn't going to let them have the last word either. He promptly started singing again, "I am leaving on a jet plane; I don't know when I will be back again"—John Denver's composition sung by Peter, Paul, and Mary.

He loves music, he sings ghazals, he sings American pop songs, he can stand up to these girls, he is such a sport, and charming. . . . I was on cloud ten in my own heaven. And it showed.

"See how she is glowing!" Ami Jan remarked.

"She looks so happy."

"She is blushing."

I heard the chatter, and all was well in my world.

Next morning Khalid was to leave for Multan. We were seated at breakfast, and then they were all out in the car headed for the airport, with me seated alone at the table staring at the empty plates.

Until this moment, "*Assalam Alaikum*" was the only one-sided dialogue I had had with my prospective.

But then there was the hug. But then again, he left without saying goodbye.

I was still sorting out my conflicting thoughts when Khalid walked back in—alone.

"I came to say good-bye."

"Good-bye." I looked up to meet his eye.

Just as quickly, he was gone.

He came back to say goodbye.

YES!

Six days later, on November 21, 1971, we were married. Three weeks later, I was in New York.

But first, the wedding.

2.

I Never Said, "I Do"
The Marriage Contract

It was one of those non-technical glitches. In his excitement, Uncle, my appointed guardian for the marriage ceremony, forgot to ask me, "Do you agree to marry Khalid Rehman?" Too submissive to remind him, I signed the marriage contract and was married off without an "I do."

OK, so let me step back.

Grounded

"We will start your *mayoon* two days prior to your wedding," Mummy said to me.

"What's a *mayoon*?" Salman, my ten-year-old brother, asked.

"It's when the bride-to-be can no longer leave the house and stays in the same clothes until her wedding day."

"You mean Baji Jan cannot change for two whole days?" My younger siblings and cousins called me Baji Jan, as in "dear elder sister."

"That's right."

"*Uf!*" He wrinkled his nose. "Why can't she change?"

Daddy took over. "Because when she stays in the same clothes day after day, she starts looking crumply, and then on the wedding day, she is transformed."

"You mean you make her look icky just so she looks less icky on her wedding day?" Salman teased. "Why does she have to be grounded?"

"Would you like to go out in wrinkled, stained clothes?"

Try explaining to a ten-year-old that the bride-to-be is kept home to get her into the mode, the frame of mind, to fuss over her, and to mentally prepare her.

Mummy gave me an orange cotton *shalwar kameez*, plain and simple. I was not to change into my pajamas; I was to eat, sleep, and hang out over the next two days in the same outfit. All my married friends had the *mayoon*. Some of them were grounded for an entire week. Lucky for me, last-minute preparations, such as trips to the tailor, took precedence, and I got away with a two-day sit-in. Salman was having fun at my expense. He would run up to me, sniff, wrinkle his nose, make an "ugh" sound, and run off.

Did I say, "Prepare her?" I should have said, "Embarrass her."

Embarrassing moment #1:

"Here is some *ubtan* for you." Mummy handed me a jar.

Those familiar with *ubtan* blush away. Let me explain. A concoction of the sub-continent, *ubtan* is a beauty paste reserved for brides-to-be in preparation for their wedding night. Made of gram flour, turmeric, sandalwood powder, milk, and rose water, it is known to make the skin glow and make it smooth and fragrant. In many families, a masseuse will come to the home and give the bride-to-be a body rub of the *ubtan*. In my case, I was the masseuse. I don't know if the ritual did anything for my skin, but it certainly got me thinking and wondering, and made me a slight bit nervous. If that was the idea behind preparing me, it worked.

Embarrassing moment #2:

Uncle walked in and handed me a package.

"Here, start using this." I heard the excitement in his voice.

I opened the package and took out a bottle. It had green liquid.

"What is this?"

"It's a new product. It's called mouthwash."

No! Keep a straight face.

"Rinse your mouth with it twice a day, and it will make your breath fragrant."

Subtle!

What are they going to tell me next?! Can we just stop here, please?

It didn't stop there, and much of it is too embarrassing to put in print. Understand that this was the first wedding in the family in my generation—in both families. Their Bia was getting married, and they loved Khalid. It was *their* wedding, *their* big day, and they were going to give Bia the send-off of a lifetime.

Uncle was back, giggling away. "Bia, do you know what your groom-to-be just said?"

No, and I am not sure I want to hear it. It sounded just like the mouthwash.

"Your grandmother said to him, 'Please take care of Bia, she is my little princess,' and do you know what Khalid said?"

Straight face. Straight face.

"He said, 'Don't worry, I will make her *my* little princess.'" He chuckled.

Phew!

Hmmm! Princess!

Auntie came rushing in. "Bia, do you know what Khalid just said?"

"Yes. I know, I heard."

"Let me tell you again. . . ."

Khalid was on a roll, keeping the reporters busy.

Whereas my parents had rented a house for Khalid and his family's stay, as you can gather, they spent most of their time in our home, pushing me into seclusion in my bedroom.

Trousseau: Pakistani Style

Mummy arranged my trousseau in the sunroom, and through the walls I could hear the buzz of appreciation for Mummy's talent and good taste. She had been saving material for my trousseau for over a decade. It was packed away, and every year she would remove the fabrics and air them. Neena and I would hold them longingly, feel their texture, and know that one day this would be ours. The two of us had already staked out our share. Mummy had carefully picked out the design of the gold and silver embroidery for the *shalwar kameez* and saris and the trimmings for the *dupattas*. My favorites were the pink sari with an overlay of gold ribbon and the red *gharara* with gold embroidery, which I was to wear at the *walima*, the reception given by the groom's family. Mummy had given me a piece from her wedding jewelry, a gold choker necklace put together in squares, with dangling *jhumka* earrings. But the most creative pieces in my trousseau were the linens Mummy had hand embroidered for me—a patchwork bedspread made with leftover fabrics from our outfits; crochet trolley covers; and a needlepoint wall hanging showing a man serenading a lady in the garden, which still hangs in our bedroom. She had put her heart and labor into creating beautiful artifacts, and it showed. The clothes are all gone, except for the red *gharara*; the jewelry I gifted to my daughters-in-law; but forty plus years later, Mummy's linen still adorns my home.

I Never Said, "I Do"

"Bia, we will have the *nikah* the day before the wedding reception—the same day as your *mehndi*," Mummy told me. *Mehndi* was the henna-painting ceremony. "It's best to get the paperwork out of the way before the formal reception. All the family and friends will be here for the *mehndi*, and we can combine both events in one evening."

Made sense.

"What's a *nikah*?" Salman asked.

"It's the official marriage ceremony," Daddy answered.

"Isn't the wedding reception the official marriage?"

Daddy explained that the *nikah* was the marriage contract—the legal and civil contract that makes the marriage official, whereas the wedding reception was the social occasion when the bride's parents ceremoniously give away the bride. Until then, despite the *nikah*, the two remain apart.

"Why don't we have the *nikah* the same day as the reception?" Salman was having difficulty processing this.

"If you can get the paperwork done earlier, then you can relax at the reception and enjoy the party." Salman looked confused, and to this day I remain confused between being married and married-married. What Daddy did not get into was that the marriage contract, which is akin to a prenuptial agreement, can create conflict and requires delicate negotiation. A tricky component is the *mahr* amount—the cash gift bestowed by the groom to the bride.

If you had been in Lalazar Colony, Rawalpindi, on November 21, 1971, you would have seen the bride's house from a mile away. With colored lights hanging like garlands from the rooftop, draping the walls, and twinkling into the night, the house was sparkling. It was the night of the *mehndi,* when henna will be painted on the hands of the bride-to-be and the guests; the girls will sing and dance late into the night; and the men of the family are the only male guests present. That somewhere on the agenda for an evening full of music was also the *nikah*—the most crucial component of the wedding—was of little consequence to my friends. They were going to get dressed in their finery and have a blast. Formalities such as the marriage contract would be deferred to the elders. On the lawn, the girls besieged Khalid, forming a circle around him, and to the beat of the *dholak,* danced the *luddi.* Swinging left, clapping once above the left shoulder, swinging right and clapping over the right shoulder, bending and clapping at the knees, then switching the routine to clicking the fingers, they danced around him. In seclusion, I sneaked a look from the sunroom window and watched Khalid swing his arms and perform a solo in the ring. The girls called out to Daddy to join Khalid, and Daddy, who had never performed the girlie *luddi* dance, clicked his fingers and joined in. The uncles were pulled in. I pressed my face against the cool sunroom window, overcome. At that moment, one of the girls looked up and shrieked, "Bia is watching," and everyone, including Khalid, looked up. I quickly stepped back out of sight, but the photographer had captured the moment.

"Can everyone please come in for the *nikah,*" called Uncle, summoning the guests in the drawing room. And thus began the first in a series of identity changes for me, this one, from Sabeeha Akbar to Sabeeha Rehman.

In keeping with the requirements of the *nikah,* both families had early on agreed upon the *mahr* amount. What remained was the consent of the bride and groom in the presence of two witnesses, the signing of the marriage contract stating the *mahr* amount, and a public announcement. That would seal it, and we would be legally married. The ceremony would culminate with a prayer led by the *maulvi,* a cleric—not a religious requirement, but a tradition. Photographs show the bearded *maulvi* in a Jinnah cap, wearing a white *shalwar kameez*, seated in the drawing room with Khalid in his brown tweed blazer, purple shirt, and purple printed tie, flanked by the fathers and Aba Jee. Uncle, who was handling the paperwork, is seated opposite—he must have pulled the chair up to the *maulvi* as they went over the *nikah* form. My grandmothers, Mummy, and the aunties would have taken their seats at the opposite side. Two witnesses each were appointed for Khalid and me. It is preferred that the witnesses be young men—on the assumption that they will live longer and be around to bear witness. I was seated upstairs in my bedroom, in my crumpled orange outfit. Neena, my cousins, and friends clustered around me—must have been twenty to thirty of them.

I wasn't present in the drawing room, but I presume that after the *nikah* form was filled out, the *maulvi* must have asked Khalid three times, "Do you, Khalid Rehman, son of Abdul Rehman, accept Sabeeha Akbar, daughter of Kazim Akbar, to be your wife?" I am sure Khalid said, "Yes." (On the other hand, given what happened later with me, who knows?) The *maulvi* would have asked Khalid to sign the *nikah* form; in the photos I see Khalid smiling as he signed the form. And then the witnesses would have signed. Next would be my turn to give consent. Since the bride is cloistered in her room with the young ladies, the *maulvi* would not intrude in their space, and an elder of the bride's family, serving as a proxy for the officiant, would go to her and ask for her consent. In my case—you guessed it—it was Uncle.

Uncle walked in, and making his way through the crowd of girls, came to me. I was sitting on the edge of the bed, squeezed on either side by Neena and my friends. Someone draped a red *dupatta* over my head, drawing it down, hiding me from view. I lowered my head. I sensed Uncle coming, and I braced myself for the question: "*Do you, Sabeeha Akbar, daughter of Kazim Akbar, agree to marry . . . ?*" and I would shyly nod my head in assent.

Well, I gave this away at the beginning. Uncle walked up to me, gently placed the *nikah* papers in my lap, handed me a pen, and lovingly said, "Bia, dear, please sign here."

That is not the way it was supposed to be.
He is supposed to ask for my consent.
I am supposed to cry; then give my consent; then cry again.
I signed the papers.
Uncle left.

Then I cried. I had just signed my life away from my parents. I have photographs with my friends wiping my tears, teary-eyed themselves. I have photographs with my witnesses—my witnesses—signing the *nikah* form; I have photographs of the *maulvi* downstairs, saying the prayer and everyone's hands raised in prayer: prayer for the couple, for a joyful marriage, and for their welfare. My Americanized husband had not brought a skullcap and is seen trying to balance the handkerchief resting on his head.

Mubarak, I heard the cry of congratulations from below signaling that I was officially married.

I am married.

The girls clapped and cheered their congratulations. *Mubarak.* Someone brought in *chowaras* and threw them into the crowd. Girls raised their hands to grab the dried dates in their fists. Mummy walked in, and everyone parted as she walked up to me and gave me a hug. "*Khush raho*," she said, wishing me a joyous life.

More tears.

What happened next . . . does not happen. At least not in Pakistan in the 1970s.

Khalid walked right into my bedroom.

Facebook generation would say: OMG.

He was *not* supposed to be there. He was not *allowed* in there.

He had enlisted my distant, elder cousin Nasim's support to escort him through the enemy lines of my friends, pleading that he wanted to see "his wife." Nasim's heart melted (I told you Khalid had charm). Believing that as the elder, married woman, she had clout and authority, she led Khalid to my room, made her way through the crowd, walked up to me—Khalid in tow—lifted my veil, exposed my tear-stricken face, and before anyone could count to one, Khalid had leaned down, touched my cheek and was congratulating me, "Bia, *Mubarak Ho*."

All hell broke loose.

Someone threw the *dupatta* over me. Tallat screamed at Nasim, "What are you doing? You have ruined tomorrow's surprise."

"Khalid, leave this room, now. You cannot see the bride before the wedding."

"But she is my wife now. I can see her."

Khalid's protests and logic were drowned out by tradition and the screams of my friends. Cousin Nasim was intimidated out of the room, and they both retreated. Under the veil, I chuckled.

He wanted to see me.

No more tears.

Someone lifted my *dupatta*, and the photographer caught my chuckle.

For a long time I would kid Khalid. "I never said 'I do.'"

I never let Uncle know that he didn't ask for my consent. I presume he was overwhelmed with the logistics and excitement and just forgot. A decade later, the Princess of Wales would marry the wrong Charles. Millennials, did that confuse you? Let me explain: while taking wedding vows, the nervous bride Diana repeated Charles's names in the wrong order—Philip Charles Arthur George. You can catch it on YouTube.

Mehndi: Henna Painting, Music, and Laughter

"Come on down for the *mehndi* ceremony."

In a minute, they were all gone—Neena, my cousins, my friends. I heard the beating of the *dholak*, the clapping, and the singing of the girls *Jeevay banra*—the *mehndi* festivity had begun.

"Ready?" Neena and my cousins came to escort me.

Someone adjusted the *dupatta*, pulling it well over my head and below my forehead to veil my face, and held my hand (I was totally blinded by the veil), while another held me by the arm, and walked me down the stairs. As I started descending, the sound of the singing kept getting louder; I entered the drawing room—all lit up in colored lights; every inch on the rug was taken up by the girls, one playing the *dholak*, the others clapping and singing wedding songs in Urdu and Punjabi. As I entered, they quickly changed their beat to a chant: "Bia is here;

Bia is here." I lowered my head; my escorts navigated me through the crowded floor, taking care not to step on anyone's toes, and led me to the sofa, seating me next to what had to be a man. I could tell by the shoes and pants.

Is this Khalid?

The man said something, I can't remember what. *Yes it is. It's his voice.*

Why am I sitting beside him, almost touching, when we are not even married?

Oh, we are married.

Head bowed, I took my place, eyes lowered, and silent.

Now wasn't I supposed to feel something when our knees touched? Should I pull my knee away or let it rest. If I pull it away, the girls will notice and then have some fun at my expense. Maybe if I let it rest, he will pull away. Right!

Three round trays lit up with candles were placed at my feet. One with henna paste, sprinkled with red and silver foil confetti; the second with hair oil in a small bowl that was hand-painted in a floral design; and the third laden with yellow *ladoo* sweets displayed on sparkling red paper. Seven married women—the *suhagans*—from Khalid's family, lined up to paint my hand with henna, for good luck. I was not able to see through the veil, so upon prompting, I extended my palms, placing them in my lap. The girls started chanting in Urdu, "The bride's mother-in-law puts henna on her hands," and clapped to the beat as Auntie Hameeda, the eldest *suhagan*, opened the ceremony by lifting a pinch of henna from the first tray, and placing it on my palm. She then dipped her fingers in the tiny bowl of hair oil in the second tray and lifting my veil just a little, rubbed the oil on the tip of my hair. Last, she took a pinch of the *ladoo*—for sweetness and bounty in marriage, and gave me a bite. She opened her purse, pulled out a hundred rupee bill, circled it over my head three times to ward off the evil eye, and placed it in my lap. It would be given to charity the next day. Six other married aunties lined up to repeat the ceremony, and each time the girls would sing out, "The bride's aunt-in-law puts henna . . .," calling out each of the aunties as they repeated the ceremony. If it weren't for that,

I wouldn't know who was applying henna to my hands. All I saw were shoes and a hand.

This is my husband sitting next to me. Husband. Husband. He sounds happy.

Khalid's turn: a leaf was placed on his palm to prevent the henna from reddening his palm—imagine the explaining he would have to do when he returned to New York and examined a patient with painted hands. Seven *suhagans* from my family lined up, starting with the eldest—my maternal grandmother, then Mummy, and then my aunts; and the girls chanting, "The bride's grandmother . . . The bride's mother . . ." If you didn't know who was who, now you did. Khalid got the henna—on the leaf, the oil in his curly hair, the *ladoo* to taste, and, of course, the rupees in his lap.

The aroma of *pullao* flowed through the kitchen, but with all the *ladoo* tasting, I had lost my appetite.

The *suhagans* done, the single girls descended, and everyone got to do the routine. Daddy, uncles, and male cousins—they were there, in the background. This was my bachelorette party, and the ladies commanded the field.

I sat for over an hour now, next to Khalid, my head bent, looking into my lap. My neck was hurting; my back was stiff. And it was not fun watching everyone having a blast, singing and laughing, and me just a prop. The girls were kidding around with Khalid, and he was humoring them. Of course, he couldn't talk to me—a no-no; we are still not socially married—so, no talking.

I can feel him smile, and he has a nice laugh. I guess he is not a cologne or after-shave guy. I kind of wish I could take a peek at him, but a sideways glance would be too risky. If the girls caught me stealing a glance, they would roar it out to the world, and my in-laws would be mortified, not to mention a scolding by my mother.

No one noticed that I was fidgeting and shifting, trying to stretch. I must have bumped into Khalid. I bet he didn't mind. And that was the other thing. I was so, so conscious of him beside me, our knees touching. I stole a glance at his knee.

Nice pants.

"Bia, are you tired?" my friend Ruby asked.

Finally!

I nodded.

"Oh, poor thing. Do you want to go upstairs?"

I nodded.

"Oh, sweet!" they cooed. "Come, let's take her."

Holding my hands, they led me upstairs, my head bent, deposited me on the makeshift floor mattress that was laid out for me and my friends in the sunroom, and off they all went back down to join the party. Someone brought me dinner, and I sat alone. I had no appetite. Someone kept coming up to check on me and then rushing downstairs to join the fun. I don't recall if I said my prayers that night. I may have been too distracted. But if I did, I know what I would have prayed for. The singing and laughter continued long after I fell asleep. Sometime late at night, I was awakened when the girls came up to sleep, sardined around me on the floor, and continued their chatter—there was too much adrenaline flowing. I pretended to be asleep. I needed to be by myself with my thoughts.

Tomorrow by this time—Shhh! Just go to sleep.

Sweet dreams—watch it—not too sweet.

The next night, at this time, I was with Khalid.

3.

A Silver Watch
My Splendid Pakistani Wedding

November 22, 1971

I fell in love with my husband on the night we were married.

It wasn't his looks. He was handsome for sure—tall, dark, no less. It was his manner—the little things; how he talked, and how he felt when he spoke—that put me at ease. He wasn't romantic; that would have made me nervous. Listening to him talk, I felt myself relax. It was simple as that. Was it his sincerity, his compassionate side, or his thoughtful nature that warmed me to him? It is hard to tell. I remember that in that moment, this was the person I wanted to be with. And that is how it has been for the rest of our lives together. I am relaxed when I am with him, and in his own thoughtful and gentle way, he puts me at ease. I still love listening to him talk; and he loves to talk.

Our wedding was the stuff fantasies are made of. Honest! It was as if God had sat at the drafting board and chiseled out every detail to make it fit for me. It was the perfect gift—of a lifetime.

I wore red. My *gharara* of tissue fabric gave off a golden shimmer through the red. I wore all my jewelry, as was the custom. My friend Tasneem did my make-up—I was hopeless when it came to makeup. She pinned the *tikka* string into my hair, letting the gold pendant rest on my forehead. She draped the *dupatta*—a red-and-gold long veil over my head, tacked it on my shoulder, and showed me how to hold it over my arms. I wore gold bangles on my right wrist and a bracelet on my left.

With the *tikka* on my forehead and the *dupatta* draped over my head, I now looked the Bride.

Don't think about the wedding night. Just focus on being a bride.

"Bia, are you ready? The *baraat* has arrived, let's go." The groom's wedding party had arrived at Hotel Intercontinental, and guests had assembled. Uncle and auntie had come to get me.

Every bride remembers the moment when she made an entrance. I stepped out of the car; uncle and auntie held me by the arms and escorted me through the doors. My head lowered and veiled by the *dupatta,* I entered the hallway. I heard Daddy's voice, then Mummy's. I felt them hold me by the arms on either side and walk me down to the ballroom.

I will miss Mummy and Daddy.

I heard my friends running toward me. "Here she is, here she is."

I love them. How I will miss them!

I was led through the hallway to the tune of the brass band, down the aisle, and up the stage. I saw a gentleman's shoes and a pair of pants; and I sensed that person stand to receive me.

That must be Khalid.

I was seated, someone arranged my attire, and I felt Khalid take a seat beside me.

Nice shoes!

I heard Auntie Hameeda's voice, and felt her put a garland of roses over my bent head, draping down my shoulders. Fragrant and heavy. The next instant, I felt the stage crowded with family and friends.

"Lovely."

"Beautiful."

"So innocent looking."

"She is glowing."

"May they be happy together. *Ameen.*"

Cameras snapped—the Kodak film cameras. Khalid had brought a camera with slide film and had charged his brother Arshed with taking photographs. Arshed, with an eye for photography, took beautiful pictures, and for decades, often when we had a gathering, we would put up the slide show. Thank you, Arshed, for your lasting gift. I now have these slides converted into a DVD and they often play on my TV screen. But we have no videos of the wedding—this was 1971. That's OK.

Someone brought a large mirror to the stage. With our garlands removed, we were made to face one another, the mirror was placed, face up, between us, and we were asked to look down into the mirror. An old tradition, *Arsi Mushuf* was the ritual where the bride and groom saw one another for the first time through the mirror. Of course, Khalid and I had seen each other, but tradition prevailed. I saw Khalid in a dark blue suit and a dark blue necktie. Arshed took a photo of our reflection in the mirror—Khalid is smiling. To this day, I love seeing Khalid in a dark blue suit.

"Thank you," I heard Khalid say to my grandparents as they handed him the *salami*, a cash gift that the bride's family gives to the groom, to welcome him in the family.

"Thank you," to my parents.

"Thank you," to auntie and uncle.

"Thank you," "thank you," "thank you."

Getting rich? Wait till the next ceremony, Khalid. You will lose your shirt.

Khalid lost his shoe.

Neena and my girl cousins seated themselves on the rug at Khalid's feet and in the blink of an eye, got hold of his shoe and pulled it off. Now they were demanding ransom. This was *Joota chupai*—a tradition where the sisters of the bride won't let the groom take the bride away until he buys back his shoe.

"I will give you a hundred rupees for it," Khalid said.

"No way," my friends had joined the looters. "We want at least a thousand rupees."

"I will give you five hundred," Khalid negotiated.

"No way," they shrieked.

The elders smiled, and the girls bargained away. I was enjoying this, smiling under the veil. Finally, Khalid pulled out an envelope, handed it to the girls, and then handed out tiny jewelry boxes to Neena and my cousins. He had come prepared. My friend Tallat opened the envelope and gaped.

"All this for us!"

Khalid nodded.

She reached out and took his face in her hands and shouted, "I love you!"

Smile.

Somewhere during that time dinner was served. My dear, dear out-of-town-married-friends showed up. One by one, they lifted my veil, peered under it, I saw their face, smiled at them, and then the veil was dropped. I got warm hugs—but I couldn't tell whom from. All I could see was shoes. I would peek out when I thought no one was watching. Later, looking through photographs, I could tell who was there, what they wore.

Sometimes after dinner, someone lifted up my veil and told me to raise my head.

Thank God.

My neck had started to hurt.

Ah, I get it. Group photos are being taken. Makes no sense if you can't see the bride's face. Right!

I, of course, kept my eyes lowered, but unlike many brides, kept my eyes open. I mean, literally.

The band started playing "Auld Lang Syne."

"It's time for you to go," Mummy said, coming up to me.

So this is when I will cry.

I was ready to cry, but the moment never came.

Khalid stood up with me, and Mummy and Auntie Hameeda started escorting me out of the ballroom. Photos show Khalid, Aba Jee, Daddy, and Uncle Rehman behind and all the rest in a procession trailing; my friends lined up showering rose petals as I pass; my maternal uncle, Jedi Mamoon, holding a copy of the Qur'an over my head.

"Slow down," Mummy said.

I walk too fast. Mummy had been warning me all along that when it is time for my *rukhsati*—the time the bride departs—I should be mindful and walk, not run. "A bride should walk in dignity and be in no rush to run off," she had told me.

I slowed down.

We reached the doors on the left, leading out, where I expected a car would be waiting, and before I sat in the car, I would hug my parents good-bye, and break down in tears. Every bride did that. And at every friend's wedding, I would cry at that "car moment"; and each time I knew that when my time came, I would fall apart, sob my heart out, and not let go of Mummy and Daddy. That dreaded moment had arrived, and my tears had already started to well up.

Mummy turned me right.

What's going on? The doors are on the left. Where are we going?

The procession stopped at the elevator.

Are they taking me straight up to the bridal suite? Whatever happened to the good-bye in the car? My send-off?

I don't want to leave without crying!

The elevator door opened, and I was led inside, Khalid too, standing right in front of me.

We are going up. What about my send-off—my tearful good-bye? The car scene!

Doors opened, I was led into the hallway, passed the threshold, into the bridal suite, and deposited onto the sofa.

I guess this is it.

Oh well!

At least I could see around me, with my *dupatta* no longer veiling my face. There was pitter-patter; someone was checking out the suite; each time the elevator door opened, more family came in; and then all my friends. The suite was full of chatter. In that moment, I felt a longing to be alone with Khalid. I was ready. And in a few minutes, everyone was gone. Daddy was the last to leave.

Khalid was to tell me later that when he saw Daddy to the door, Daddy gave him a bear hug, held him tight, held on, and then quickly left.

Dear Daddy!

Now, I will pause.

If you are looking forward to a detailed description of what followed, you might as well stop reading and go no further. But if you continue, I promise, you won't be disappointed.

There are moments in your life you never forget.

Khalid walked toward the sofa and sat down next to me.

"Bia, I have a present for you." He pulled out a watch.

A silver watch.

How much stuff was he carrying in his suit pockets anyhow?

"Thank you," I remember saying, and smiling.

It was delicate, stylish, and sparkling. I tried to put it on.

"May I?" He leaned forward.

I smiled again. I watched him put the watch on my left wrist, pushing my bangles aside.

"It's pretty," I said, keeping my eyes on the watch, too shy to look at him.

Khalid started talking.

And then I looked up. He kept talking, about the wedding, how well it went, stuff like that; and I kept listening, watching his face. He talked about America, what life is like, what it will be like for me, and just— stuff. I don't remember much of what he said. I only remember how it made me feel. I was charmed.

It must have been hours, or maybe not.

The more I listened to him talk, the more at ease I felt; the more I warmed up to him; and by the end of the evening, I was falling in love. I have loved him deeply since that first night. He is my soul mate, my best friend, my companion; he is my source of energy, inspiration, and motivation; from him I seek comfort, solace, and joy; and with him, I am calm and at ease. We grew together to fill our life with adventure; were blessed with two beautiful sons; and are now basking in the delightful company of four grandchildren. Aba Jee was right; grandpa knows best.

I wore the silver watch for decades. Forty-four years later, when I started writing this chapter, I was startled. OMG! Whatever happened to that silver watch? I stopped typing and went running for my jewelry box. It wasn't there. Maybe it got used up and I discarded it? I couldn't have! It must be somewhere.

It was nowhere.

"I will get you another silver watch," Khalid said.

"But it won't be the same. I don't need another watch. I want *my* silver watch."

And we left it at that.

Months later, when Khalid needed to replace the battery in his watch, we stopped by the SWATCH store in Grand Central Terminal. While he waited for the technician to put in the battery, I hung around, casually checking the stock. A watch caught my eye, and I held it. I draped it on my wrist. I looked at it again.

"Did you find your silver watch?"

"I just did."

4.

Marital Advice

Marital advice was coming in droves. This was Pakistan, where unsolicited, free advice is in abundance. The elder ladies of the family, the aunties, friends of aunties, and friends of friends of aunties, impart years and years of earned wisdom to the bride.

"Give a portion of your money to charity every month," Daadee Amma said.

"Don't use birth control. It leads to infertility," auntie pulled me into a quiet room and whispered.

"Here is a recipe book for you"—another auntie.

I am embarrassed to say that I don't recall most of the pearls of wisdom, but what Khalid's father had to say has stuck with me. The night before we were to depart for America, he sat us both down. The room was crowded with family—this was no one-on-one counseling.

First, the preamble:

"You are both sensible people, so I trust you to . . ." I don't recall precisely, but it had something to do with trusting us to be sensible in our dealing with one another. "And now I want to give you both a piece of advice." He turned toward Khalid.

"Khalid, my son. Every month when you bring home your salary, hand over the entire amount to your wife."

"Acha Jee," Khalid nodded dutifully.

"And second," he said, looking at us. "Don't argue with each other."

Over the decades, I have pondered over the wisdom of his words. A conservative Muslim man of a patriarchal society, asking Khalid to trust his wife, trust her with all his earnings, his hard-earned earnings from standing on his feet for sometimes thirty-six hours at a stretch, dealing with the stresses of life and death. He was expressing his confidence in me to honor that trust. He was asking us both to put respect for one another above all. He was defining the boundary beyond which words can chip away and diminish the level of respect.

Asking married couples not to argue is not as tall an order as it seems. Try it. When you see the tone shifting from a discussion toward a possible argument, stop. Just stop.

It works.

PART TWO

A Pakistani Muslim in New York

5.

A Pakistani Bride in New York
"I Wouldn't Do That If I Were You"

December 3, 1971. Amsterdam Airport en route to New York
"War has broken out in Pakistan," the Pan Am official at the gate informed us. "Your flight was the last to leave the country."

Did a bomb just drop on me!

Oh God, NO!

What war?

India, she explained.

It can't be! How did a civil war in East Pakistan lead to war with India? Did Daddy get sent off to war? My uncles too? Will Rawalpindi get bombed? Mummy and auntie must be panicking. Dear God, please, please, please keep them safe. Please end this war. Please.

As we followed the official, I felt myself stagger. I had stepped onto a path without realizing that it was moving—my first step into the world of moving platforms, escalators, and sliding doors. I felt Khalid hold my arm to steer me off the platform. I moved in a daze; my moment of wonder and awe snatched away.

Did I run over to the first public telephone? No. This was December 1971, and this E.T. couldn't "phone home." An overseas call had to be booked weeks in advance. I would have to wait to get to New York and hope to receive a telegram.

It was less than seven hours ago that I had left my family standing at Rawalpindi airport, waving good-bye in the morning sun. Then turning back again to wave. Sitting next to Khalid, flying into a new future, my hopes soared as the plane rose. I saw the rooftops descending, my home being pulled away.

Where on top of the world was I when war broke out?

Two years later when I visited Pakistan, Daddy told me that when he waved me good-bye, war had already broken out, and he had known that he was sending his little girl off on the last flight out.

New York, New York

The Pan Am flight descended through the clouds, and the waters of Jamaica Bay glistened in the afternoon sun. Dollhouses appeared, with slanting rooftops, rows and rows of them.

Is that New York? I don't see the skyscrapers? This looks like the countryside in the movies.

"When we get home, we have to go out and get some groceries for dinner," Khalid told me as the plane descended into JFK.

That didn't sound appetizing. Good-bye comfy life in Pakistan; no more Aurangzeb to buy groceries; no more Razia to cook dinner.

Khalid's friends were at the airport to receive us, one of them with his American fiancée, who quickly put out her hand to show Khalid her ring.

I guess American girls are not shy.

"Hi," she greeted me.

"Hello," I replied. "Hi" was too American for the British in me. Did I mention that Pakistan was once a British colony and part of India? In Pakistan, we spoke the Queen's English.

Looking back at that day, I am grateful for their generosity. They gave up their Sunday, drove to the airport to welcome me and drive us home. They were all resident physicians with a grueling schedule. It was the Pakistani hospitality. The fiancée, she was to tell me later, was also curious—who is this girl who Khalid married without knowing her; she had expected to see a girl with long hair, sweeping to her knees.

The roads are so clean, smooth, and wide. . . . So many road signs; so many cars moving fast in straight lines; roads turning into bridges over roads; a left light blinking at the tail when a car changes lanes (that's a great idea); such big cars, but no convertibles as in the movies. No horns honking. Why was there only one person in each car? Such big cars could pack in two families, right? Why don't I see any skyscrapers? I suppose American girls are not demure—for a fiancée, she is rather chatty.

As we approached what I later learned was Jamaica, it started to feel crowded and the buildings grew taller, but not in a glitzy way—rather drab. The car pulled up in front of a tall building.

"Would you like to come in?" Khalid asked them.

The fiancée declined—something about another engagement. *For a fiancée, she is pretty much running the show. I guess that's America.*

It was a walk-up. The stairwells were scribbled with odd designs. *But this is America! More civilized. Why are they scribbling on walls?*

Khalid opened the door to the apartment, and I froze. Two of his friends had gotten there ahead of us to bring our suitcases and stood there in the apartment with stuff strewn around, trying to make room to place the bags. My face must have said it all; so did their apologetic looks.

No carrying over the threshold for me.

They handed Khalid the keys and said their good-byes. Khalid said something about having to leave in a rush with no time to tidy up. A sofa against one wall; a tiny table with two chairs at the other wall—which I guessed was the dining table; a closet against the third; a kitchen against the fourth; and in the corner, a door leading to the bathroom.

Where is the sleeping area?

The blushing bride was too embarrassed to ask.

This was to be my new home; but at that moment I felt like a guest.

The apartment was warm—actually a bit hot for a December afternoon. How did it get hot so quick—his friends had arrived only minutes before us? Khalid explained central heating to me. *What a luxury!* And that the apartment had stayed heated all the time he was in Pakistan. *What a waste!*

"Let's go get groceries," Khalid reminded me.

Ah yes, groceries. No rest for the weary bride.

Khalid walked me across the street to what he called the Super Market.

Is this Super indeed! That much food! Even the supermarket is centrally heated.

Khalid pulled out a cart.

"What is this for?" I asked.

"For our groceries."

That big a cart just for food?

No one welcomed us at the supermarket. There was no owner to greet us. No one saying, "Hello, you are back, this must be your bride...."

All this food!

Khalid sped over to a section that said "Dairy." "We need milk."

I picked up a carton. It felt cool. I could feel the blast of cool air coming from the back. It was an open refrigerator.

Beats having fresh milk delivered daily, warm off the cow. But isn't this open refrigerator such a waste? Daddy always used to say, "Don't open the fridge door and just stand there; it's a waste of electricity."

"Let's get this one. It has Vitamin D in it." I tried to impress.

Khalid played along, and put it in the cart.

The eggs are not lying loose in a pile but are in this box with egg holders. That's smart; they won't break. But I wonder how one can make use of the boxes after the eggs are eaten.

"We don't need a *dozen* eggs," I said.

"That is how they sell them."

Oh.

Khalid picked up a couple of onions—perfectly round without blemishes.

How do they make them perfectly round? The apples are labeled "delicious." All that canned food—potatoes, beets, corn, peas—peas—I won't have to labor over shelling pea pods.

As I turned around the bend, it suddenly got freezing cold.

Even the sign says "Frozen Section." An entire wall lined with freezers. So many kinds of ice cream! Now if the frozen section can have doors on the freezer, why can't the refrigerated section?

Khalid swooped out Butter Pecan.

"My favorite," he said

Butter?

No one in the supermarket is talking with one another. All these people in one place but shopping alone. Maybe they are in a hurry.

Khalid rolled the cart to a counter to pay the bill.

Why isn't he bargaining? I guess the marked prices are not negotiable. All the sales people are ladies. The salesgirl isn't chatting with us; she didn't even greet us. Rather unfriendly—just got right down to business. Instead of writing out the prices on a piece of paper, she is pressing buttons on a machine, and it's adding the numbers. Great idea! This way you don't make mistakes, unless of course you enter the incorrect price. She must have a lot of practice—see her fingers fly.

Putting the groceries in a large brown paper bag, she handed it to Khalid. That was the most silent transaction I had ever encountered.

Who is going to carry the bag home for us?

Dummy, this is not Pakistan.

The war was on my mind when we walked back home. I noticed a woman on the street.

Poor woman, her jeans are torn at the knees. Another woman with tattered jeans! A lot of poor in this neighborhood.

Khalid asked me to freshen up, relax, write my letters, and he will make dinner for me.

He will make dinner for me? But he is a gentleman.

We put away the groceries, and as I took out the carton of milk, I asked Khalid where I could find a large saucepan. Asking no questions, he handed me one. I took the milk carton and tried to open it, as I held it over the saucepan.

"Let me open it for you." He pulled open the spout.

The carton has a spout!

"We have to boil the milk." I was taking charge.

Khalid must have smiled.

"Here in America, the milk is pasteurized."

Oh again.

I sat at the table and wrote to Mummy and Daddy, totally distracted in the presence of a gentleman cooking. This was a first for me—seeing a gentleman peel an onion. Watching him gently, caringly, peel away the layers, crack the eggshells, sprinkle the seasoning, stir the eggs—I loved him.

Why did he do that? He had just torn off a piece of something from a roll, wiped the counter, and thrown whatever it was, in the rubbish ("garbage" will follow). Just threw it away. Then he did it again. *He is wasting it.* After dinner, he wiped out the leftovers and threw them in the rubbish—sorry, garbage.

"Why are you throwing away food? On the Day of Judgment you will be made to pick up every wasted morsel with your eyes." That is what I believed happened to people who waste food.

"Here if you start picking up every discarded morsel with your eyes, you will never stop."

Oh.

I curled up next to him on the sofa as he went through his mail.

Look at how many people write to him.

He was doing it again, throwing away envelopes and their contents in the garbage.

"Why are you throwing away letters people write to you?"

He had to explain "junk mail" to his Pakistani, just-off-the-plane bride.

Seems like such a waste, all that good paper.

Ready for bed?

Yes, but where?

The closet door opened and out flipped the bed.

Wow!

How clever!

Americans are so clever ("smart" will follow).

I Wouldn't Do That If I Were You

It was my first morning in New York. Khalid gave me directions to the post office, some cash, and keys and took off for work. Just as all newly-wed brides, I put on my shimmering outfit, gold jewelry, golden pumps, golden evening purse ("pocketbook" will follow) and stepped out into the crime-ridden streets of Jamaica, walking on air. I was off to the post office.

Stopping for directions, which passersby graciously offered, I made it to the post office. I fumbled with my change. *The small coin says,*

"Dime"; the large coin says, "Five Cents"; so the smaller dime must be less than five cents in value, right?

"Just give me the nickel." He was patient.

Nickel? I just put the change on the counter and let him pick whatever a nickel was.

If a ten-cent coin reads, "Dime," then why doesn't a five-cent coin say, "Nickel"? And why is five larger in size than ten?

Ah, a drugstore. Let me see what they have. A nice old man with spectacles ("eyeglasses" will follow), behind the counter, beamed at me with a benevolent smile.

"You must be new in town," he said, giving me a grandfatherly look.

"Yes."

"A bride?"

"Yes."

"I can always tell a bride. She has that starry-eyed look." Now he was talking to some little old ladies already in the shop ("store" will follow).

"Young lady," he said, turning toward me. "I wouldn't be walking around the streets of New York with a pocketbook in hand."

I am not carrying a pocket-sized book, or any book for that matter.

"A pocketbook?"

He pointed toward my golden purse.

Americans have ruined the English language. How does "purse" translate into "pocketbook"?

"Why not?" I can picture the naïve look on my face.

"Because you will get mugged."

"Mugged?" Remember, the British say "robbed."

He smiled.

"Someone will snatch it."

Horror.

"New York is a decaying city. No one is safe walking the streets."

Did I walk home, or did I run in shoes not meant for running?

"Khalid, why didn't you tell me?" Khalid got an earful when he returned.

"I had no idea you would get all dressed up."

"Brides get dressed up."

In Pakistan, not in America. And certainly not on the streets of Jamaica, Queens.

This is not the America I had seen in movies and TV serials.

That evening we received two telegrams. "We are all OK. Do not worry."

I worried.

In the days to follow, Pakistan suffered a humiliating defeat—lost half its territory. East Pakistan was now Bangla Desh, my cousin was a prisoner-of-war, and the country went into a downward tailspin. It never recovered. The glorious era of the sixties was over. Over the next many days, months, years, and decades, I would be confronted with the escalating anti-Pakistan sentiment in the media and political arena. The pain I felt for my motherland, the guilt at having abandoned it, the love for the promise it held remained potent. In due time, we would become active in promoting Pakistani culture in the US, but remain conflicted over the shifting boundaries of cultural assimilation.

In the forty years that followed, I would make over twenty trips to Pakistan. I buried Daddy, then Mummy, and I still go back.

But in those early years as I reeled from culture shock, spun around in dizzying confusion, I felt my identity slipping away. The hardest part in those first few months was surviving the unflattering inquiries about my culture and my homeland.

6.

Where Are You From?

Where Are You From?

Forty-four years later, I am still asked this question.

Fresh off the plane, I would say with pride, "Pakistan."

"Where is that?"

Insulted.

"Is it in the Middle East?"

Shocked.

Isn't this the most advanced country? Don't they study geography in school? I was ten when we would play capitals of the world. I had a world map on my bedroom wall, and we friends would trace our fingers over it, gathering the capitals of new nations in Africa. And Americans have never heard of Pakistan!

I was unable to reconcile ignorance with progress.

It got worse.

I was reeling with grief when Pakistan lost the war, while TV anchormen were delirious in their Pakistan-bashing rhetoric.

Whoever coined the phrase "add insult to injury" must have experienced what I am going through.

The next time someone asked me, "Where are you from?"

"Pakistan."

"Ah! The ones who lost the war."

We did lose the war; so what am I to say? Get into a discourse on "this was a war that could not have been won" with a passerby on the street?

I couldn't be rude and say, "Guess who is losing the war in Vietnam."
Where is the culture of consideration of the other's feelings? Americans are
honest, and I appreciate that, but this is being blunt with a sharp-edged
sword. At least I know what they are thinking.

I was now labeled a loser.

How Could You!

"How could you! How could you marry someone you didn't know?"
She shook her head, narrowing her eyes.

I had been in America only a few weeks, when an American wife of
Khalid's Pakistani colleague confronted me.

Insulted again.

"Why not?" I raised my voice. I tried explaining that this is our way
of life. . . . We don't date. . . . Parents know best. . . . Besides, love is blind,
and love marriages end up in failure. . . . Arranged marriages dignify the
girl, who is sought after. . . . It has its charm.

"I don't see what's charming about it. You girls don't have any individuality. You are led to the altar and you just go along."

Can't American women argue without being rude? I am not going
to tell her what I think about women sleeping with men out of wedlock.
That would be rude. Besides, I am sure she is not that kind of a girl.

"Do I look devoid of individuality? Do I look unhappy in marriage?"

"Well you just got lucky."

"And all the other Pakistani wives around you, did they also just
get lucky?" I argued that it is our mindset. We go into marriage with an
attitude that has been cultivated through conditioning and culture—
that we are going to make our marriage work. And then we work at it.
Somewhere along the line, we grow to love one another.

"It's weird." She shook her head.

Uhhh!

On the way home, Khalid asked me why I looked so upset.

"She insulted me, insulted our traditions."

Khalid laughed, rubbed his hand through my hair, one hand off
the steering wheel. "Don't let her get to you. Just understand that she
doesn't understand."

I was still fuming when I got home.

I wish I could tell her what I think of their culture, but it wouldn't be polite. Besides, I am a guest in her house. I cannot insult my host. And if she comes visiting me, I still can't say it because now she would be a guest in my house and I cannot insult my guest.

"It's OK." Khalid ruffled his hand through my hair. I loved it when he did that. He still does, and I still do.

Two score and four years later, I am still asked this question, only now it is phrased delicately, almost in a complimentary tone. "Tell me about the wisdom of arranged marriages," someone recently asked. And I have learned to be more understanding and less defensive.

Sleepovers

Dr. Zhivago was playing at the movies. Omar Sharif and Julie Christie kiss passionately; the scene changes, and they are in bed, clothes off.

I gasp.

But they are not married! And they are showing this on the screen!

I felt myself tighten. I felt people watching me through the darkness of the movie theater. I flushed at the thought of Khalid knowing that I had seen a man, half-undressed, in bed with a woman, also bare shouldered. Later I talked about how gorgeous the photography was, how sad the story was . . . and pretended that the bed scene never happened.

Another movie. *Love Story*. There they go again. In bed, out of wedlock.

Is this how it is in America? Or is it just in the movies? I can't ask Khalid. It's too embarrassing.

I was watching *Dating Game* on TV. A man and a woman, who have never met, are paired up to go off to go on vacation.

An out-of-wedlock vacation? Maybe it's just a game.

One evening Khalid and I visited one of his Pakistani friends, a doctor. His American girlfriend was there. We chatted, had tea. As we were leaving, and they both walked us to the door, Khalid asked her, "Are you leaving too?"

"I am staying," she said.

Staying where?

That night, I asked Khalid.

"She said she was staying. He has only one bedroom. Where is she going to sleep? On the couch?"

"With him." Khalid was incredulous, like, what a question.

"NO!"

"Bia, this is America. Girlfriends and boyfriends sleep together."

"But *he* is not American. Pakistani boys don't do such things."

"Well, he is Americanized."

"But this is a betrayal of one's culture. How could he! I am not sure if I want to visit him again. You see, if I socialize with them, I will feel that I am endorsing such behavior."

"Bia!" Khalid looked at me lovingly, with a get-real look.

We did continue to visit him and other Pakistani friends with their girlfriends, sleepovers notwithstanding. I was getting assimilated, and I didn't like it. But I had made up my mind.

I am not raising my children here. If mature Pakistani men, who grew up in Pakistan, with Pakistani values, can veer off-course, what hope do I have for children who are raised in America? We are going back after two years.

No Titles of Respect Here

Tremors: a neighbor's child addresses my husband by his first name, not "uncle."

That is disrespectful. You never call an elder by their first name. It's "uncle" or "auntie" for an adult; and "baji" or "bhai jan" for anyone older than you. Come to think of it, there is no equivalent title of respect in the English language for elder sibling. Whenever my grandfather entered a room, Mummy would cover her hair with her dupatta, *and Uncle would stand up and quickly extinguish his cigarette out of respect.*

Decades later, Khalid now a senior attending physician, could still not bring himself to call the director of medicine by his first name. He always addressed him as Dr. Bloomfield, never Dennis. I was an assistant vice president at Interfaith Medical Center, when the CEO, sitting across the desk from me, said, "What is this Mr. Jamison thing?! Call me Ted."

"OK, Mr. Jamison."

I never could call him Ted. He was older than me, senior to me.

Old and Alone

Aftershocks: my neighbor told me that her mother lives in a nursing home.

"What is a nursing home?" I asked Khalid that evening. I had been too embarrassed to ask my neighbor, lest this foreigner appear ignorant.

Khalid explained.

"They leave their parents in an old peoples' home in the hands of strangers? Why don't they take care of them at home, just like we do in Pakistan?"

Khalid explained that here women work and there is no twenty-four-hour live-in household help. It's not practical.

I don't want to grow old here.

Four decades later, I flew back to Pakistan to take care of my father, terminally ill with leukemia. Even as I tried to talk Daddy into coming to the US for medical treatment—after all, Khalid is an oncologist—I could tell the weakness in my argument. He was enveloped by all the comforts that America could not buy: a house full of family, children, grandchildren, extended family down the block; live-in domestic help of loyal, long-time Aurangzeb and Razia; someone to drive him, someone to help him out of the car, someone to park the car; friends coming and going, and Daddy relishing their company. He never had a moment alone. I watched his end-of-life days in heaven. *What will it be like for me when I am dying of cancer, alone in my apartment in New York?*

Terrorists

I switch on the TV. "Muslim terrorists blew up . . . Muslim suicide bombers . . . Islamic terrorists . . ."

My religion has no respect in this country. Their point of reference for Islam is terrorism. What will this do to the self-esteem of my yet-to-be-born children?! I cannot raise my children here.

Anonymous

No one knows me; no one knows my family name; no one knows that I can sing; that I was the head girl in college; or that my mother stitches beautiful clothes. No one knows where I came from or cares. I am a foreigner.

Yet . . .

I am falling in love with America. I won't be swept away. I will enjoy it to the fullest for the next two years and then return to Pakistan for good. I am not letting my parents down. I will go back.

Yet, my love grew into respect and I ended up marrying America. I marveled at the ease of "getting things done"; the absence of corruption (in daily activities); the culture of honesty (even though it felt rude at times); having a clean life (despite the polluted air); the dignity of labor (the mailman owned a car); the opportunity to be anything you wanted (not just doctor or engineer); the freedom to express oneself (even though the press sometimes went too far); and the sheer excitement in the air.

In less than a year, I had decided to make America my home, and "these Americans" became "my fellow Americans."

7.

A Muslim Girl in New York
A Holiday Muslim

Why is it that when it comes to celebrating holidays, we suddenly find religion? Is it possible to transplant a Pakistani-style holiday in New York?

January 1972
At first it seemed as though I was the only Muslim on the streets of New York. If they didn't look like me, didn't speak like me, they weren't Muslim. I have since forgiven myself for my stereotyping. Nowhere were the sounds and sights to be found—the muezzin's call to prayer, *Allah-o-Akbar*; the minarets of the mosques towering above the sky-line; signs displaying Qur'anic verses of prayer in Arabic calligraphy; the greetings of *Assalam Alaikum*; the good-byes—*Allah Hafiz*, God willing, and *Insha'Allah*; and I am embarrassed to say I didn't miss it, so distracted was I by the excitement of discovering New York all dressed up in Christmas lights, so self-absorbed in making a blissful new life and being deeply, totally, wholeheartedly in love. Standing by the window, waiting to see Khalid's blue Maverick pull up to the curb; watching him look up to the window, flashing his gleaming white teeth; rushing to open the door for him; these moments were all I cared to live for. I was a bride in heaven, and the only place religion had in my life in those first few months was saying the night prayer before going to bed, and, of course, the holidays. That is, before I found out that I was pregnant.

But first, the holidays.

It was the festival of Eid-ul-Adha, the holiday commemorating Prophet Abraham's willingness to sacrifice his son at God's command (the directive was rescinded) and to mark the annual hajj (pilgrimage). This was my first Eid with Khalid, and I wanted it to be special. The yearning to capture the spirit and the celebration of Eid was intense.

The bleating goats and lambs are paraded through the markets of Pakistan, as buyers line up to select the sacrificial lamb. It must be at least one year old, healthy, and not disabled. Buyers are seen stretching open the mouths of the lamb, counting teeth to confirm their age. In our backyard in Rawalpindi, the lamb is stringed to a hook in the wall, and for the next many weeks, is fed, fattened, petted, caressed, talked to, played with, and sometimes even given a name by the children. I get to love that woolly thing, its sad bleating a reminder of the countdown to Eid. On the morning of Eid, the butcher comes to the house, sharpens his knife on the stone slab, and—with the servants holding the lamb down—says a prayer asking God's permission before he slaughters the lamb. The darling lamb is sacrificed. Children weep.

A child of the tender age of eight, unable to comprehend the slaughter, I had asked Daddy, "Why?"

Eid was not an official holiday in the US—still isn't. That was a first for me—a holiday without a holiday! There was no way I could have survived Eid if Khalid had not taken the day off. Once again, his friend Izhar, chief resident, saved the day. He had worked it out in advance—the Muslim doctors worked Christmas and got Eid off; but it was taken out of their vacation days. OK, so Khalid had the day off, but how do I create the festivity? How do I recreate the traditions? It's not as if I had a lamb tied to a pole in my nonexistent backyard. Nor was Khalid going to be walking down the block to the nonexistent mosque. No Mummy or Daddy to give me a hug; no family we could go visiting; no neighbors to stop by; no families to distribute meat to.

But I did have friends.

I got on the phone. "Eid celebration is at my apartment," I invited them all. "Come dressed in your finest of finest." I got that squared away—we wouldn't be alone.

Daddy explains that it teaches us to make sacrifices, to give up what we love, and to share with the poor and others what is dear to us.

The butcher ties the hind legs of the poor dead lamb and hangs it on a tree limb in the backyard, allowing the blood to drain out, the dirt below absorbing it. He places himself on a stool, skillfully stripping off the skin into one whole furry piece, which he will keep for himself and sell at a handsome price. He places large portions of the pink meat on the gray stone slab, slicing, chopping. The bones and fat are put in a container for the stray cats and dogs. He makes three portions of the lamb meat: one for charity; one for family, friends, and neighbors; and one for us, the household. Aurangzeb pays him, and then he is off to the next house, for the next slaughter.

Early that morning, before the butcher arrives, Daddy and my brother Salman, in freshly laundered and starched white shalwar kameez, *head out to the community Eid Gah for Eid prayers. Mummy gets the house ready, supervising the help. A hand-embroidered beige tablecloth is draped over the dining table; Razia has cooked up a feast; Aurangzeb has arranged the table with* sheer khorma, *carefully layering the vermicelli dish with* warq—*the shiny paper-thin layer of pounded silver—and ribbon sandwiches before accompanying Daddy for prayers. By the time Daddy and all the male members return, we are all dressed up in our new, brightly colored* shalwar kameez, *ready to receive Daddy.*

"Eid Mubarak," Daddy calls out, wishing everyone a blessed Eid.

"Khair mubarak, jeetey raho." Daadee Amma says a prayer for their long life, opens her arms, and gives Daddy and Salman a hug.

Now, what do we do about Eid prayers? Can't have Eid without prayers. There was no mosque in New York. Khalid solved that one. Apparently, there was a Muslim organization in New York that had organized Eid prayers at the Americana Hotel (now Sheraton, Times Square) in Manhattan.

"We will leave at 7:00 a.m. for Eid prayers," Khalid announced.

"We? But women don't go to the mosque!" I didn't catch myself in time.

"We are not going to a mosque."

"But women don't go to Eid prayers."

"Here they do."

"Oh!"

I suppose there is nothing wrong with that. I mean—it's prayer. Actually, I wonder what that would be like—women at Eid prayers. Wait till I tell Mummy and Daddy.

"Eid Mubarak," we all squeal and run down to Daddy's arms. Daddy opens his wallet and hands us our eidee—*crisp rupee bills for each of us. We gleefully count the money and rush off to stash it away. We dig into the* sheer khorma, *fishing for the coconut shavings, sliced almonds, and oversized raisins, and slurp away as we try to suck in the last strand of vermicelli, inhaling the aroma of rosewater.*

It was a cold January morning, and I got all dressed up for Eid in my pale blue *gharara* with silver embroidery, a trailing *dupatta* with silver trimmings, and silver shoes, and got onto the subway. It was Eid, and no one was going to talk me out of getting dressed up. I did yield to Khalid's caution against wearing jewelry when riding the subways—this was 1972, and New York did not rate well on crime statistics. Khalid dressed "regular"—a suit. The trip to Manhattan took some doing. We had moved to a one-bedroom garden apartment in Glen Oaks at the farthest end of Queens, bordering Long Island. Grand Central Parkway was bumper-to-bumper on this weekday morning; we parked at the subway station somewhere in Queens where our Pakistani friends were waiting for us, took the train into Manhattan, and walked through the then-seedy Times Square, cluttered with peep-show posters, to the ballroom of the Americana Hotel. Not many subway riders took notice of my flowing, glittering outfit, and when they did gawk, I took it as a compliment. Inside, Khalid escorted me to the "ladies' section" in the back before making his way to the men's section up front. There were fewer than twenty ladies. *Why are ladies in the back? Why am I not with Khalid?* I don't remember the details of my introduction to congregational prayer; I do remember that the ballroom was huge, with crystal chandeliers and gold and red carpeting, and was full with people. Khalid later told me that people had come from all over the Tri-State area. I lingered alone in that cluster of ladies with unfamiliar faces. Khalid's friends were either single or had married American women who had embraced Islam but had chosen not to join the prayers. I was too shy to start a conversation, a trait that has endured. My glittering attire finally got attention, and a few Pakistani-looking women called out, asking if I was a newlywed. Smiling demurely, I said yes. I was hoping the question would be a prelude to an introduction, a dialogue, and we would part having exchanged phone numbers.

"That's nice."

And they moved on.

The tea trolley is wheeled out and stocked for the guests—tea set on the top tray, quarter plates and forks on the lower tray, and samosas, kebabs, and jelebi *on the lowest tray. When guests arrive, hugging us with greetings of "Eid Mubarak," Razia pours steaming tea in the preheated teapot and hot milk in the milk pot, and covers the teapot with the tea cozy. Aurangzeb wheels the trolley in the drawing room, placing it in front of Mummy, who with oh such grace pours out the tea for the guests after it has steeped for ten minutes, and the tea cozy, decked in round mirrors sparkling as they catch the sunrays filtering in the drawing room, has been gently removed. "How much sugar?" she asks, as I hand out the quarter plates and embroidered napkins, balancing the forks, and Neena serves the crisp samosas. The elder ladies are served first, then the elder men, followed by the younger ladies, and then younger men, and finally, the children. We, the hosts, are the last to help ourselves.*

Aurangzeb is busy in the backyard, apportioning the meat into plastic bags, and will soon start making the rounds in the neighborhood, distributing meat. Razia watches the gate, handing out meat packs to the poor who have lined up. She has already stocked the household's one-third share of the meat and has quickened her pace to start cooking it. The kitchen smells of a butcher shop. Freezer space will be taken up by meat we receive from family, friends, and neighbors. Razia is busy socializing, exchanging greetings with the neighborhood help who stop by to deliver meat and trading neighborhood happenings. We inevitably end up with two-thirds of the lamb meat—neighbor's share replaced by our share of the neighbor's.

As soon as there is a lull in between visitors, we pile up in the car and go visiting. The elders in the family are the first stop; we leave with our purses fattened with eidees. By the end of the day, the parents have emptied their wallets, and we all sit gleefully, counting our loot.

The high tea brought the flavor of Eid into my home—a little. Khalid's friends with their American wives and girlfriends brought food, fun, and laughter. But I missed the sounds and the familiarity of communion of shared background. The men in the living room chatted in Urdu and Punjabi, and the girls and I cleared the kitchen, in English. This day, I didn't want to explain my customs—I wanted to share them. I didn't want to make these friends understand; I wanted it to be understood. And I certainly didn't want to deal with looks of horror over the sacrificial lamb. I didn't want to repeat myself to make my British-Pakistani-English accent understood to the American ear. I longed for the freedom to speak Urdu, to have someone talk back to me in the language of Eid. Sara Lee cake didn't have the sweet-and-sticky texture of swirling *jelebi*; hash browns didn't have the spicy sting of samosas; *sheer khorma* made with spaghetti lacked the fine, slurpy feel of vermicelli; vanilla flavoring couldn't replace the refreshing flowery fragrance of rosewater; and *Eid Mubarak* with an American accent felt foreign. Ah, what I would have given for a layer of *warq* on the *sheer khorma* for that touch of sparkle. I yearned to share the nostalgia of knowing what we were missing.

I would write to Mummy and Daddy about the wonderful Eid party I had and Eid prayers. I would enclose photographs of us partying in the living room. And I would leave out the rest.

8.

Pakistani Pregnancy, American Delivery
A Baptism of Sorts, Plus a Circumcision

The next time I found religion was when I learned I was pregnant.

Glen Oaks, New York. 1972
How I wished my mother were with me! I couldn't stomach food; morning sickness was nauseating; and, finally, I was beginning to feel lonely. Khalid was on ICU rotation and on night call every third night, which meant he would put in a full day of work, work all evening, all night, all day again, and come home after thirty-six hours of being on his feet with critically ill patients. All this time I was home alone, filling space with my thoughts and thrilling anticipation of a baby, and sick to my stomach. I had Pakistani friends, but they were in the same situation—pregnant, throwing up, waiting at home for their husbands to return after a night call. We would chat daily on the phone, but that was the extent of it. It was too cold to take a walk, and I was afraid to slip on the ice and miscarry. I could picture myself lying in the snow—alone. I stayed closeted in that one-bedroom apartment, our wedding photos on every wall, writing letters, waiting for the mailman, reading *Dr. Spock's Baby and Child Care*, and watching Nixon and McGovern battle it out. I played the same two LPs of Mukesh and Lata's love songs over and over again. I had a room with a view: bare trees, gray skies, rows of garden apartments with shades pulled down and no sign of existence. Occasionally a car would pass by and be gone. Winter was as noiseless as a snowflake

falling. The only sounds I heard were the muffled thuds of footsteps of the lady above. I longed to see a face, hear a voice. Khalid would come home exhausted, immediately attend to me, chatting, heating the food to spare me the nauseating experience of the whiff of chilled curry that hit my nostrils each time I took the lid off the Tupperware, and just plain keeping me company and comforting me—it will pass, only one more month to go and you will be craving food; only a couple of weeks to go. I couldn't comprehend what life would be like without vomiting trips to the bathroom. If only Mummy were here—she would see to it that I was taken care of, tell me what to eat, what to do.

I had spoken to my parents on the phone only once. I had to call the overseas operator and request a call; she had called me back the next day to give me a date and time—three weeks out; I had then written to my parents, advising them of the call date and time. The entire family had assembled at our house in Rawalpindi to join the call, including Khalid's family who traveled from Multan (they did not have a phone). Daddy had engineered a speakerphone by wiring the phone into his music system. It was a three-minute call; and as soon as pleasantries were exchanged with the two-dozen people in the room, the call time ended. And it was expensive—expensive for a resident physician with an annual salary of $7,500.

I was too bashful to tell my parents about my pregnancy. What will I say? I can't say, "I am going to have a baby"—that would be *so* forward. Someone other than me had to break the news, and Khalid, being a doctor, wrote to my parents.

No sooner is a couple in Pakistan married than the expectant elders exchange greetings in hushed tones. How are the newlyweds? Any good news? Not yet? Don't worry, Insha'Allah it will happen soon. Ah, there is good news! Congratulations! May Allah grant them a son. And good news is celebrated quietly—only the elder ladies talk about it, referring to the mother-to-be as being in a "family way" or "expecting." The phrase "having a baby" is too graphic to be considered appropriate, and the word "pregnant" is off-limits and reserved for doctors only. Mother informs father—behind closed doors—that their daughter or daughter-in-law is to be a mother.

One day I came home after spending a few days with my newly-wed uncle and aunt. Mummy asked me how everyone was doing, and I told her that my aunt had been vomiting. The next moment Mummy was on the phone with my uncle, who confirmed the vomiting. Excited, Mummy called my grandmother: "Congratulations, your daughter-in-law is vomiting."

The expectant mom remains silent. When elder aunts wish her well, she will blush and lower her gaze. Once she starts showing, she will drape a dupatta *or shawl over her abdomen, concealing her growing pleasure, and could carry through full term without anyone noticing that she was pregnant.*

Khalid never noticed his mother's pregnancies. He was the oldest of ten siblings; eight made it to adulthood. One morning his mother asked him to stop by the missionary nurses on his way to college and tell them that she would need them today. That was code word for "I am in labor." He came home that evening to a newborn baby.

Mothers and mothers-in-law fuss over the expectant mother to no end. In her final weeks, the expectant mother will move to her mother's home for her delivery and stay there until six weeks after the baby's birth. The mother attends to her diet, makes sure she rests and does her walks, indulges her moods, fulfills her cravings, and hovers over her day and night. Sometimes a masseuse will come to the house and massage her legs. Special prayers are said for an easy pregnancy and for the health of the child and, of course, for a boy.

I yearned for the comfort of that special prayer—without the boy part—although perhaps deep down I too wanted a boy. I never admitted that.

Mummy wrote back. As soon as she had read Khalid's letter she was on the phone with Daddy, "My baby is going to have a baby," and then with my mother-in-law, who said, "I was waiting for the good news"; then my uncles and aunts; then the friends, the neighbors. . . . The annunciation of the first grandchild in both families burst like a piñata of excitement and joy, tempered with worry for me being by myself. Mummy sent me those special prayers. Read the Qur'an every morning; recite the chapter of Mary, mother of Jesus, and pray for an easy childbirth; and recite the chapter of Joseph, and your baby will be *beautiful.*

I didn't have a Qur'an. Bookstores didn't carry it. Khalid asked around among some conservative religious Muslim doctors and was told of a store in Manhattan. We drove out, found parking space—oh, how I dreaded trying to park in Manhattan—and bought a copy of the Qur'an in Abdullah Yusuf Ali's English translation. I purchased brown velvet material and stitched a book cover. Thus began my daily recitation of the chapters of Mary and Joseph. I resumed my daily prayers but only four of the required five. I found the daybreak prayer too early for me to give up my sleep. And I fell in love with my unborn baby, buoyant with his every kick.

My prayers were granted—all of them. On the morning of October 3, 1972, I woke up with mild contractions. I was two days past my due date and had had a breezy, blissful second and third trimester, consumed with longing for my baby's arrival. Khalid called my obstetrician—I will call him Dr. Roberts—who said to bring her in right away. Dr. Roberts was a male obstetrician, and that was the other thing. In Pakistan, women had their babies delivered by female obstetricians, or "lady doctors" as they called them. With all the segregation of the sexes, exposing one's genitalia to a male was unthinkable. When I first got pregnant, Khalid asked around and told me that his colleague had recommended this doctor.

"I can't go to a male doctor!" I was horrified.

"There are no female obstetricians in New York."

"How come?" If Pakistan, a third-world country, is loaded with female obstetricians, how is it that . . . ?

Khalid sat me down and gently counseled me, rationalizing the professionalism of a doctor-patient relationship. Having no choice, I went along. That both the doctors in this practice were old enough to be my father—older, actually—made it less awkward. After the first visit, I got over my hesitation. Dr. Roberts was a rounded figure with a balding head and a stern look who never smiled—and I was afraid of him. On one of my prenatal visits, when the nurse took my weight, I had put on six pounds. "We keep telling you ladies to watch your salt." He had never told me that, but I was too meek to speak up. Of course, I stopped the salt, and on my next visit I was hoping I'd get to see his nice partner instead. No such luck, but he did acknowledge that I had done well with the weight.

Long Island Jewish Hospital was barely a mile away. A lady in white greeted me and filled out some forms.

"Would you like to have the baby circumcised if it is a boy?"

"Yes. How old will he be when you circumcise him?" I asked.

"On the second day of his birth."

Thank God it's a Jewish hospital.

Khalid had briefed me earlier that Jews also circumcise their boys. Later I was to learn that all hospitals offer that service.

How fortunate that my baby boy—if it's a boy—will get circumcised right away, and in a clean hospital setting.

When my brother was born, I remember Mummy pleading with the British doctor to please circumcise him while he was still in the hospital. He refused, saying it was too risky. My brother ended up getting circumcised at age five, the typical age for boys in Pakistan. I still recall how uncomfortable he was post-procedure. He had the procedure done in a hospital, but in most homes the barber would come to the house to perform it.

Dr. Roberts was waiting. "What took you so long? I thought you had the baby at home."

Getting a scolding in labor.

He told me that he was going to put me to sleep.

"But I want a natural childbirth."

"You should have taken classes."

No one told me that. I suppose I should have told the doctor ahead of time, but in all fairness, the choice was not offered. I relented, he put me to sleep, and I woke up to see Khalid through blurred eyes in a blue gown.

"Baby is here—a boy."

Can't be. My labor has only just begun. Let me just sleep.

He caressed my shoulder. "Baby is here."

Groggy, foggy, and uncomprehending.

But I had no labor, no pains, no pushing. I hadn't heard the baby cry. It can't be, just let me sleep.

They brought baby Saqib to me, wrapped up in a blue and pink-striped receiving blanket. I was propped up. The nurse handed me a baby. He opened his eyes for me, big dark eyes, a fine nose, baby pink skin with blotches of red on his forehead and eyelids, jet-black tuft of hair, soft and warm in my hands. I looked up.

"He is mine?" I asked.

She smiled. "He is all yours."

I looked down at what I held. Small, light, real—a baby.

My baby! This is what I carried! Is this what I carried! My baby?

Upon a baby's birth, a male elder in the family will bring the baby in the fold of Islam by reciting the *adhan* in the baby's right ear. The call to prayer invokes the glory of God.

It was Father's Hour. Khalid gently picked up Saqib, cradled him, lowered his head to bring it close, and recited the *adhan* in Saqib's right ear. Saqib was baptized a Muslim.

I don't believe I thanked God. He had answered my prayers. I had a painless delivery—slept through the entire labor—a beautiful, healthy baby; a doting husband by my side; was surrounded by friends; nurses hovered. . . . I was swept away by the wonder of it all and forgot all about God. And that is precisely what God says in the Qur'an, that you will reach out to Me when you are in need, but once you have what you want, you will no longer remember Me.

Three years later I went through the same prayer ritual when pregnant with my son Asim. His birth was not that easy, but he was a beautiful baby. The nurses kept telling me, "What a clean looking baby he is." I wasn't sure what to make of it until they brought him to me. A perfect, round face, not a blotch of red, same dark hair, small chiseled nose, fine lips, and bright dark eyes. In three years the world had shrunk—phone connectivity, ease of travel, affordability—and there was more traffic between Pakistan and the US. Uncle sent auntie to stay with me for four months. She chased Saqib when I was too slow on my feet; stayed home with Saqib when Khalid took me to the hospital; cooked when I fed Asim; and watched them when I napped. A Godsend. Did I thank God?

I could not keep up with my prayers after entering the realm of motherhood. It was not that I didn't have the time; I couldn't take my eyes off my children. Prayer required me to enter into a state of total focus where I am standing in the presence of God, silently reciting verses of the Qur'an in Arabic, bowing, prostrating, sitting, and remaining in that state of submission until the ritual is complete. Now try doing that with a child crawling around and going off to who knows where. Or when you go into prostration, he comes and sits on your head. Or he starts wailing and you wonder if he is hurt. It was just not doable. I was left with the night prayer only, which I performed when the children were fast asleep and Khalid was thankfully home. Then it became a habit. The next time I thought of prayer was when my boys grew up and I had to inject religion into their lives. Until then, the colors in my prayer rug had faded, and the threads unraveled.

9.

Ramadan without Ramadan
Why I Stopped Fasting

I continued to lose my grip on religion.

Glen Oaks, New York. 1972

Saqib was barely a week old when Ramadan began. Neither Khalid nor I fasted. God had given me a temporary exemption—a benefit of nursing a baby; and Khalid took a personal exemption—he played hooky. We were just not in the mood. New York City did not rejoice in welcoming the holy month of Ramadan: TV news was silent; there were no special Ramadan programs; missing were the sounds of Qur'an recitation; absent were the green and white RAM ADAN MUB ARAK signs on stores; I did not hear the sounds of the *adhan* resonating from the minarets of the nonexistent mosques announcing the beginning of the fast at daybreak; and restaurants remained open. At home, there was no domestic help to cook the predawn *suhoor* meal; no murmurs of the elders reciting the Qur'an during the afternoon hours; and no chatter of the family gathering for the *iftar*—breaking of the fast at sundown. The communal sense that goes with fasting was not there. It was just I, home by myself with a newborn baby, fully immersed in diapers and feedings—stealing a lucky nap, totally flustered over my inept mothering skills and convinced that Dr. Spock didn't get it. Islamic rituals had taken a seat in the last row on the bus journeying through child-rearing. We were adrift.

* * *

A gentle knock on my bedroom door in Rawalpindi, Pakistan. It's 3:00 a.m. Razia, our cook calls out to me, "It's time for suhoor." I stumble out of bed, brush my teeth, put on my dressing gown, and, knotting its belt, head downstairs. Razia has laid out the table, and Mummy and Daddy are already eating. I break a piece of the greasy, crispy paratha, and scoop the ginger- and garlic-flavored chicken curry. A steaming cup of tea jolts open my sleepy eyes. The clink of forks on china is the only sound as we eat in silence. Razia and Aurangzeb eat in the kitchen and clear away after we have retreated upstairs to recite the Qur'an. Now I start hearing the voices of men singing in chorus, glorifying God and the Prophet, resonating from the mosque down the street. A chorus from the second mosque joins in, then a third, the closer ones louder, the farther ones fainter, each drumming their own song in a competition of sorts. Voices from the street call out again and again, "For those fasting, it's time to wake up," rousing those who have no intention of fasting. I keep drinking water until the melancholic cry of the adhan rings out, signaling the beginning of the fast. The naat singing has ceased. We quickly gulp a last sip of water and, in our hearts, declare to God our intention to fast. The sky has lost its pitch-blackness with a break of grayish hue. I perform the ritual ablution to purify myself, washing my hands, face, arms, and feet three times, drape the dupatta over my head, remove my shoes, spread my prayer rug in my bedroom, and stand in the presence of God to offer my morning prayers. Mummy prays in her bedroom. A few minutes later I am struggling to fall asleep, but that cup of tea won't let me. I could forego the tea, but then I would have to go through withdrawal with a ten-hour piercing headache. I do fall asleep, just before it is time to wake up again.

There will be no eating or drinking until sundown. No water either. No lunch hour in offices, and no ladies' coffee parties. Restaurants display signs, Open for Non-Muslims, the Sick, and Travelers. Thankfully, the sign does not list menstruating women. A girl seen eating in a college cafeteria is a dead giveaway: she is having her period. Or playing hooky. At home, we let Razia know in hushed tones that as of tomorrow, one of us will not be fasting, and she gives us the understanding nod. Lunch is brought up to her bedroom to avoid the stares of the male help in the house. I would rather fast than be exempt. Once Ramadan is over, I am supposed to make up the fasts for each day missed. I am unable to do that. The world has moved on, people are back into the swing of eating, and trying to get up at 3:00 a.m. and have suhoor all alone, fast when everyone else is eating, break your fast when everyone else has already had dinner, is not easy. I honestly don't know why girls are not allowed to fast during their period. Daadee Amma, suffering from multiple chronic ailments, is exempt. She will never be able to do make-up fasts and therefore gives charity as compensation.

We are getting a little woozy by late afternoon. It's dehydration more than hunger. Iftar won't be until 8:00 p.m. We start counting the hours, and then the minutes, to sundown. I perform my ablution, retrieve a copy of the Qur'an—wrapped in green velvet—from the highest shelf of the mantle where it has been placed out of reverence, kiss it, place it against my forehead, and take my place on the diwan next to Mummy. I cover my hair with the dupatta and start reciting. My goal is to complete the recitation of the Qur'an by the end of Ramadan. With thirty chapters to cover in thirty days, if I can recite one and a quarter chapter a day—the quarter makes up for days lost due to that stupid period—I can be done. Downstairs, we can hear the clatter of Razia's cooking, the aroma of spices whiffing up the stairs, whetting my appetite. With minutes to go, we gather downstairs for iftar at the dinner table. We take our places, pray in silence for God to accept our fast—and, between God and I, to make the seconds go faster. And then the sound we have been yearning for—the adhan. Bismillah! I start in the name of God, and we reach out for the dates. Prophet Muhammad would break his fast with a date. Razia has made rooh afza–flavored pink milkshakes—the fruity rosewater-flavored cool and refreshing drink. The fruit chaat gives me the sugary oomph—the battery charger getting plugged into the outlet. At this time, I am not thinking of all the hunger in the world—the idea behind fasting—I am conversing with my grateful taste buds over those crispy pakoras. Razia and Aurangzeb break their fast in the kitchen. A sip and a bite of each, and I am full. A pity—fasting has killed my appetite. All those pakoras beckoning!

I retreat to my bedroom for evening prayers. When I emerge in the sunroom, Aurangzeb has wheeled in the tea trolley. The cup-a-tea I have been yearning for. I sit cross-legged on the diwan *and inhale the aroma of cardamom-flavored tea. I warm my hands, holding the cup with both palms. I am feeling lazy and sleepy. But wait; there is dinner—at 10:00 p.m. Then night prayer made longer with the Ramadan Taraweeh prayer. To bed at midnight; then up again at 3:00 a.m.—the daily ritual for thirty days.*

Now that you have had a glimpse of Ramadan in Pakistan, do you blame me for chickening out? OK, so the days are not that long in October—daybreak at 5:30 a.m., sundown at 6:30 p.m. But still, think of it: a sleep-deprived new mom nursing a week-old baby, having to wake up at that odd hour, cook, eat, try to sleep; and when she finally sleeps, baby wakes up; then she is hungry and thirsty all day. . . . Thank you, God, for exempting nursing mothers. But what was Khalid's excuse? And what was my excuse a year later? Or the year after? Or the year after that? Let's just say that the environment and the support system were not there. There was no flow to go along with. And we did not have the wherewithal to create that flow. Not yet. Unable to integrate our religious rituals into our new lifestyle, we put religion on hold.

It was the birth of my children that created that gap. Later it would be concern for my children that would close the gap—with religion reinvented. For now, I had folded my prayer rug and placed it deep down at the bottom of the pile.

10.

The Christmas-ization of Eid

"Mummy, why can't we have a Christmas tree?"

I had been expecting this question since the first Christmas lights went up after Saqib's birth. I, the perfect planner, anticipator of all scenarios, had laid the groundwork and would be ready to deal with this question when asked. In fact, if I played my cards right, he might never ask the question.

Within six months of Saqib's birth, we had a critical mass of Muslim families. A total of three. My friend Rabia, Kausar, and me—three Urdu-speaking families from the subcontinent, with three baby boys. We were all worried. How are we going to explain to our children why we don't celebrate Christmas? How does one explain to a child that, yes, as Muslims, we believe in the miracle of Jesus's birth, we believe he was a prophet, but we don't celebrate his birth with a tree or gift giving. That is not good enough for a child. Who doesn't love the festivities of lights, Santa Claus ringing the bell, shoppers walking out of Macy's with piles of gifts, children lined up at the windows of Saks Fifth Avenue, the Radio City Christmas Spectacular, the towering tree in Rockefeller Center, and the city as decked up as a Pakistani bride. Well, if we love it, won't our children? Won't they wish they were part of it? Wouldn't they want a Christmas tree in their home? Wouldn't they want gifts? Won't they feel that they are missing out on life? Won't they wish they were born Christian? Oh, dear! Well, don't just stand there and wring your hands—do something!

I reached out to my Jewish friend, Nancy. Minorities reaching out to minorities.

"You have to come up with a substitute. When is your religious holiday? Make a big deal out of it."

We will Chrismas-ize Eid, give it a makeover. We set the ground rules: (1) all three families have to take the day off. No excuses. (2) We adopt one another as family, get dressed in traditional shimmering *shalwar kameez*—baby boys included—without the shimmer. (3) We all go to Manhattan for Eid prayers. (4) We converge back home for a potluck feast. (5) We dress up the apartment inside and out in colored lights (never mind that we will have to explain to the neighbors when they ask, "Christmas in October?"). (6) There is no sixth—we are not going to put up a tree. (7) We exchange gifts for the children; replacing the traditional *eidee* of cash gift; and make a noisy fuss over tearing open the crackling gift wrap and going, "Yeah," "Oooh," "Aaah." Just as Christmas. Brilliant! Of course, we pulled it off, Eid after Eid, year after year. More babies came along, more families joined the trio, houses replaced apartments, Eid parties moved from living rooms into basements and eventually into rented halls. We were smug: our children will never miss Christmas.

I was wrong.

Asim was six when, on Christmas morning, he woke up crying with muffled sobs.

"What is it, Asim?" I rushed over to his room.

"I wish we had a Christmas tree."

Mommies, did that tear your heart out?

Why couldn't we have had a Christmas tree? It's just a tree. What was I afraid of? That we will lose our children to another faith? That somehow their identity as Muslims will get compromised? Over a tree! He is crying, for crying out loud! What was my problem?! Depriving my child because I couldn't handle my insecurities!

I called Nancy.

"So get him one."

I never got him the tree. By the time next Christmas rolled around, I had convinced myself that he had grown out of it.

Decades later, when I walked into Saqib's home during the holi-days, I saw to my surprise and relief a mini Christmas tree in the fam-ily room. Saadia, my conservative, nice Muslim daughter-in-law, had demonstrated more sense than I.

11.

A Muslim among Orthodox Jews

The first time I saw a Jewish person was when I came to America. There were no Jewish families in Pakistan. I had never come face to face with a Hindu either—same reason. Pakistanis were pro-Palestinian, and the country had fought three wars with India. I had been in New York for less than a week when Khalid took me to his hospital's Christmas party. The medical residents were Pakistani, Indian, and Jewish.

The Indian and Jewish people seem to be rather nice—they are welcoming, friendly, and chatty—just like regular people.

Next week Khalid's colleague—Jewish—brought his family over to visit us. His wife, Nancy, took me under her wing and showed me the ropes. She became my lifeline. To her I owe her my child-rearing skills. Ruth Jaffe, the nice old lady upstairs who would invite me in for coffee, hand me recipes, and take me grocery shopping—you got it—was Jewish. My obstetrician—Jewish. Dr. Orlicker, Saqib's pediatrician, whom I revered—Jewish. Khalid's boss, whose reference got him his next job—Jewish. Khalid's hospital: Long Island Jewish. It didn't take long for my mind and heart to pop open. On my first visit back to Pakistan, when Saqib was a year old, my family kept hearing the word "Jewish" in my discourse. Sensing the sensitivity, I switched my ambassadorial role, from promoting Muslims with my American friends to promoting Jewish folks with my Pakistani brethren. Think of it this way: if you don't have Muslim friends, you are likely to believe what you hear.

Young Israel Community. Staten Island, New York. 1976

I didn't know what I was getting into when we bought our first house in Willowbrook, Staten Island, a neighborhood of semidetached, tree-lined houses. Gerald Ford sat in the Oval Office, and Zulfiqar Ali Bhutto was president in Pakistan. Khalid had completed his Fellowship in Hematology/Oncology and was employed by the Staten Island Medical Group. The three-bedroom split-colonial was within our reach. An eat-in kitchen with glass sliding doors opened onto the deck; a formal dining room and a sunken living room with southern exposure was perfect for hosting parties; and the family room on the ground level opened onto the fenced backyard for the children to play in. Asim and Saqib, now ages one and four, shared a bedroom, and we set up the third bedroom as a study and guest room. One Saturday morning I decided to go introduce myself to my neighbors. This was, after all, a homeowners' neighborhood and would have a more welcoming mindset. I started ringing doorbells. No answer. The cars were parked in the driveway—they had to be home. You got it: it was the Sabbath. And this was the Young Israel Community, clustered around the synagogue only two blocks down—an Orthodox Jewish community.

One of Khalid's Jewish colleagues who had invited us to their house asked, "Why did you buy a house in an Orthodox Jewish neighborhood? How will you fit in?" Daddy was visiting us from Pakistan and had noticed, looking out the window, the procession of families, well dressed, well groomed, walking their strollers to Sabbath services. He said to me, "People of faith, no matter what their faith, make good neighbors. They live by the rules, they are disciplined in their way of life, and it's bound to have a positive influence on your children." He was right. And I got a bonus out of it. I no longer had to explain to my children why we don't eat pork and why we eat halal meat (the equivalent of Kosher). I didn't have to get into the circumcision part—yet. The first time I told my children, "We don't eat pork," they said, "My friend Jason doesn't eat pork either." At Saqib's fifth birthday party, while all other children were savoring the cupcakes, Jason stood by. He did not touch a crumb. Mummy pointed it out to me, "See that little boy. He is watching everyone eat and is not eating. Such restraint, and he is only five." I seized the opportunity.

After the party is over, I will have a talk with Saqib. I will draw attention to Jason, explain the whys and why nots in the Jewish faith, then segue into, "Likewise, Muslims have their dos and don'ts." My intelligent son will see the light.

"Saqib, did you notice that Jason didn't eat anything?" I delicately introduced my preamble.

"Yeah. He's Jewish. Only Kosher food." And he ran off to play.

Mummy remembered the little boy Jason and would often tell the story to her friends in Pakistan.

That holiday season, I didn't have to explain the whole "why we are different" bit. Menorahs did the explaining. What comfort being a minority among a minority. And I didn't even plan it that way.

I had started homeschooling Saqib in Islamic teachings, which I will get to later. I knew this was a start, and I also knew that it wasn't enough. But I didn't have an answer. One evening, I was hanging out with my neighbors on the sidewalk, when one of them took her leave saying that she had to pick up her child from Hebrew school.

"You have a Hebrew school?" I asked, feeling envious and deprived.

"Of course. Don't you have a religious school for your children?"

A meek "no."

"You need to start one. Don't do it for yourselves; do it for your children."

Embarrassed, I tried to make excuses—we were new, didn't know many Muslim families on Staten Island, not many with children, definitely no teachers, where are we going to get a place, how would we get started, etc.

Even as I heard myself, it was clear to me that all that stood between a Muslim school and me was me. She was right. I had to get started.

It didn't happen the next day, but it did happen. Khalid and I would go on to become part of a team that established a mosque and Sunday school on Staten Island. Our children grew up to become devout Muslims, bridge builders, and torchbearers. My Jewish neighbor ignited the spark in my mind, but it was the American spirit of pluralism that provided the fertile ground for our efforts to take root and flourish.

As I embarked on finding the pathway to Islamic teachings, I realized that I was no longer the girl who had grown up in Pakistan. I had become Americanized big-time. Would the two go hand in hand?

12.

The Americanization of Yours Truly

Would You Like Something to Drink?

Here is how it goes in Pakistan:

You go visiting—it could be anybody—family, friend, stranger . . .

You are immediately served a drink—juice or soda.

The host never asks you if you would like a drink. It is a given that you will be served a drink.

A little later, the help will wheel the trolley in, and you are served tea, *mithai*, or cake, and some kebabs, samosas, or fruit *chaat*. Again, the host didn't ask if you wanted some.

"Have some cake," the host says.

"No. No, thank you," you say. You have to say, "No, thank you," or you will appear to be greedy.

"Oh, please, do have some," the host insists.

"No, I really am fine."

"I insist. Please have some."

"Oh, well. OK, if you insist." Then, and only then, will you take a small piece or helping.

"Please, have some more. Take another kebab."

"No. One is fine."

"Just one more," and she puts it in your plate.

Once you are done eating, she insists that you have seconds, and the back and forth starts all over again.

Here is what happened in New York in 1971:

I pay my first visit to an American friend.

"Would you like something to drink?" the host asked.

"No. No, thank you."

"OK," said the host.

And that was that.

I had not eaten all afternoon, thinking: I am going visiting, surely she will be serving tea and snacks, and I don't want to end up overeating. I was also thirsty. Now what? I couldn't backtrack—what's done is done. She had asked me an honest question, and I had given a not-so-honest but Pakistani-culturally-appropriate answer, and I got what I asked for. I stayed hungry and thirsty, feeling rather stupid.

Did I learn fast.

Here is what happened in New York in 2015:

Some friends from Pakistan were in town, and we met over coffee at a café. Later we walked over to my apartment, and I asked them.

"Would you like something to drink?"

"No, thank you," they said.

"OK."

You Look Lovely

In Pakistan, when someone offered you a compliment, humility required you to decline it very politely so as not to sound self-assured or flattered. One responded with a gesture that conveyed: I am not worthy of your generous compliment.

"You look lovely."

"No, I don't," with a shy smile, I would demure.

"You have a beautiful voice."

"No, no." I'd wave my hand. "You are very kind," was my standard response.

Got it?

Transplant to the US. Picture the look on someone's face when she praised my dress: "What a pretty outfit!"

"No, it isn't."

Accepting commendation was hard. It took years, maybe more, for me to recalibrate my thinking—that accepting a compliment was an indication of pride or superiority—and say, "Why, thank you."

1980s
Working Girl (Home-Ec or Homework)
My mother was a housewife, and that was the norm in Pakistan in the fifties and sixties. Among working women, the leading professions were teacher and doctor. And that is because of the segregation of the sexes. All-girl schools had to have women teachers, and women wanted a "lady doctor." I was raised to be a housewife—the perfect housewife—like my mother. Mummy taught me to sew, embroider, knit, and cook. By age twelve, I was sewing my clothes and knitting my sweaters. In Pakistan, all clothing was custom-tailored at home or at the tailor's. We shopped for the fabric after the shopkeeper had unrolled reams of fabric for our perusal, picked out the trimmings and buttons, had the *dupatta* dyed in matching color, and then stitched the clothes at home. I was in high school when my maternal uncle, Jedi Mamoon, who was an engineering student in Lahore, told my parents of the perfect college for me: "The College of Home Economics in Lahore will groom her to perfection." Just eleven years my senior, we were best friends; he was my surrogate elder brother, and his opinion, in my opinion, was paramount. So I was going to Home-Ec. Mummy bought into it, the rationale being that if my career was to be a homemaker, then my college education should be along those lines. I had done well in high school and could have gone anywhere, including a career in medicine. But Mummy was against my becoming a doctor. "Lady doctors do not make good housewives," she would say. Daddy wanted me to pursue a career in medicine, and he tried. He took me to visit Kinnaird College, a prestigious college in Lahore. They wanted me, but I was hung up on Home-Ec, and he let me have my way.

I came to the States, all committed to being a homemaker. One of the first items on my shopping list was a Singer sewing machine. I started stitching my pantsuits, and when pregnant, knitted a newborn-sized yellow sweater, but cooking stressed me out. Home all day, going to kiddie movies, reading kiddie books, and playing kiddie games—after a few years I yearned for adult company and some life outside the home.

When Khalid left his job at the medical group to set up his private practice in Hematology/Oncology, a colleague advised him: "Have your wife manage the office," and I leaped. The colleague's office manager trained me, and a week later, I had donned a white uniform and was answering the phone, "Dr. Rehman's office." I enrolled Asim at the Alphabetland Nursery School and went to work part-time. Mummy was tickled; she thought my being Khalid's secretary was rather romantic. Just like the movies.

Back to School

Two years later, I was yearning for more. Other than new patients coming in, it was the same work, day after day: reception, scheduling, billing, and that was the extent of it.

Maybe I will be a hospital administrator. I know enough of healthcare to give me a jump-start; and I do have some leadership and people skills. Actually, I would like that.

Khalid thought it was a great idea. As soon as Asim started kindergarten, I went back to school, enrolling at the New School for Social Research in the master's program in health services administration.

Only in rare circumstances did married women in Pakistan go back to school—at least in my day. Domestic responsibilities and child-rearing took precedence. Besides, there was an age limit for enrollment.

Mummy wasn't happy. She was visiting when I announced my plans.

"You won't be able to handle it. It's a long commute into Manhattan, and at home you will busy with homework. Your children, your husband, and your home will be neglected. Don't forget, you also tire easily. You have been out of college for nine years. It won't be easy to get back into a school routine. Why can't you continue to work in Khalid's office?"

I didn't have an answer. But I didn't budge either. So Mummy went to Khalid and repeated the same script, adding, "The only thing working for her is her strong willpower. She may be able to muster the energy. But, practically speaking, she cannot do it all."

Back in our bedroom, I was in tears. Mummy was right, but I wanted to do this. Khalid was smiling. "Your mother knows you."

That evening, I saw Khalid pondering over some bills, checkbook in hand.

"What are you doing?" I asked.

"Paying the bills. You won't have the time, and I can take this over."

And that was just the beginning. He took charge of all my duties: finances, children, shopping, parent-teacher conferences. . . . All I did was commute, attend classes, and study. When I had an exam, he would take the children to the park. When I started working on my thesis, he bought me a then-state-of-the-art typewriter, with memory and auto-correct. (I had taken evening typing classes at the community college when pregnant with Asim.) When I did well, he beamed with pride and broadcast it to the world. When I graduated two years later, he took the day off, and looking at him, you would think it was he who was getting the degree.

Mummy, after casting her nay vote, got behind me. She stayed with me to babysit the children until I could find someone. I couldn't. We had moved again, to a four-bedroom house on Lighthouse Hill, across from a working lighthouse, on a cliff overlooking the valley, with a living room that had a southern exposure bringing in the light and a view to brighten your day even on a cloudy, rainy morning. Problem: no babysitters. Khalid wrote to his mother and asked if she could send his sister Farhana to live with us for a year. Auntie Hameeda agreed. Farhana was engaged to be married in a year, had completed her education, and was free to take an extended leave of absence from home. She would play with Saqib and Asim, help them with their homework, and I would walk in from school to the aroma of chicken curry and steaming rice. Bless her. Getting me through school had become a family project, extending from New York to Pakistan.

When Farhana left to get married, Khalid's parents agreed to send his youngest sister, Nyla, to get me through my second year of college. The American embassy turned down her visa request, and that was that.

I panicked.

"Don't worry. I will change my office hours to be home when the children come home from school," Khalid said.

That is how I got through. Bless him.

Hospital Administrator

In 1982, at age thirty, I started my career as a hospital administrator at The Brooklyn Hospital. Mummy would later say, "If I'd known you would become a career girl, I would have sent you to medical school." But then, it was my Home-Ec background that Khalid had been attracted to.

Hospital administration was a man's world. At management meetings, the director of nursing and I were the only two women present. Sometimes it was just me. In fact, at the weekend planning retreat, it was just the guys and me. For cost-saving purposes, they all had to be paired in rooms; I, being the only female, had a room to myself. Did I feel intimidated—the only woman in the presence of these high-powered men? Not for a moment. The age of Mad Men was history, and though Anita Hill had not yet surfaced, I was among a cadre of polished and sophisticated professionals. The staff welcomed me, supported me, mentored me, and, as their resident, took me under their wing. That I spoke with a foreign accent, looked foreign, and was a woman was not an issue. They had hired me—how could it? If I never felt conscious of my gender, it was because of the corporate culture. They knew what it took to groom a professional. I completed my residency feeling comfortable in my skin and ready and equipped to slash the Emergency Room waiting time.

Skirts, Pants, or *Shalwar Kameez*

Somewhere along the line, I crossed the cultural divide. In donning a business suit, as in skirt and blazer, I committed the first violation. Mummy was not just upset, she was angry. "Muslim girls don't reveal their legs," she told me. I retreated into my bedroom and burst into tears. I dealt with it the only way I knew how. I started leading a double life. When Mummy visited, the skirts were packed away and out came the pantsuits. Eventually, Mummy came around. I faced the same dilemma with the Muslim community. With my liberal friends, we would go to the beach in beach attire and blend in, but the conservatives would stare me down if they caught me wearing skirts. One of them confronted me. I had stopped by her house on my way home from work to pick up something.

"You should not wear skirts," she said.

I said nothing. I did not want to get into an argument.

The next time she met me, she asked, "Have you stopped wearing skirts?"

There are people who believe that "enjoining good and forbidding evil" is not just their calling, it is their responsibility.

"No, I have not," I said. "I don't believe my attire is immodest."

"Your legs should not be visible."

"I wear long skirts, way below my knees, and colored stockings. A few inches of colored-stockinged legs is not indecent."

Defensive?

"Just wear pants."

Gloves off, I argued. Our religion requires us to dress modestly. Aren't pants more revealing than a flared, long skirt? Aren't the contours of hips and thighs more visible in pants?

"No, no, no," disarmed, she was protesting.

Seeing that I had her cornered, I plugged away and attacked the sari blouse. Was revealing the midriff acceptable, I asked?

"No. No. No. Just stop wearing skirts."

We left it at that. But I knew that she spoke for many who didn't have the nerve or were too polite to confront me. So, I applied the same technique. When in their company, I avoided wearing skirts, and it saved everyone the discomfort.

Double life.

Friends: Women—and Men?

That wasn't all. I had male friends. Students from school, colleagues from work. Khalid welcomed them all; the boys loved playing with them, and our home became the place to get together for my "single" friends. This was highly unusual for a woman of Pakistani origin. You know by now that women in Pakistan did not have male friends; and even after marriage, when couples got together, men and women would gravitate into separate parts of the room. One-on-one man-woman relationships, however platonic, were nonexistent—at least in the public eye. And here I was, hanging out with the boys. Bob and John, my classmates, would walk me to the bus stop after classes at the New School and wait with me on 14th Street until I was safely on the bus. One day, class ran late, and Bob and John insisted on driving me home, from Manhattan to Staten Island. They didn't want to risk me riding the bus at night. Remember, this was Union Square in 1980—not a pretty place. I remember Bob telling Khalid, "We can't trust Bia to be standing alone at the bus stop. She is so gullible that if a mugger asked her, 'May I please see your wallet?' she would say, 'Here.'" Another time, walking out after class, I looked at my watch and muttered, "Oh, dear! I missed the bus." A gentleman walked up to me and said, "I couldn't help overhearing. I can drive you home." I walked off with him. He was a classmate, and I knew that he lived on Staten Island. I saw Bob give me this look, but I made nothing of it. No sooner had I got home than the phone rang. It was Bob.

"Who was that guy you went off with?"

"Oh. That's my classmate in my hospital administration class." Bob was not in that class.

"Why did you take a ride with him? Do you know him well enough? Do you realize how scared I was? It's the oldest trick in the book: 'I couldn't help overhearing. I can give you a ride.' You know, I followed you to the car, just to make sure. Do you realize the trouble you could have gotten into?"

"Oh, you shouldn't worry. I was fine."

"Let me talk to Khalid."

I put Khalid on.

"Do you know what Bia did? She took a ride with a stranger. And she doesn't realize the risk she put herself in. Talk to her. Make her understand."

"Well, I don't have to worry; I have you looking out for her."

Didn't I just make you fall in love with Bob? I loved my friends. That some of them were of the male gender was irrelevant. Khalid liked them, my children got to know them, and together we built friendships that endure to this day. When they married, we were at the weddings; when their children were baptized, we were there; and when Saqib and Asim got married, they were there. But at the time, knowing that some would frown upon my friendship with members of the opposite sex, I had to keep my American social life separate from my Muslim community social life.

Double life?

A Handshake, a Hug, and a Kiss
Now I was really crossing the line. Worse, it didn't feel that way. In Pakistan, women did not even shake hands with men. A hug and a kiss would be scandalous! You just don't do that. Period. I remember the first kiss: I had just given birth to Saqib and was in the hospital bed. A colleague of Khalid's and his wife came to visit, and the colleague walked over to me and planted a kiss on my cheek.

A fleeting moment of awkwardness—for me.

This is their culture. There is nothing more to it. It's OK. Relax.

The moment passed. Years later, when I started entertaining Khalid's colleagues in our home, they would greet me, shake my hand, and give me a kiss.

This is their culture; take it in stride.

After the first few kisses, I stopped taking notice. And, finally, one day, I shocked myself by initiating the peck.

One evening, as my fellow student friends were leaving after dinner, one of them said to me, "Would it be against your religion if I give you a hug?"

And there I was, handshaked, kissed, and hugged.

A Double Standard?
Were we setting a double standard for my children? They saw their mother wearing skirts to work, shorts in the summer, beach attire at the beach, but a *shalwar kameez* at Pakistani-Indian parties and her hair covered at the mosque. I tried to rationalize it as a dress-code thing. I was holding American parties in English, in pants, with Western music,

and Pakistani parties in Urdu, in *shalwar kameez*, and with Urdu songs. Khalid and I would greet our Muslim friends with a nod, our American friends with a hug and a kiss. The only common denominator was food—Pakistani spicy, spicy food and no alcohol. And, of course, no pork either.

Alcohol, Pork, Halal, Kosher, or None of the Above

We never crossed the line when it came to alcohol and pork. I was Americanized in many ways, but this is where we drew the line. Alcohol consumption and pork are forbidden in Islam. There are no two ways about it. Our parents never drank, we didn't drink, our children don't drink, and I hope that my grandchildren never will. I have never tasted alcohol, except by accident at an event. The same is true for pork and pork products—by accident, that is.

Halal meat was another story. When I first came to the US, I didn't even know the difference. For me, meat is meat is meat, as long as it isn't pork. Then I started hearing the word "halal." Someone at a party explained that Islam requires an animal to be slaughtered in a humane way, with God's permission, and the blood drained out. That is considered halal, or permissible. The meat sold in supermarkets is not halal. However, kosher meat, prepared in the Jewish tradition, meets the Islamic requirement and therefore is permissible. I asked where one could get halal meat and was told that halal meat stores are few and far between. I dismissed the whole halal meat idea as extremist. I wasn't even going to consider kosher as an alternative. As far as I was concerned, one shouldn't complicate life with dos and don'ts. So I continued to buy meat right out of the cooler at Pathmark. I had opted for the "none of the above" option.

Beer was another story. One day my college friends, Bob, John, and his lovely fiancée, Tina, decided to play a prank. We were at a diner. They told me that they had ordered a special drink for me that I would find interesting. "Don't worry, it's not alcohol." Drinks arrived. I took a sip.

"How do you like it?" they asked.

"It's different. OK, I guess."

"It's called root beer," they said, chuckling.

"Oh, my God! Beer! You said it wasn't alcohol."

More chuckles. I felt myself choke.

"It's not alcohol. It's just root beer."

These are good kids. They wouldn't do that to me.

The joke went on and on, until one of them felt sorry for me and explained, "It's not beer, it's only called that."

I had forgotten all about this episode, until John and Tina, now parents of adults, reminded me. "Don't forget to mention the root beer incident in your memoir."

Ladies First. All Rise

Would you be surprised if I told you that in Pakistan, the Ladies First rule applies? When a man holds open a door, it's ladies first. When men are lined up at the counter and a woman approaches, it's ladies first—she moves to the front of the line. When dinner is served, it's ladies first. When a lady enters a room, men stand up and remain standing until she takes a seat. When she approaches her seat at the table, a gentleman will pull out the chair and seat her. If both approach a door, he will hold open the door for her. If it's a revolving door, he goes first so that he does the pushing. Got it! And where do I land? In the land of women's equality. No more preferential treatment for me. Not only do I have to scrub, clean, wash, cook, and shop, I get treated like a man. Sorry feminists, but inequality has its privileges.

Decades later, at work, I walked into the office of the chief operating officer at the hospital to greet him on his first day at the job. He was seated.

"Good morning," I said.

He stood up.

My jaw dropped.

Waltz, Twist, and Disco

Daddy taught me to waltz when I was ten. For a Pakistani family, this was unusual. Girls in Pakistan did not dance (now they do), and fathers certainly didn't teach them. But Daddy loved to dance and in England had won a silver medal in a dance contest. He and Mummy would dance at the Army parties and made an elegant couple on the dance floor. My friends and I rock 'n' rolled in the fifties—in girls' schools—and twisted away in the sixties in girls' college. When Khalid took me to hospital dinner dances, I would dance the night away. Then disco hit the scene. Not wanting to be left behind, we enrolled at the YMCA for disco classes and became a hit on the dance floor. People would part to watch Khalid and me twirl. Imagine Daddy's delight.

I crossed the line again. At my hospital's dinner dance, after I had exhausted Khalid on the dance floor, I noticed one of my colleagues sitting alone. Poor guy had no one to dance with. I ran up to him, beckoned, and raced back to the dance floor. We didn't hold hands, just danced. Khalid didn't mind. My liberal Muslim friends wouldn't have objected. But there were others who would have raised eyebrows.

With an Accent

I clung to my British accent. I was not letting go. It was too much a part of my identity. Imagine my surprise when on my first visit to Pakistan, Mummy remarked, "She said 'skedule' instead of 'sheydule,' and 'aawer' instead of 'our' (hour), 'fla-wer' instead of 'flaar' (flower)."

Every time I said "can't," my cousins giggled.

I guess I was losing it.

Today, when someone remarks, "You have an accent," I beam.

A Suburban, a Dog, and a House in the Country

Well not quite, but close. We got a Ford Taurus station wagon, Bob gave Mao, his Siamese cat, to the boys, and we bought a country house in Hemlock Farms in the Poconos along with a sailboat. With that, and a dose of apple pie, we were now the All-American Family.

So

How do I make Islam fit into all this? How do I introduce Islam into the lives of my children?

PART THREE

Creating a Muslim Space

13.

Where Do I Begin?

Circa 1970s

Saqib is now six. How do I make a Muslim out of him?

How do I teach him:

To believe: I can just tell him about the Oneness of God.

To pray: I can help him memorize the Arabic prayer.

To fast: It can wait. He is just six.

To be charitable: hmmm!

To make the hajj: deferred.

To study the Qur'an in Arabic: yikes!

He is only six.

How do I transmit the religious values I was raised with? Faith in God—trusting that He knows best what is right for us; God consciousness—that He is watching over us and will protect us; our responsibility toward God and our fellow human beings—do the right thing and avoid what is forbidden; that we are accountable for our deeds; that charity and compassion toward our fellow human beings is paramount. How can I teach him that through prayer one can give thanks for countless blessings; that God has given us a precious gift—a book of guidance—of divine revelation showing us the right way, a way of life that is pious and filled with love. How do I inculcate the value of respect for elders? How do I get him to understand that out-of-wedlock dating and sex are not permissible? Hold off on the last one—he's only six.

How did *I* learn to be a Muslim?

Perhaps it was the environment: I had grown up in a predominantly Muslim country. But wait! I had started my schooling at the Presentation Convent Girls School, a missionary run by European nuns—in habits—and remained in the convent system until high school. We started our day with the Lord's Prayer, "Our Father who art in Heaven . . ." Sister, I still remember it. When Christian students went for Catechism, we Muslim girls attended class in "Moral Science," teachings that left a permanent imprint on my values and sense of ethics. At an early age, we learned to coexist. My friends went to the same schools—a privilege afforded to daughters of army officers. And yes, it was considered a privilege. So scrap the external environment factor.

Was it the home environment? No and yes. First the no. My parents were secular. Daddy did not observe the rituals. I don't recall seeing him pray or fast. He never learned to read the Qur'an in Arabic, which was unusual. The only time Daddy went to the mosque was on Eid; and women never went to the mosque at all. Mummy would pray every now and then, would sometimes fast, and, like most of her contemporaries, would embrace religious rituals later in life. The Qur'an had a place on the uppermost shelf and almost out of sight. It was brought down at the first sign of an impending calamity, when Mummy would assemble ladies' prayer groups. Mummy did not wear the hijab, and no one—as in no one—in her circle of army wives did, but legs were always covered. The only time they covered their hair was when praying or reciting the Qur'an. I don't believe I ever heard the term "Islamic"—honest.

Now the yes. My religious education did indeed begin at home and remained in the home. It began with bedtime stories. One hot summer night, as we slept outdoors with a mosquito net covering all four beds, Daddy told his two little girls, ages seven and five, the story of Adam and Eve. Think of it: creation, man and woman, heaven and earth, angels and Satan, temptation and sin, punishment and reward, expulsion and exile, repentance, separation and unification, and genealogy—all in one story. From Daddy, I first heard the story of Prophet Moses. The next morning, Mummy showed me the *surma* bottle, a kohl powder eyeliner. "This is made from the ashes of the mountain that burned down when God showed a glimpse of Himself to Prophet Moses," Mummy told us. It may have been soon after that Aba Jee, my maternal grandfather, started telling us stories—stories of Prophets Abraham, Jesus, Jacob, Joseph, Noah, and Muhammad. Ami Jan, my grandmother, taught me the prayer. Together, they taught me to observe the faith. Grandparents were a religious breed, either because they had the time or due to their sense of impending mortality. Aba Jee was the exception. A religious scholar—self-taught—he was conservative, devout, and open-minded. Tall and well built, he had a short, gray beard, sharp, handsome features, and a refined manner and was always immaculately dressed. When telling us bedtime stories, he would fall asleep. We would nudge him; he would wake up with a start, continue the story, and then fall asleep again. This went on until Ami Jan would come in and shoo us off to bed.

At age ten, I learned to read Arabic—which was the norm. The *maulvi* would come to our house and teach me to recite the Qur'an. By age eleven, I had completed the recital—in Arabic. With this, my religious education was considered complete. The fact that I could not understand Arabic was considered inconsequential. I had recited God's revelation, in His words, from A to Z, or rather, from *alif* to *ye*, no worries if I couldn't comprehend what I read. Daddy was one of those rare people who had studied the translation of the Qur'an. As for me, I grew up strong in faith but lacking in knowledge of the sacred text. It was in that state that I started making Muslims out of Saqib and Asim. *Good luck!*

Do Unto My Children, as Daddy and Grandpa Did Unto Me

You guessed it! I started with bedtime stories. But my memory was vague. I needed a storybook, and there weren't any Islamic bookstores. Searching in the children's section of Waldenbooks, I found one: *Stories from the Bible*. There it was, the stories of Adam and Eve, Abraham, Moses, Jesus. Only Prophet Muhammad was missing. No worries; I can cover that from memory. The belief in all the prophets is an essential part of the Islamic creed, so this book would do—

notwithstanding that each faith has its own interpretation. Bedtime stories became daytime stories. With Saqib and Asim on either side, I would sit on the brown velvet sofa by the window, with the sun streaming in, and read to them. Seeing the wonder in their eyes, I was reliving my childhood. Did I ask Daddy the same questions? "Why did Joseph's brothers throw him in the well? Why did God make so many people drown in the flood?" I didn't have the answers, but I took comfort in believing that I was laying a foundation, inculcating faith in the One God and the belief that good triumphs over evil.

What about Arabic?

There were no *maulvis* on Staten Island, of course. Bookstores didn't sell *Teach Your Child Arabic* or *Arabic for Dummies*, nor was this the age of Rosetta Stone. Dead end. But Pakistan was only halfway across the world. I started making a list of all the books I would bring back on my next trip to Pakistan, where General Zia had overthrown President Bhutto and declared martial law. Armed, I put on my brand-new Arabic teacher hat and began the daily sessions with dear little Saqib. He was such a good boy. Not once did he protest, as in, "Do I have to?" He would sit with me on the brown sofa and learn. He was diligent. He would bend over the book and studiously, with effort, work at learning. What a precious gift! It was a slow process. I could teach only what I knew, which was "read only," minus the comprehension. At the time, this is what I believed was necessary—evincing an appalling sense of comfort in the limitations of ignorance. Decades later, I would wake up to become a student of Arabic and would study it for five years. Asim would go on to take a semester abroad at American University in Cairo and study classical Arabic. He picked up enough Arabic to make his way with a group of students to the Sinai desert, camping at the mountaintop and offering his prayers at daybreak at the pinnacle of Mt. Sinai.

Where Do I Go from Here?

So my children are getting the basics in Islam. But is that enough? As they grow older, won't they lose their religious identity if they don't experience a sense of belonging? They see their friends and neighbors go in clusters to the synagogue and church. Won't they feel the desire to have a sacred place of their own—a community to belong to, where they can bond with peers, gain comfort through association, and grow confident in their faith and their heritage?

How in God's name am I going to pull this one off?

14.

Building a Muslim Community

How does one build a community from scratch?

Circa 1970s
Let Your Fingers Do the Walking

I knew no one. When I first moved to Staten Island, I didn't know any Muslim families. Khalid and I would go through the Yellow Pages looking for Muslim-sounding names. Millennials, that was the telephone directory—in hard copy. We found one name but were too shy to call and say, "Hello, this is your friendly Muslim family." We put word out to our friends in Queens and Long Island, "Does anyone know any Muslim families on Staten Island?" Eventually, through word of mouth, we found one, then two, and then three. Yeah! One Pakistani, one Indian, and one Sri Lankan. She knew someone; he knew someone; and then we were six. Six Muslim families on Staten Island—a dream come true. We now had a network. Not a critical mass to establish a religious center, but enough to get something going.

Like what?

How about a party!

Eid Eve

There is Christmas Eve—why not an Eid Eve? Why not indeed! The sighting of the new moon signals the end of the month of Ramadan and the celebration of Eid the next day. Let's celebrate the moon-sighting night as our Eid Eve.

I got on the phone and called the five families.

"Let's have a music party."

"Henna-painting for the girls."

"Make it pot-luck."

"Everyone gets dressed up in traditional, glittering outfits."

Someone dubbed it Chaand Raat, or night of the new moon.

And a tradition was started. That year, and for many years to come, we gathered in our home for the moon-sighting night until the community grew so large that I could no longer accommodate them and the venue moved to a larger space. This was by no means a religious event; rather it was a means to bring Muslim children together for a fun-filled evening and to heighten the joy associated with Eid.

One Dish

The party bug caught on. Why wait for Eid when we have weekends? We filled up the rest of the year with parties. All we needed was an excuse, and we'd have a party. Meet-my-visiting-parents-from-Pakistan party; honor-your-visiting-parents party; new-baby party; started-private-practice party—you get the picture. Staten Island, Long Island, Queens, and New Jersey: if there was a party, we were there. Our network was branching off like a date tree on growth hormones—excuse the cliché. Average occupancy in these parties: thirty, not including children, would be conservative. Too many for the lady of the house to cook? No worries; everyone bring a dish. We dubbed these the one-dish parties.

Men and women started self-segregating. As the guests arrived, they would sit together in the living room, chatting comfortably. Once the room started filling up, men would gravitate to one end, women to the other, in a rather seamless transition. Chattering in Urdu, the men talked politics—Gerald Ford and Jimmy Carter were running neck and neck, and President Zia in Pakistan had hanged Bhutto, the ex-president. The women talked fashion.

That wasn't fair. I am sorry.

Whereas there is some truth to it, it was more perception than reality. These women were doctors, businesswomen, designers, artists, and, of course, housewives like myself. But let's be honest. Doesn't every woman's face light up on seeing a dazzling piece of jewelry or a stylish *shalwar kameez*? Won't she say, "What a beautiful outfit! Where did you get it?" Now do the math: fifteen women, each complimenting one another, and you've got the fashion buzz going. I will tell you a secret. Parties became the platform for us to display our latest *shalwar kameez*. Trips to Pakistan became shopping sprees. Every time a woman walked in donning a new style, it was a given that she had just returned from Pakistan. Mommies back home were kept busy getting new outfits for their daughters, packaged and ready to send with whomever was willing to carry it back to the States. "What will I wear?" topped our list of worries. A discrete inquiry of the guest list was made, because God forbid that people should see you in the same outfit. We were in our twenties, so cut us some slack.

Ever been to a Pakistani dinner party? Forget about the French. "Lavish" is an understatement. It's not your one main dish with one side dish menu. Picture this: dining table buffet style, covered edge-to-edge with serving dishes and no room to place even a fork. Chicken biryani, kebab, *haleem*, chicken curry, ground meat curry, *palak paneer*, potato *bhughia*, *raita*, salad, naan. A separate table for the drinks: Coke, Sprite, 7-UP . . . did I tell you that Muslims don't drink alcohol? These were dry parties and have remained that way to this day, at least in the company I keep.

The fun began after dinner. We sang. We sang solo, Khalid and I sang duets, we sang in chorus, and, of course, we all sang in Urdu. An oversize cooking pot, placed upside down, served as a tabla, and singers roused their hibernating talent, practicing new Urdu songs for the upcoming parties. Down came the barriers of segregation. Children would sit around or run off to play, but they cultivated an ear for Pakistani music.

Our children made Muslim friends, dressed traditional Pakistani, and indulged in the taste and flavor of kebabs and biryani. They were being immersed in the Pakistani culture, and somewhere in the subtle undercurrent was the awareness that they were Muslims among Muslims. One day one of my Pakistani friends asked, "Are there any Pakistanis in your neighborhood or are they all foreigners?"

Get the joke?

We had built a Muslim community along cultural lines, based on national origin. But partying and singing alone weren't going to make Muslims out of the children. They needed a community based along religious lines.

All Religion Is Local

What are we going to do for Eid prayers? It's not easy to bundle up two children and drive all the way into Manhattan on a weekday. They say politics is local. I say: religion has to be local too. Long distance can work only up to a point.

Khalid came home one day and told me that the Albanian mosque on Staten Island was holding Eid prayers. Now, my geography is pretty good, but I had to squint to recall Albania on the map. I had no idea that Albania had a Muslim population, let alone enough Muslim immigrants in New York to have a mosque on, of all places, Staten Island. No wonder I hadn't found them in the *Yellow Pages*; my world of Muslim names was limited to the nomenclature of the subcontinent—Khan, Ahmed, Rehman, Saleem—not Strelic, Velic, Govic. Talk about a humbling moment. Anyhow, the Albanians, bless them, held the Eid prayers, and the place was packed. Albanian women, all dressed in flowing white garb, with serene faces, meditating in unison, prayer beads clicking rhythmically to the imam's note, looked like a flock of angels. There was more good news: we found new Pakistani/Indian families there. But here was the problem: the sermon was in Albanian. It didn't matter to us adults—we were not at risk (or so we thought), but we wanted our children to understand the sermon.

Now what?

Cultural Divide

We had to have our own place, a place where we could hold the sermon in English. But where? And how do we find an imam to give the sermon? Who will lead the prayers? And do we have a critical mass to hold and support a congregation? We did not have an answer and so kept going back to the Albanian Mosque for Eid prayers.

Our life had taken on a new trajectory. With Khalid in private practice, me in school, and partying off the calendar, we let another few years slip by. Jimmy Carter lost to Ronald Reagan, and General Zia ul Haq tightened his grip on Pakistan.

God was watching over us. We got a call. Eid prayers were being held in Burgher Hall, and the sermon would be in English. Apparently, one of the Indian/Pakistani doctors had rented the hall; another doctor gave the sermon and led the prayers; someone went around collecting donations; and there it was. Someone had made it happen. The small hall was full. New faces—all of Pakistani/Indian descent.

Muslims on Staten Island were now separated by boundaries of national origin, language being the driver. And we had a forum for Eid prayers.

But we parents knew that congregating twice a year on Eid wasn't going to do it. We needed a schooling system for our children. Something along the model of an American Sunday school.

15.

A Muslim Sunday School and a Mosque

I had never been inside a mosque in Pakistan, and there was no such thing as a Sunday school. Religion was a home-based department, and every family did it their own way. And here we were, a bunch of religiously ignorant mothers, trying to model religion the American way. Was there anybody out there who could show us the way?

Circa 1980s
In a House
I wasn't doing anything about it. I was in a full-time job with a long commute to Brooklyn, adjusting to a new life, and could barely handle the basics. Children's religious education got back-burnered, and I was no longer home-schooling them in religion either. I did worry, but that is where it stopped.

A godsend. A phone call: "A doctor has bought a house for a Muslim Sunday School for children, and classes are starting on Sunday." Think of it. Someone actually bought a house and just gave it to whomever to run a Sunday school. I had no idea who this generous doctor was, what the arrangement was, or who was teaching classes. I was just grateful it had happened.

For sure, we were there on Sunday. Staten Islanders, if you are reading this, it was on Gansevoort Boulevard, right off the Staten Island Expressway. I walked into the living room and saw children sitting on the rug and an Indian doctor teaching them. *Thank you, thank you.*

Downstairs in the basement, an Indian doctor had set up classes for adults. *Who cares about the adult classes?* Looking back, I wish I had cared, because I had to self-teach when, years later during the first Gulf war, I found my back against the wall. In the kitchen, a lady had taken charge and was serving tea and goodies. Saqib and Asim fell right into it, and all I could do was feel grateful.

Within weeks, Sunday school took on the feel of a community center. Someone brought a cake—it was her child's birthday. Someone didn't show up because one of them was sick—and everyone rallied around to help them out. Children were setting play dates; Ramadan *iftar* invitations for dinner were being issued; and on and on. My boys now had Muslim friends on Staten Island. In those first few weeks, for the first time, I felt that I belonged.

I belong to a community. There are people who know I exist, people whom I see every week, who care about what is happening in my life, who will call me when my child is sick, celebrate with me, be there for me. Khalid and I are not alone.

Saqib and Asim were now reading Arabic, with an Arabic accent (I read it with an Urdu accent that would make an Arab want to scream), they knew their prayers, and they were learning about the values of Islam. Above all, they were schooling with Muslim children, a prerequisite for confidence building. Khalid and I went with them every Sunday, and stayed. The first time I heard my children say, "Prophet Muhammad, peace be upon him," I wanted to fall on my knees.

One summer Sunday, I handed Asim his shorts.

"Mummy, teacher says we cannot wear shorts to Sunday school."

Ouch! I didn't know that. Khalid then explained that in the mosques in Pakistan men had to be covered from the waist down to the ankles.

"What about the waist up?" I asked.

"It doesn't have to be covered."

Oh.

In a Mosque

We outgrew the space—within months.

Another godsend: the Albanian Mosque offered us space, free of charge, to hold our Sunday school. They are a blessed community; they take care of their people; they have preserved their culture and faith; and now they have the most beautiful mosque on Staten Island. Years later when Asim was to marry, it was the imam of the Albanian mosque who would perform the *nikah*.

Khalid and I were now committed, committed to clearing our calendar every Sunday. No more weekend trips to the Poconos, no more drives out to Long Island to huddle with friends, no more Sunday matinees, no more walks in the park. Sunday school was not going to be a place where our children went only when they had nothing else to do, and it was not going to be a place where we dropped off the children and drove off to run errands. For me personally, it was not the adult classes that were the draw, it was the adults. I wanted to get to know the mothers, whose children my boys would be socializing with. I wanted this socializing to be a family event, hoping to create and nurture a Muslim community. Every mother who parked her car and got off to stay had the same drive. Children made friends at the drop of a *dupatta*. Private home parties became community parties as Sunday school families merged into our social groups. Saturday night parties closed with, "See you at Sunday school tomorrow." Good-byes at Sunday school were punctuated with, "See you at dinner tonight." And everyone was invited. That was the unwritten rule. If someone wasn't your type, too bad. The distinction between friends and acquaintances was erased. You had to open your home to everyone. This gift-wrapped package was all-inclusive.

Reach for the Crescent

One day Khalid and I got a call from one of the Pakistani doctors from Sunday school, inviting us to attend a meeting at the school. He explained that our Muslim community would soon outgrow this space and we needed to start planning for a place of our own—a mosque.

Build a mosque! A few families will build a mosque! How thrilling is that!

I counted the days to Sunday.

We were going to plan a mosque for our children. Where would we even start? Where will we get the money? Would it look like a mosque, as in domes and minarets? I told the children, showing them photos of mosques. *I want them to feel the pioneering spirit.* As a young hospital administrator, I did have some exposure to planning, construction management, and community outreach, enough to appreciate the complexity of our undertaking.

Muslim readers in the US know how this story unfolds. It is a shared narrative. Interest is forbidden so you cannot take a mortgage—has to be a cash purchase—which means fundraising. Khalid, all pumped up, agreed to serve as chairman of the building committee. The committee's charge was to look for a property—buy or build. Khalid took this project by the throttle and flew with it. I inserted myself somewhere between the role of a copilot and a flight attendant. From then on, mosque building was all we talked about—well, almost all. We talked about it on the way home from the Sunday school; we talked about it over dinner; we talked about it after dinner; and we talked about it in bed.

On weekdays, when I got home from work, as I busied myself preparing dinner while the boys did their homework, Khalid would give me his building committee report.

"The mosque has to be beautiful. Our children should take pride in their place of worship. . . . It should have a community center on the grounds, a place where children can have their activities, apart and separate from a mosque," he said.

I like that. Take the gatherings out of the home parties into a community center. Create a space where children can play sports, have a library, do teen activities, maybe even have a gym, in the company of Muslim friends, within the boundaries of Islamic values.

Khalid always got home before I, the commuter. As I entered through the garage downstairs, making my way up to the kitchen, and heard the excitement in Khalid's *Salaam Alaikum* from above, I would know that he had a good mosque-finding day.

"I saw a piece of property today. It's an old church." He helped me with my coat and gloves.

"Will the church owners be OK with us converting it into a mosque?" I asked, as I made my way to the bedroom to put away my briefcase.

"They are OK with that. The problem is the price. They are in a hurry to sell, and we need more time to raise the funds." He had followed me back into the kitchen.

"Mummy's home," I called out. "What is the property like?" I was heating whatever it was that I had cooked—probably chicken curry or *keema matar*. I would cook for the whole week on weekends. Khalid was setting the table, and I was having a mommy moment with Saqib and Asim.

Khalid continued his story over dinner. Saqib and Asim wanted to know what changes would be made to the interior of a church to make it more mosque-ish. Khalid promised to drive us all after Sunday school to show us the church.

"When did you make the time to see the church?" I asked.

"In the afternoon, between hospital rounds and office hours."

Thank God for Khalid. Only he can squeeze hours out of minutes. Somewhere between rounds at two hospitals at both ends of Staten Island, seeing patients in his office, and making house calls, he goes mosque hunting.

The church deal did not go through.

Meanwhile, Khalid kept coming up with bright ideas, one of which was to approach the borough president of Staten Island. It started with a conversation in the doctor's lounge of St. Vincent's Hospital. Khalid made his pitch to a colleague, whose father was a former borough president. "I want my children to grow strong in their beliefs. . . . I want to preserve our religious traditions. . . . They need a place where they can congregate, pray together, play together . . . a mosque, a place they can be proud of . . . We first-generation immigrants have no experience in establishing a house of worship." And then he put forward his ask: "Can your father help?" This Catholic Italian doctor was so moved that he promised to speak to his dad. True to his word, he arranged for Khalid to meet his father. A gentle elder statesman, the former borough president was magnanimous. He got Khalid an appointment and accompanied him to the office of the Hon. Ralph Lamberti, borough president of Staten Island.

A man with a gracious and humble demeanor, committed to diversity, he listened with interest.

"How did it go?" I asked that evening.

"He says he will help in any way he can. Apparently, the city has designated parcels of land for religious organizations to purchase. Someone will get back to me."

I bet this was the first in the borough president's career. A respected elder statesman comes to his office and asks him to help this handsome Pakistani Muslim doctor build a mosque. I bet he couldn't resist Khalid's charm.

This was the mid-1980s, not the world we live in now, and the toxin of Islamophobia had not infected the American psyche. The borough president said yes. Would that happen today, in the post-9/11 era?

"I have invited him to come to our Sunday school graduation," Khalid said to Saqib and Asim. "The borough president will be awarding you your certificates."

I didn't know what surprised me more: Khalid's audacity in inviting him, or the borough president's acceptance.

"You invited the borough president!" The board was in utter disbelief.

"How are we going to pull this off? We don't have a venue, we don't have an audience, we can't invite the borough president to an empty hall."

"It'll get done." Khalid was calm.

Reach for the crescent.

My children will be proud of being Muslims. The borough president handing them certificates, recognizing them as young Muslims. We are going to make this the most beautiful, organized, and well-attended ceremony. And we will fill the hall. The borough president will not be disappointed.

Graduation day came—June 30, 1985. The auditorium in the Staten Island Academy was packed. Families in traditional garb—*shalwar kameez*, saris, *jalabeeya*, African headdresses, pantsuits, and long skirts; women with headscarves, women without headscarves, and men in suits. We had organized a combined graduation for three Sunday schools on Staten Island: Albanian, Egyptian, and ours. To the marching tune, the students filed in, girls in white dresses and white leggings, the boys in white shirts, neckties, and gray slacks. Mr. Lamberti handed each child their certificate, shook hands, and smiled into the camera. When he took the podium to speak and offered his support to the Muslim community, the audience rose to an applause that resounded beyond the walls of the auditorium, all the way to the ballot box. I stole a look at the children.

Relish your proud Muslim moment.

A decade later, when Mr. Lamberti, now out of office, visited our home for a holiday party, Khalid pointed out two photos on the mantle: Saqib and Asim receiving certificates from him. He looked at Asim and said, "See how I am bending down to hand you the certificate, and now you are bending down to shake my hand."

Mosque Hunting

I had just returned home from work, and walking up the stairs, I sensed a wistful note in Khalid's greeting.

"I wish I had the money!" he said.

"What happened?" I knew it was mosque-related. That was all we thought about.

He followed me to the bedroom. He had met with someone at Borough Hall, who had gone over parcels of land designated for religious organizations. The prices were discounted, but the tracts were so large that the price was out of our reach.

"These are solid properties and a great location," he told me. "The tracts cannot be broken up to meet our budget. We are back to the start."

He is trying so hard. For his sake, I pray that we get the mosque.

Over the next six months, Khalid and a member of the board looked at houses, a church, land, more houses, and finally settled on a warehouse. We could raise the funds to purchase it, but then it would sit for a long time until we had the funds to make it functional. In December 1985, the deal was closed.

Where did the money come from? Every Muslim community in the United States that has built a mosque knows the formula: fundraising parties, fundraising picnics, fundraising auctions, fundraising. . . . You go to the same trough again and again and again until people stop looking you in the eye. Mosque fundraising is local. Forget about reaching out to the donor in the next town; he has his own mosque to give to. I was up to my expanding waist in fundraising events. As we got close to wrapping the deal, Khalid got on the phone and called the board members: "Board members are committed to donating $5,000 each. I am coming to pick up the check." He was ringing doorbells that evening. I sat on edge, at home, hoping we'd make the down payment. "Children, Daddy is out collecting money for the mosque." I told them.

They should see what it takes—torchbearers of the future. They should know that Daddy is making history, and they can too.

One of the board members complained that Khalid was being heavy-handed. Years later, he would recount this episode with a footnote: "Things got done because Khalid rang doorbells."

Construction started. Our living room became the forum for meetings with the architect. On my way to work, I would drive by the site, sit in the car, and watch the cranes lift steel beams. *It's actually happening!* One morning so very close to the finish line, we ran out of funds. We had wanted to hold the opening on Eid, which was fast approaching. The community coffers were exhausted. Khalid suggested that we reach out to members of the Association of Physicians of Pakistani Descent of North America (APPNA) and ask for a small amount. I typed the appeal letter: it's Eid, we are inches away, please send us just $50, that's all we are asking, and we will have a mosque. Families congregated in our living room that evening to stuff the envelopes, hundreds of them. It worked. Checks started pouring in, and we completed the construction. I would later mail the donors a thank-you letter with two photos: the interior of the mosque before your check, and the completed mosque with people praying, after your check. Thank you, APPNA members.

The mosque opened its doors on March 5, 1989, and my children witnessed a dream realized. It had taken three years to bring that vision from an idea to a warehouse to a mosque, and on the way we banged our heads going over many a speed bump.

Meanwhile, I found myself reintroducing Islamic rituals in my daily routines and in my home, compelled not by my religious beliefs, but by my children. And I found myself questioning some of our practices. The edges of the motifs in my prayer rug were getting blurred.

PART FOUR

Rediscovering Islam:
Religion or Culture?

16.

Born-Again Muslim

Bringing my children into the fold of Islam had a prerequisite. I myself had to start practicing the rituals that had fallen off my schedule. I retrieved my prayer rug. I didn't know how to reboot. My children showed me the path—in many ways it contrasted with the Pakistani Islam, some of which I welcomed and some of which I was uneasy with. I had to restart, relearn, reinvent, and question.

Submission
"Mummy, we are supposed to say our prayers five times a day," Saqib said.
    I better start praying.
    "It will be prayer time in ten minutes," Saqib said.
    How does he know the prayer timings?
    "Asim, have you done your *wudu*?" Saqib asked.
    I saw Asim go into the bathroom and perform ablution, the ritual purification, before offering prayers. If you have had the chance to notice Muslims performing ablution in public bathrooms at rest stops, you will recall seeing them wash their extremities, i.e. hands, face, arms, and feet. I must confess that washing one's feet in a sink is awkward. I once lost my balance. You also get the floor wet, risking a fall. At rest stops, I symbolically rub a damp hand over my socks—God will understand. Mosques have ablution areas, designed for washing feet while comfortably seated on a stool.

"Daddy, can I give the *adhan*?" Saqib said.

Oh, my God! My children know the Call to Prayer. Thank you, Sunday school. Thank you teacher.

He stood in a corner, put his right hand to his ear, and called out in a melodious voice, *"Allahu Akbar . . ."*

God is Great,

There is only one God,

Muhammad is His Messenger,

Come to Prayer,

Come to Success,

God is Great,

There is only one God.

Saqib was perfect. *Oh, God! Thank you.*

In Pakistan, no one had ever given the adhan *in the house. It was broadcast from the minarets of the mosque five times a day, and if there were five mosques in the neighborhood, you would hear twenty-five* adhans *a day. I don't believe I even paid attention to the wording of the* adhan. *Etiquette, however, required that as soon as we heard the* adhan, *women would cover their heads with the* dupatta *and stop talking. As soon as the* adhan *was over, off came the* dupatta, *and the chatter resumed. Some men would head out to the mosque; no one in our home went to the mosque.*

"Teacher said it is better to pray in congregation," said Saqib.

"Yes, of course."

I didn't know that.

We obeyed. I handed Khalid the prayer rug, a two-by-four-foot rug threaded in red, gold, and green, patterned with an arch, with floral designs on the edges, and a soft and silky feel. Khalid placed the rug facing northeast, orienting us toward the Kaaba, the shrine in Mecca built by Abraham. The teacher had told us that though Mecca is southeast of New York, we calculate the shortest distance between where we stand and the Kaaba, which is over the North Pole. I spread a bed sheet behind him; Saqib and Asim stood behind Khalid; and I stood behind them all, covering my hair.

I have to get more prayer rugs on my next trip to Pakistan. And can someone explain to me why women have to stand behind men? It makes me feel secondary—relegated to the back. What will my children think? How do we explain it to them?

Khalid led the prayer, and we followed in unison. For the first time, we were offering congregational prayers in our home. Khalid recited the opening chapter of the Qur'an in Arabic, asking for God's guidance, then a short chapter of the Qur'an. We bowed together, kneeled with our foreheads to the ground in submission to God's will, sat in silent prayer, stood up again, and repeated the cycle until the prayer was over. We said, "Peace," to the angel on our right shoulder recording our good deeds and to the angel on our left shoulder recording our not-so-good deeds. Holding a *tasbeeh*, we recited the names of God over the prayer beads, glorifying Him. Khalid raised his hands and began the supplication—a personal conversation with God, in English, thanking him for His blessings, for the health of his family, their well-being, asking for them to be good Muslims, for the children to do well in school. I cupped my hands and silently added a few more items on my wish list to God. We hugged each other, folded the prayer rug and sheet, and put them away until the next prayer.

In Pakistan, I never prayed in congregation. That was reserved for the mosques. I would pray in a quiet private area of the house, usually a bedroom. And we prayed facing west, toward Mecca.

"Saqib, how did you know that it was prayer time?" I asked.

"Teacher gave us a *salat* timetable."

"Really! Can I have a look, please?"

Sure enough, a prayer schedule for each day of the month, for each of the five daily prayers. Daybreak, noon, afternoon, sunset, and night. Daybreak was at 5:40 a.m. on the first, 5:41 a.m. on the second, and so on. In Pakistan we never used a timetable. One knew it was prayer time when one heard the *adhan*. In the US, one had to figure out the approximate time by the movement of the sun.

What a great idea to have a schedule! How did the teacher get this information? And for that matter, how did the muezzin in Pakistan know the exact time for the prayer?

Khalid surmised that the teacher must have contacted the observatory.

I learned later that morning prayer begins when the morning light starts spreading horizontally and ends when the tip of the sun becomes visible; noon prayer, after the sun has reached its zenith and our shadow is shortest in length; afternoon prayer, when our shadow is longest; evening prayer, when the upper tip of the sun sinks below the horizon; and night prayer, when the sun loses its redness. In the short days of winter, the interval between the midday prayers is short. If you are out Christmas shopping between noon and 5:00 p.m. in December, chances are you will miss your noon, afternoon, and evening prayers. Likewise, in June, you can come home from work at 6:00 p.m. and still make it on time for your afternoon prayer. I liked the feeling of prayer time keeping us in sync with the cosmos—just follow the movement of the sun across the sky.

"What will happen if I miss my prayer?" Asim asked.

Aha! This I can answer.

"Sweetheart, you can make up for missed prayers. Just state your intention and offer the prayer you missed." Aba Jee had told me that.

One day, the dreaded question was asked.

"How come Mummy isn't praying with us?" Congregational prayers at home had become the norm—during the evening hours and on weekends. Khalid was left with the task of making an excuse for me. I don't know what he said, but I do know what he did not say: "She is having her period."

Don't ask me why. It is just the way it is. The practice of rituals—in my opinion—has its hang-ups, which beg to be sorted out.

I am twelve, saying my prayers in the drawing room in Pakistan, when I sense my aunt come and stand beside me. As soon as I finish, she beckons me to get up and follow her. In her bedroom, she whispers, "You don't say your prayers when you are menstruating."

"Why not?"

"Because you are impure."

"Can I read the Qur'an?"

"*No.*"

I didn't question it.

Isn't it remarkable how the irrational interpretation of the sacred text—striking a week off the girl's monthly prayer schedule—goes unchallenged, is embraced, universally adopted, and passed on from aunt to niece? Why did women just accept the edict that they were impure? Did they really believe that God did not want to hear from them? Or were they just relieved to be on prayer vacation? Sorry, ladies, but I hold women responsible for allowing this, including me. If only they had studied the Qur'an. If only I had.

I am happy to report that the position on this practice has finally been elevated from certainty to controversial. Too late for me—post-menopause.

"Khalid, what is this business of women praying behind men?" I asked one day. I made sure the children were out of range.

"It's all about control. Some men decided that it is best to keep women at the back, and it became the rule." Others told me that it was to protect the privacy of women while prostrating. *What about the privacy of men?* Some explained that women prefer to be together in their own space. *Did anyone ask the women?*

My children didn't question it openly, but they must have thought about it. Two years later, when we performed the hajj—the pilgrimage to Mecca—we noticed that at prayer time men and women were separated but women were not relegated to the back. Here, in the holiest place in the Muslim world! *Can someone explain this discrepancy to me?*

Back in New York, I started speaking up. The organizers agreed but placed a moveable wall to separate men from women. We had our own space, in the front, but were visibly cut off and could not see the imam leading the prayer on the other side of the divide, and thus could not follow him in the movements. One evening, in the midst of prayer, we women realized that we had been standing instead of sitting, and bending instead of kneeling. As soon as the prayer was over, I and another woman walked over to the men's section, spoke up, and spoke out: "Tear down this wall. You have ruined our prayer."

The wall came down.

A Time to Reflect

"Mummy, Ramadan starts tomorrow. Teacher said children don't have to fast, but all grownups should fast. Aren't you going to fast?"

"Yes, yes, of course I am."

Vacation over. Start fasting.

I hadn't fasted in a decade. Neither had Khalid. But there we were, an hour before the crack of dawn, having *suhoor. Thank you, children, for making Muslims out of us.* The first day was hard. It wasn't the hunger or the thirst; it was the splitting headaches from caffeine withdrawal. The second day was easier, and by the third day, the headaches were gone. *Iftar* wasn't until 8:00 p.m. When I came home from work at 6:00 p.m., I would give the children their dinner, and Khalid and I would eat at sundown.

"Can we fast for just a day? Please, please," Saqib asked.

"Tell you what. How about if you fast for half a day on Sunday."

"Yeah!"

So every Sunday, Saqib and Asim would wake up at 3:00 a.m., have breakfast, and break their fast at lunchtime. They loved it. At Sunday school they would show off.

"Half-a-day fast is not fasting," said one of the boys.

"My mother says it is for children."

That's right. Stand up for your mother.

"What happens if I eat when I am fasting?"

"If you eat accidentally, because you forgot, then just ask God for forgiveness and continue with your fast. If you intentionally eat, then your fast is broken, and you have to make up for it."

Please, let them not ask the next question: how do you make up for it? I have no idea. How am I going to make a good Muslim out of them if I don't know the rules?

I called my friends. I got three different answers:

You have to fast an extra day;

You have to feed the poor for a day;

You ask God for forgiveness.

The right answer? None of the above. The teacher confirmed that if you deliberately break your fast, you have to fast for two consecutive months or feed sixty people. If you don't have the means, then give whatever charity you can.

You live and learn. Take your fasting seriously.

The time of the day I relished was after *suhoor* and before the daybreak. I would curl up with the Qur'an and recite it in Arabic and study its translation. The house was quiet, it was still dark outside, and I could feel the power and beauty of the Qur'anic verses. God revealed these verses to Prophet Muhammad. This was God speaking to me, urging, comforting, and guiding me. The verses gave me pause as I reflected on the simplicity of the message. By the end of Ramadan, I had completed the recitation of the entire Qur'an. My mother told me that we fast so that we know what it is like for those who live in hunger. For a child, that was an appropriate answer. But I was beginning to see that Ramadan was much more than an exercise in restraint, that if you can control your appetite, you can control other impulses. It was a time to appreciate the blessings we take for granted, and to give to those in need. It was a time for reflection, a time to spiritually cleanse oneself and connect with the divine.

Fasting at Work

This wasn't going to be easy. Daylight Savings Time was in effect, and the fasting days were long. Each evening, Khalid and I would make our silent intent to fast the following day, set the alarm for 3:00 a.m., drag ourselves out of bed, prepare breakfast, force-feed ourselves with cold cereal—remember, who has an appetite at 3:00 a.m.?—wait for the clock to strike 4:15 a.m. for daybreak, say our prayers, and then head back to bed at 4:30 a.m. Now that we were fully awake, good luck falling asleep.

I have to get some sleep. I am not used to lying in bed with a full stomach. If I don't fall asleep quickly, I will be dozing off at my desk, or fade out in a meeting. Stop thinking—just blank out and let your mind rest. Count camels.

An hour later, I would fall asleep, only to have to rouse myself at 7:00 a.m. Rush hour: get dressed, wake up the children, get them breakfast, off to school, off to work. I'd walk into the office looking like I had been up since 3:00 a.m.

At lunch time, my colleagues invited me, and the conversation went something like this:

"Want to join us for lunch?" my colleague asked. I was now working at the Health and Hospitals Corporation in Manhattan.

"No thank you." *Should I tell them?*

"Having a late lunch?"

"Actually, I am fasting. It's Ramadan."

"Oh, I am sorry."

So polite!

"Maybe tomorrow?" she asked.

"Actually, it's for a whole month."

"A whole month! You can't eat for a whole month?"

"It's not like that. I break my fast at sundown, and then I can eat until daybreak the next day."

"It's a long day. Well, at least you can drink."

"No. I can't drink either. No eating, no drinking."

"Not even water?"

"Not even water."

"Bless you."

And No Sex

What? I didn't know that! Fasting was "No eating and no drinking." Where did "No sex" come from?

I was at Sunday school and had dropped in on the adult classes. The teacher was giving a lecture on—you guessed it—Ramadan. "From daybreak to sundown, Muslims refrain from eating, drinking, and marital relations."

All those years in Pakistan, nobody ever told me that. Not my parents, not my grandparents. Of course, they didn't. It wasn't applicable. Unmarried girls and boys didn't have sex. Why bother telling them to abstain from what they already abstain from. I could not picture my parents and grandparents waving their finger at me, "And no sex." Besides, talking about sex was off limits. What confounds me is that my friends didn't tell me either. Girls talked and eagerly imparted any new information on the forbidden topic. Every now and then, a steamy book was brought into the hostel—*Valley of the Dolls* was a favorite—and we girls talked about the dreaded wedding night, yet no "wise" girl ever offered this bit of information. We were not just naïve; we were ignorant. To test my hypothesis, I did a poll while writing my memoir. I got on the phone and called my friends in the US.

Voicemail.

I left messages.

"This is Sabeeha. I have a juicy question. I cannot say it to voicemail or text it. Just call me."

In minutes, my friends were calling.

"What's the juicy question?"

"Tell me, when we were in college, did you know that sex was forbidden during fasting?"

Pause.

"Let me think. No. I didn't know. How could I? Sex was already off limits."

Here is what one of them said:

"I am sure I knew."

"How did you know? Did your parents tell you?"

"No, of course not. Parents didn't talk about sex."

"How did you know?"

"Well, maybe my elder sister? No, she never talked about these things. Talking about sex was taboo. No one ever prepared us for sex in marriage either. And now that I am having this discussion, I am beginning to doubt that I knew."

Hypothesis confirmed. We were ignorant.

A few days later I was having lunch with my Jewish friend, Toni. I related this story.

"So that means that Muslim women don't give birth nine months after Ramadan," she said.

"Right. No, wrong. You have to abstain only when you are fasting, which is from daybreak to sundown. But you *can* eat, drink, and be merry between sundown and daybreak."

"Ah, just no daytime sex."

Luncheon Meetings—without the Lunch

The aroma of coffee in the office didn't help. At luncheon meetings, I would be the only one not helping myself to the spread.

"Sabeeha, you are not eating?"

Just say it.

"I am fasting."

"I am sorry. We shouldn't be eating when you are fasting," said my boss, Ted Jamison. I was now working at the Interfaith Medical Center in Brooklyn.

"No. No. It's perfectly all right. Please go ahead."

He must have said something to his secretary. The next time a meeting was scheduled, she asked me if I was fasting. I was. She moved the time to avoid lunch, and I noticed that coffee was off the table.

Only in America.

In years to come, I would try to keep my fasting low profile, so as not to disrupt the flow of the workplace. But as awareness about Ramadan increased, it became a moot point.

"Coming for lunch?"

"No, thank you."

"Ah, it's Ramadan, isn't it?"

Years later, when Ramadan moved into the winter months and sundown was as early as 4:30 p.m., I had to break my fast at work. Delaying the breaking of the fast is not an option. I would keep a few dates in my desk drawer, watch the clock, and break my fast with dates and a cup of water, and then, ahhh—coffee. If my boss or staff walked into my office, their standard response was, "I'm sorry. I'll come back." And then someone would bring me a cookie, a muffin. . . .

Several times, when meetings ran late, I would be sitting at the conference table, and as it got close to sundown, I would start checking my watch every minute. If you had been at the table, you would have seen me fumble into my briefcase, retrieve something, and pop a date in my mouth. My boss would give me a knowing nod with a smile.

"Sabeeha had to break her fast. It's Ramadan," he'd say.

"Shall we take a ten-minute break?" came a gracious offer from a participant.

"Thank you, but I'm fine."

Only in America.

It was harder when sundown was on my way home, as in 5:30 p.m. I had my car stocked with dates and water, but breaking the fast at the exact minute was a challenge. I could be at the tollbooth fishing out change—this was before the days of EZPass—or speeding away on the highway or just lose track of time.

People in Pakistan have it easy. Halfway across the world, they adjust working hours during Ramadan, have iftar *breaks at the office, no luncheon meetings. At* iftar *time, everything stops—businesses, offices, traffic, movie theaters—and people stop to break fast. Here in New York, I am going against the flow, and my goodness, it is a struggle. I suppose this is what is meant by jihad—the inner struggle—the struggle to overcome obstacles for the higher purpose of submitting to God. I don't see it as a hardship, rather as a challenge. I feel a stirring of pride, a feeling that is foreign to my friends in Pakistan. I no longer miss Ramadan in Pakistan—I sort of like the version of American Ramadan we have crafted. So what if it isn't entirely convenient?*

Is Ramadan in Summer or in Winter?

Were you wondering how it is that Ramadan moved into the winter months? Muslim readers, this question is not for you. So here is a one-paragraph course in Islam 101. I promise not to bore you.

The Islamic calendar is based on the lunar cycle. The new moon signals the beginning of the month. A lunar year is shorter—just 355 days. The Muslim New Year therefore begins ten days earlier each year. If Ramadan began on June 30 this year, next year it would begin around June 20, and the year after around June 10, and twelve years later, in the winter months. Thus one gets to experience fasting in all seasons. On one sunny Eid day in New York in July, I called my cousin in Australia.

It was the middle of winter there, and she was having a white-snowy Eid. "Your turn will come," she said to me. "In eighteen years, you too will have snow on your doorsteps on Eid."

Summers are a challenge, because the days are long and one can be fasting for as long as sixteen hours. Managing thirst is hard, and one has to be cautious and avoid dehydration. No jogging in Central Park.

Period Break

I mentioned earlier that when a woman has her period, she is exempt from fasting but has to make it up later. You also know how I feel about both the break and the exemption. Try explaining this at the workplace: It's Ramadan, I am fasting. It's Ramadan, I am not fasting.

If I don't understand why women cannot fast during the menstrual cycle, how can I explain it to my coworkers? Besides, who wants to advertise "that time of the month"?

Do I keep a low profile?

Do I pretend I am fasting and avoid the explanation?

Do I appear to be noncompliant, which I am not?

Do I tell it like it is?

"Coming to lunch? Sorry, didn't realize it's Ramadan."

"I'll come. I'm taking a break."

No questions asked.

Phew! Thank God Americans are not as nosy as Pakistanis.

What about the children? During the long summer days, when *iftar* was late in the evenings, say around 8:00 p.m., I would have dinner with the children at 6:00 p.m. Khalid would wait until sundown.

"Isn't Mummy fasting?"

"Mummy is taking a break," Khalid would explain.

Living in the college hostel in Pakistan, taking a break during Ramadan is everybody's business. I am serious. On the bulletin board of the dining room is a roster titled, "Students Not Fasting." Girls on a break put down their names for the next day. The kitchen plans the meals according to the head count. One day, I forget to put down my name (yes, it was that time of the month). At the stroke of the deadline, the roster is removed and there I am, locked out of the dining room. Some girls are too embarrassed to advertise their break and forego the meals, eating in the privacy of their rooms on an overextended budget. There are always a few girls who do not fast by choice. But by and large, this is an open advertisement of who is having their period.

If you can come up with a better privacy-protection system, I'd love to hear it.

Communal Iftars

Think of it this way: in Ramadan, every Friday, Saturday, and Sunday you and all your friends, as in "all" your friends, get together for huge dinner parties. Have you ever done that? By the way, this question is for non-Muslim readers. Monday through Thursday, we would eat at home, but on weekends we got together with friends for a communal *iftar*. No sooner had Ramadan started than friends would start calling.

"I am hosting the first Saturday of Ramadan. *Iftar* at my place."

"I am hosting the first Sunday."

Everyone was invited to the home. If you weren't among the first twelve to book the weekend, you were out of luck. Hosting an *iftar* was a privilege. In the *iftar* package was: (1) reading of the Qur'an—all thirty volumes; (2) *iftar*—breaking of the fast with refreshments; (3) evening prayer in congregation; (4) dinner; (5) night prayer in congregation; and (6) *taraweeh*—a special Ramadan night prayer, a long congregational prayer.

It's my turn to host the *iftar*. I try to be organized, planning my menu a week in advance and doing my grocery shopping the night before, running through the aisles of Pathmark on Richmond Avenue, list in hand. Khalid picks up the meat from the halal grocer on his way home from the hospital.

"Don't cook too much food. People are not very hungry after breaking their fast," says Khalid.

"Yes, but I don't want to be short on food."

If there is one thing Khalid and I disagree on, this is it. At every party I have hosted, he always cautions me: "Don't cook too much," and

I always insist on making sure I don't run out, which I never do, and we end up eating leftovers for a week.

On the day of, I can barely sleep after dawn, my to-do list running through my mind.

Did I forget to buy something? Will I have enough food? I hope the children do not make much noise when everyone is praying. Oh dear, I forgot to get the recipe for palak gosht. *It's no use, I might as well get up and get started.*

Khalid and I get the house ready. Sofas are moved against the wall to create floor space for guests to sit on. Sheets are spread on the rug— pale yellow king-size flat sheets I found at Macys. Colorful pillows are placed against the wall for back support, incense burners are lit, and thirty volumes of the Qur'an are placed on the coffee table with the sign To Be Read. Next to the stack, I place another sign: Com p leted. Once a volume is read, it will be placed in the "completed" section. It takes me all day to cook, with Khalid helping chop the onions (he cannot bear to see my tears), crush the garlic (he likes my hands fragrant), skin the potatoes, cube the meat, wash the pots, and do anything I need a hand with.

I hope I didn't put in too much salt or make it too spicy. I wish I could taste the food, just to be sure. Oh, the aroma is making me so hungry. Oh, I am so tired. My feet ache.

"Sit down. Put your feet up. Let me give you a foot massage," says Khalid.

Ahhh!

I put the food in the oven; I will turn it on half an hour before serving. And I go take a shower.

"Saqib and Asim, time to get ready," I call out.

"What should I wear?" Asim asks.

"*Shalwar kameez.*" I wait to hear a groan. I don't hear one. Aha! They know that their friends will be dressed traditional as well.

Precisely an hour before *iftar*, guests start arriving, giving themselves an hour or so to read a volume of the Qur'an. I have invited the Sunday school teachers, one of whom I regard as our spiritual leader. I shall call him Imam. Adults and young adults remove their shoes, enter in silence, say, "*Salaam Alaikum,*" to the assembled guests, pick up a volume of the Qur'an next to the sign To Be Read, take a place on the rug, and silently start reciting. Women cover their hair with the *dupatta.* Children play outside or cluster in the bedroom. If a child were to run in to ask mom something, he would first stumble over the shoes in the foyer, and, making his way to the living room, he would see a room full of people seated on the rug, against the wall, heads lowered, reading the Qur'an, and swaying back and forth, mommies on one side, daddies on the other, the late afternoon sun streaming through the floor-to-ceiling windows. He'd hear a buzz in the air, of whispered chanting, and inhale the fragrance of incense.

It takes me an hour to recite one volume of the Qur'an. I hope enough guests come on time to finish all thirty volumes. Only forty-five minutes left for iftar, *and the pile of "completed" is way lower than the "to be read" pile. Look, she just got up and is walking over to the completed sign, placing her volume in the pile. She is picking up another from the "to be read." That look of devout accomplishment! Maybe we will complete the Qur'an by* iftar *after all.*

Thirty minutes to *iftar.* The "completed" pile is getting taller.

I better get into the kitchen and start preparing the individual dishes for iftar.

Like birds in a flock, the ladies who are done reading join me in the kitchen, and we start chatting in loud whispers.

"Can we help?"

"Yes, please. Here, just put two dates and the fruit *chaat* in the dessert bowls." I point to the stack of foam plates stacked on the counter (I am embarrassed to recall) and watch as the assembly line of ladies gets going. From the living room, I can hear the hum of the recital.

"Here, the *roof afza* has to be poured in these cups." I take the drink out of the fridge and hand them the cups, as the assembly line goes into motion again.

Twenty minutes to *iftar.*

I take a peek in the living room, and the "to be read" pile is almost gone. Some of the men who are done are sitting back and reciting the names of Allah on a *tasbeeh*, and by now all the women are in the kitchen. I turn on the oven to 250.

Fifteen minutes to *iftar*.

Khalid walks into the kitchen, picks up the individual dessert bowls, and starts carefully placing them on the rug in front of each guest; along with the *rooh afza—no tipping over, please.*

"Children, come on in. *Iftar* time. Shoes off."

In my tiny foyer, you have shoes flying all over. Every inch on the floor is carpeted with sneakers, sandals, high heels, pumps, and loafers. Try walking out—you first have to navigate the shoes.

Ten minutes to *iftar*.

The ladies rush back in the living room; the children squeeze in. Every inch on the rug is taken. I look at the To Be Read sign—nothing there. *Ah! The Qur'an is completed.*

Imam starts reciting the last chapters of the Qur'an, and like a curtain call, the room goes quiet.

Even the children are quiet.

Heads are bent. Everyone raises his or her hands in supplication.

Oh, look at the little one, raising her tiny hands in prayer. Adorable.

Imam prays: "May God accept our fasting, may He keep us in good health so that we can continue to fast, guide us on the right path, make us charitable...." *Ameen*, says Imam. *Ameen*, everyone responds in chorus. Some people continue with their private prayer. He starts watching the time. At the precise minute of sundown, he announces, "You may break your fast."

"*Bismillah*," In the name of God, says everyone and picks up the date and then takes a sip of the drink. No one talks—everyone is eating, quietly. It's been a long, hungry, and thirsty day.

I hope we put enough fruit in the bowls for the guests. I hope the drink is not too sweet. Please, don't let the pink drink spill on the rug.

Khalid asks Saqib to give the *adhan*, the call for the evening prayer. Guests line up outside the bathrooms to perform ablution.

I am sure I put enough towels in the bathroom. I did, didn't I?

Someone removes the plates and cups. Someone picks up the sheets and folds them.

Thank you, angels, whoever you are.

Then I notice a guest picking up one of the sheets and draping it over the photographs on the wall.

Yikes! I should have taken care of that ahead of time.

If you have been inside a mosque, you will notice that there are no images of human figures or statues. I remember an elder once telling me that it is to prevent idolatry, i.e., when praying, one is facing God, not the pictures. This was the tradition, and I was going along with it. Later in life, I would question the practice of covering the pictures.

Imam leads the prayer, the men lined up behind, and the women at the back.

You see? No woman questions this practice. We all just line up and do as expected. I can't worry about that right now, I have a dinner to serve.

I can barely concentrate, worrying about the next step—setting out the food and getting everyone through dinner, dessert, and tea before the night prayer.

Maybe I should have turned on the oven sooner—I hope the food heated well. Did I get ice? Allah, forgive me.

Can't I just get the food out of my mind for five minutes!

After prayer, we ladies rush to the kitchen and the men rearrange the room.

Guests compliment me on the delicious food. Not too salty, not too peppery. *Thank God.* The best part of the meal comes after dessert—a hot cup of tea. I make the best tea, so everyone tells me. We barely clean up when I hear Saqib give the *adhan*. It's the night prayer, and the special Ramadan *Taraweeh* prayer. Line up again.

It seems like everyone is not staying for the prayer.

"Thank you for having us. We do have to leave. It's late, and the children need to get to bed." They line up to say good-bye.

Taraweeh prayer is long, and in the summer months it can end as late as 11:00 p.m. By the time you get home, you can barely get three hours of sleep before it's time for *suhoor.*

Next day, if it's Sunday, another communal *iftar.*

One year, when Mummy and Daddy were visiting during Ramadan, Daddy remarked, "I have never spent a Ramadan like this in Pakistan."

He was referring to the communal spirit and activity. In Pakistan, Ramadan was a family affair. There were no weekend communal *iftars*, communal readings of the Qur'an, or congregational prayers in the homes. In New York, being a minority, we were compelled to build a community for our children to belong to, and communal *iftars* were the perfect setting for children to break bread, develop reverence for their faith, and get comfortable in their skin.

I beamed. *Mummy and Daddy are approving of my new lifestyle. They will go back feeling good.*

Saqib took the ritual with him when he went away to Haverford College. He simply spoke to the person in charge of the dining room, who, saying, "No problem," had a breakfast box prepared for him every day for *suhoor*.

Only in America.

A Time to Give

"During Ramadan you should give to charity. Do you give to charity?" Saqib asked.

I didn't have an answer.

Khalid has been supporting his parents generously since day one of his employment. Does that count for charity? Charity does begin at home, but checking off that line item as charity doesn't feel right. Other than giving a solicited donation every now and then, we really have not been into the business of charity. Daadee Amma had advised me to give to charity every month, and I didn't pay heed. How much can we afford to give? There is the mortgage, private school, taxes, car loans. . . . Is there a minimum requirement?

"Muslims are required to pay two and a half percent of their savings in *zakah*," Imam answered my question in his Sunday lecture. "Ramadan is the month of giving. Calculate your annual charity obligation and give before the end of the month."

I looked at the handout, which defined who is eligible for receiving charity. Parents were not listed. It described the method for calculating *zakah*, listing the items on which two and a half percent *zakah* is obligatory: savings, gold, commercial property, etc. It explained that God has made us the vessel for redistribution of wealth to the needy. He urges us to spend out of what He has given us, and discourages us from hoarding.

So zakah is obligatory only on hoarded items, which prevent money from circulating.

How does one figure out the two and a half percent on gold? I have all this jewelry but have no idea of its gold value.

I got my jewelry out of the bank safe deposit, weighed it on a kitchen scale, deducted what I estimated was the weight of precious stones—a conservative estimate— looked up the value of gold on the market, and calculated the two and a half percent. Done. That plus the savings, and I had a number.

Who to give to? The Pakistan model didn't apply. There are no beggars lined up outside the house or on the streets of Staten Island, nor any orphanages or domestic help whose children need an education. I should ask around.

"I send the money to Pakistan. There is so much poverty there. With the dollar value so high, a little money goes a long way to feed the poor."

"I send the money to India."

"How about the Red Cross?"

"Are non-Muslims eligible for *zakat*?"

I was clueless, and time was running out. I asked Daddy, and he told me about Abdul Sattar Edhi, a man who single-handedly started operating ambulances for the poor in Karachi, Pakistan. Eventually, Edhi's work would expand throughout Pakistan and internationally, with an office in New York.

Over the years, as I continued to study Islam, our attitude toward charity shifted. I learned that there was a pecking order to giving:

Family and kin,

Neighborhood,

Local community,

Country,

World.

What Khalid and I understood was that supporting worldly causes while family members suffer in poverty does not foster kinship. Likewise, take care of your neighbors before you take care of the world. Khalid and I embraced the concept that a strong family and stable neighborhood make a stronger nation. We reprioritized our charity list. We choose not to follow the annual reconciling of the books during Ramadan. Instead, we spread the giving throughout the year through auto-deduction from the bank. I also vowed never to turn down a request for a donation. Those were the days when one did not have to vet each organization to rule out links to terrorists.

The Fifth Pillar—1986

"Let's go for hajj," my friend said to me one day. Just like that. "I have family in Jeddah. They can take care of all the arrangements."

Until that moment, the thought of performing hajj hadn't entered my mind. I knew that all Muslims who can afford to are required to perform the hajj once in a lifetime, but I also knew that in Pakistan people performed the hajj when they got old. Once people had discharged all their obligations, as in marrying off their children, settling their debts, they would go for hajj, and by that time they were well into their platinum years. Mummy and Daddy had performed the hajj just a couple of years ago. I just assumed that Khalid and I would perform the hajj when we were old.

Wouldn't it be much easier if we perform the hajj while we are still young? Everyone talks about the physical hardships of the pilgrimage.

I spoke to Khalid.

"What about the children?" he asked.

"They can go to Pakistan and stay with our parents."

Mummy and Daddy were ecstatic.

"With God's blessings, go perform the hajj. It is better to go with friends, particularly those who have family in Saudi Arabia, just in case you run into difficulties," Mummy said.

"Don't postpone it. Better to do it while you are in good health," Daddy said.

And that settled it. My parents came over, coached us on the rituals, gave us books to read and travel tips, and, before we departed, took the boys with them to Pakistan.

"You need to get your mind ready for hajj," Mummy said before she left. "Start studying the rituals, read the Qur'an, talk about the preparations, and ask your family and friends for forgiveness." This was Mummy advising me on getting into the spiritual mode for hajj. It was not going to be a vacation or a sightseeing trip; this was a pilgrimage to Mecca, to the house of God, where we would immerse ourselves in communion with our Creator and return spiritually cleansed and rejuvenated.

"In the Prophet's Mosque in Medina, make sure you perform forty prayers," Mummy advised. "Walk in his footsteps; visit the places where he made history."

We waved good-bye to Saqib and Asim. It was the first time they were getting on a plane without us.

Be safe. Be well.

Two days before we were to depart, one of our friends held a have-a-blessed-hajj party for us. Everyone was wishing us a blessed pilgrimage and asking us to pray for them. They were handing me their prayer wish lists: pray for my son to get into a good college, pray for my husband's health. . . . One of the women called me out.

"You cannot perform the hajj," she said.

A hush fell into the room.

"Why is that?" I asked.

"Because you have a mortgage on your house."

Is she serious?

"I cannot perform the hajj because I have a mortgage?"

"You are supposed to settle your debts before you go for hajj," she said.

"Ability to afford is the only requirement for eligibility. I can afford the journey."

"No, you cannot. You are in debt."

If I let this go, those watching are going to walk away with the wrong idea. Push back.

My discourse went something like this: settling debt is an Indian-Pakistani tradition, not a religious requirement. There was a time when the hajj was a journey that took months and sometimes years. People traveled on horseback and camelback from places as far as China. Some never made it back home. For them, it was important that they settle their affairs before leaving. In my case, I will get on a plane and be back within two weeks, *Insha'Allah*. Why should I have to pay off my mortgage if I am leaving home for ten days? Don't we take long vacations? How is this different, other than the spiritual aspect?

"This is your interpretation," she said.

"As is yours," I said.

It didn't end there. We continued to argue until someone called for dinner and we stopped. I fumed all the way home.

Hajj was a life-changing experience for me. Arm-in-arm with Khalid, I circumambulated the Kaaba—the black stone structure that Abraham and Ishmael built, and prayed to God for forgiveness. Among a sea of hundreds and thousands of pilgrims, we retraced the path that Hagar took, running seven times between the hills looking for water for baby Ishmael until the spring of Zamzam erupted. A million people walking the walk, commemorating a mother's struggle for her child, honoring a woman. I wondered if they were aware of the esteemed place of a woman. We stood on the plain of Arafat and held out our hands in prayer; we slept under the stars in Muzdalifa; we stoned the devil symbolized in pillars; and in the comfort of shared space, with no space to share, standing shoulder-to-shoulder, we prayed. At every prayer time, someone in our group would stand and lead the prayer—a Nigerian, a Malaysian, an American—reciting the same prayer of guidance that I have been reciting since childhood. We were all the same in prayer, in faith. The lines of nationality and color were erased when we stood in prayer. I noticed something else. None of the women had their face covered. Women are forbidden from covering their face at the Kaaba. Think about it.

By the time I returned to New York, I had made a resolution—my hajj resolution. *I will commit to saying all five prayers every day for the rest of my life.* I had come to the conclusion that the only thing that stood between my prayers and me was me. I equipped my office with the essentials: a prayer rug, a scarf, a gown to drape over my skirt, and bathroom equipment for ablution. At prayer time, I would tell my secretary, "I am closing my door to say my prayers," and no one would disturb me until I opened the door. And that is all it took. At night, as I put my head down on the pillow, I would ask God, "Please wake me up for morning prayer." He does. It's been almost thirty years. I never set an alarm for the morning prayer. But if I am lazy and go back to sleep, saying, "God, wake me up a little later," He does not.

I made another resolution, that in two years we would bring Saqib and Asim for *umrah*, the lesser pilgrimage. *If I bring them here when they are still in high school, they will take it upon themselves to perform hajj on their own when they are adults.* We did return two years later for *umrah*—all four of us. Saqib performed *hajj* three years ago; Asim plans to go this year, *Insha'Allah*.

17.

Lower Your Gaze

I lost my footing once again. I had gotten through hajj, the largest congregation on earth, but couldn't handle the assembly in my living room. Think of a packed subway car; now multiply it ten thousand times, and you have a picture of the hajj. I made more than eye contact during hajj—at times I was skin-to-skin in the crowd—but back home I was jolted into reconciling the boundaries of gender distinction. After the sublime and spiritual experience of hajj, these demarcations felt superficial.

Circa 1980s

I was hosting event-planning meetings for the mosque in my home, where members of the board were present. I was aware of being the only woman in the room, and knew I had to be sensitive to the sensibilities of the men. A few were conservative and may not have been comfortable having a woman in their midst. My work environment had conditioned me, so I wasn't fazed. I am sure they had similar situations in their workplaces. But in this setting, in my living room, we were all Muslims doing the Muslim thing, and Muslim rules applied. A physical distance had to be maintained. So I always took my place on a chair. Were I to sit on a sofa, I would be sitting next to a man, and that would not be acceptable, unless, of course, the man was Khalid. When conversing, some men would look me in the eye; others would lower their gaze. Now, there is a reason for the lowering of the gaze.

It says in the Qur'an: "Tell the believing men to lower their gaze and be mindful of their chastity . . . and tell the believing women to lower their gaze and be mindful of their chastity. . . ."[1] The purpose—as I understand it—is to encourage modesty in exchanges between men and women. I have to confess: I get very uncomfortable when men lower their gaze when talking to me. I feel it's as if I am a threat, and if the man dares makes eye contact he will fall under my spell. Give men more credit than that! I couldn't force myself to lower my gaze and fix it on the static pattern of the rug. The men in attendance were going by the book; I was not. But I found an acceptable medium. Each time I had to speak to someone who did not make eye contact, I would turn to Khalid and make my point. We would exchange a complicit look. I was conversing through my male guardian, a chaperone of sorts. Understand that I had a stake in this. If I wanted to influence decisions, I had to abide by the rules of decorum. I wasn't the only one making compromises; they were too. For the conservative men in our meeting, my presence was a major departure from the norm; yet they accepted it (I'm not saying they welcomed it); they listened when I spoke and agreed with my suggestions. All that without an air of condescension. I owe that to the leadership of the mosque, who had set the tone for accepting me. A year later, I would get emboldened, push my luck, and fall on my face. I will talk about that later.

2014

Recently, I had an end of the bell-curve encounter on lowering the gaze. I met an old friend from college days. Her son was with her. I greeted him. He lowered his gaze. *Oh, come on! I am your mother's age—going on Medicare. Do you really believe you will get swept away?* I thought about it on the drive home. It's his conditioning. He has cultivated a manner of conversing with females, and it has become a habit, one that removes the distinction of age. I would hardly suggest the alternative: take a quick look, if you find her attractive, lower your gaze. Think of the fallout: boy meets girl; boy looks at girl; girl holds her breath; boy

---

1 Qur'an 24:30–31.

keeps looking at girl; girl is insulted. So, my dear friend's son: I understand. And to men who lower their gaze, who are abiding by God's injunction in the Qur'an, I have no business making light of it. If I have offended your sensibilities, I apologize. And if lowering the gaze makes me uncomfortable, that is my problem.

18.

Pakistani Islam or a Hybrid?

How much of what I practiced was Islamic-Islamic, and how much of it was influenced by Pakistani culture? In the beginning, I didn't even know that the distinction existed. I believed that all my practices were religion-based. Not so, it turns out. Great! That means I can change outfits, dress up my faith in an American ensemble, with American sounds, flavor, and color. A hybrid.

But first, take an oath.

Citizen Rehman

Standing by the Statue of Liberty, Khalid and I took our oath, pledging allegiance to the United States of America. It was 1981. Did I feel a lump in my throat; did my eyes well up? I had been a Pakistani all my life, and giving up Pakistani citizenship was bittersweet.

Will I have conflicting loyalties? Am I now less Pakistani? How will I feel when my new country takes up arms against Pakistan? Will I stand up for the US when Pakistanis blame it for everything? Will part of me always be Pakistani? How wrong is that? Am I the only one feeling that way?

Be Counted

We voted! How empowering is that?!

I have a voice.

I have a say.

I count.

In 1984, Khalid and I reelected Ronald Reagan. Democrats, sorry to hurt your feelings, but we were Republicans. Most Pakistanis were of Republican leaning. It dated back to the Eisenhower years and his foreign policy towards Pakistan; and then it was Nixon's leaning toward Pakistan during the war of 1971. Add to that our conservative social values. We remained committed Republicans to the shock and dismay of my colleagues, who couldn't fathom how "nice people" like us could be Republican. Years later, we would switch parties. I will talk about that conversion later.

Threading My Prayer Rug

Call it redefining: now an American, I was witnessing the Islam I grew up with undergo a transformation. The main ingredient in the recipe was the Qur'an, blended in with the coloring of Pakistani culture, accentuated with an American flavor—all folded into the sounds of Arabic. As the next generation came of age, the colors took on more and more of an American hue.

Do They Have to Recite the Entire Qur'an?

"I want my children to complete the recitation of the Qur'an. Six months later they are still on the first chapter." I spoke to the Sunday school teacher, a medical doctor of Indian descent.

The other parents chimed in.

In Pakistan, reciting the Qur'an in its entirety—all thirty volumes—was an essential part of religious education. I didn't see that happening at Sunday school.

This is how I recall his response: listen. Recitation will not educate them. They need to understand the belief system, the elements of faith, and the history. It is knowledge that will strengthen their faith and build their confidence. I understand that it gives you parents a sense of accomplishment when your child has read one volume, then two, then three, and appears to be progressing. Besides, I am the only teacher for twenty children. In the few hours that we have at school, it is impossible to give one-on-one instruction.

He was right. We parents were hung up on our tradition of recitation. We became Muslims through osmosis and blind faith—the consequence of growing up among Muslims. Our children don't have that advantage, or, rather, disadvantage. They are going to have to learn the hard way, through education.

Hold it! I still want my children to complete the recitation of the Qur'an. I cannot just dismiss that.

There was only one option. Khalid and I started coaching Saqib and Asim at home. Saqib completed the recitation at age thirteen, Asim at age ten. Children younger than Asim were completing the recitation, and each time a child reached the milestone, the parents would hold an *Ameen*—call it a "Qur'an completion ceremony." We held an *Ameen* for Asim. Saqib did not want one—he felt that he was over-age to qualify for a celebration.

Ameen

This was a first for me. In Pakistan, we didn't have *Ameen* celebrations. At least, not in my family. We had birthday parties, Eid parties, and just parties, but not an *Ameen*. When it was Asim's time, I asked Imam if he would conduct the ceremony, which he graciously agreed to.

Asim got nervous.

"Do I have to? Why do I have to have an *Ameen*? Saqib didn't have one!"

I overruled him.

I cooked up a storm—rice *pullao*, chicken curry, kebabs, and *kheer*. I had invited everyone in the Muslim community on Staten Island. As we got closer to party time, Asim's protests grew insistent. "Why do I have to?" Two cars pulled up—the first guests had arrived. Through the kitchen window, Asim watched them get out of their cars, bearing gifts.

"I am getting presents!" Eyes brimming with sheer delight, the brightest of smiles, the unexpected pleasure—oh, I wish I could have captured that Kodak moment. I heard no protests after that.

"*Mubarak*," I was congratulated by the parents. Gone was Asim's nervousness. In the living room, with windows overlooking the valley and treetops, guests took their places on the sofas and on the carpet. Asim and Imam took their place on the center of the rug. I had the children cluster around Asim—*let them be motivated.* Asim held the Qur'an. Imam asked Asim to recite the last five chapters, and as he recited the last verse, Imam said, "*Ameen.*" Everyone chanted, "*Ameen.*" We all raised our hands in prayer—prayer of thanks, prayer that all Muslim children complete the recitation and grow up to be observant Muslims. I could see Asim smiling amid all the congratulations.

I missed Aba Jee. He had passed away several years earlier. He would have rejoiced.

Bismillah

The phone rang.

"I am calling to invite you to my daughter's *Bismillah* ceremony." It was a mother from the Sunday school.

What is a Bismillah ceremony?

I know *Bismillah* means "In the name of God," and we say it before we begin something—like before we eat—to seek God's blessings. But what was a ceremony? Too embarrassed to ask, I listened.

"She is so excited to be starting the recitation of the Qur'an," the mother said.

Ah, so it's the ceremony to mark the beginning of her recitation; an initiation of sorts, I suppose.

"How old is your daughter?" I asked.

"*Masha'Allah*, she is four," she invoked God's blessing.

"*Mubarak.*"

In Pakistan I had never heard of a *Bismillah* ceremony. I am sure it was held, but not in our social circle. I was beginning to appreciate how secular our military lifestyle had been. Not knowing what to expect, what would be an appropriate gift, I called one of my Pakistani friends whose husband was rather religious. *She would know.*

"Don't ask me. Never been to one, never seen one. You are better off checking with one of the Indian ladies." She was clueless.

"Why Indian?"

"It's their culture."

Their culture? Aren't we all Muslims? So what if some are from Pakistan and others from India, or Indonesia for that matter? What is this culture stuff?

I asked Khalid, who rationalized that these ceremonies are not a religious requirement. Studying and understanding the Qur'an is what God asks of us; ceremonies associated with it are man-made add-ons for celebrating milestones. It brings people together. You break bread and, in this case, give encouragement to a child and motivate other children and their parents.

Then how come we didn't have these ceremonies in Pakistan? Wouldn't the same principle apply?

A friend explained his take: Muslims are a minority in India. As a religious minority, you tend to establish a culture of communal events. Your religious community becomes your source of strength. It's about survival. Look at what we are doing here in New York: establishing a Muslim community for the same reasons. In Pakistan—a Muslim-majority country—there was no need for us to define our Muslim identity and lifestyle. And yes, *Bismillah* ceremonies are held in Pakistan but are not as prevalent.

That would mean that Indian Muslims in the US have a head start on how to survive as a religious minority, and Pakistanis can piggyback on their model. Sorry, I didn't mean to offend the sensibilities of my Muslim readers by using a porky analogy. Camelback would be more like it. Until now, I had not paid attention to who was Indian and who was Pakistani. Come to think of it, the Sunday school teachers—Indian; the doctor who had given his house to the Sunday school—Indian.

Praising the Prophet: In English!
We were celebrating Milad un Nabi, Prophet Muhammad's birthday.

Mummy would invite all the ladies to a Milad in her home. The sunroom floor was covered with sheets, pillows placed against the wall, and incense burners placed on a small, low table in the center. Women would sit reclining against the wall, dupattas *draped over their heads. An elder religious auntie, with a gift for oratory, would open the ceremony by chanting blessings on the Prophet. Everyone would join the chant. Auntie would relate the story of the Prophet's birth and his attributes. I would sing a naat, a poem in praise of Prophet Muhammad, women swaying to the tune, their eyes closed in reverence. The cycle of chanting, reading, singing would continue for an hour. At the end, everyone would stand to pay their respects to the Prophet, and I would sing the "salaam," blessings of peace on the Prophet. We would sit again; and then as everyone raised their hands, auntie would lead the prayer, asking for God's blessings. All in Urdu. At night, the city was dressed up in lights, and Daddy would take us out just to savor the sights.*

I was to learn later that since women on the subcontinent did not go to the mosques, the ceremony of Milad was established to provide them with a space for spiritual fulfillment.

To my delight, this event was resurrected once the Sunday school took off. But here, it had a new flavor. We ladies held the Milad upstairs in the Albanian mosque, and the men had their Milad downstairs. *Men doing the Milad?* Another first for me. In Pakistan, this was a ladies' thing. Well, turns out, in India, it's a man's thing as well. OK, so why not take it a step further and include the children? After all, it's their Prophet too. So we invented the children's Milad.

The teacher gave the children an assignment to make short speeches on the life of Prophet Muhammad and taught them to sing some *naats*. Now, here is the problem. *Naats* were in Urdu; some children spoke Urdu, others did not. Bless these children, they just went along and sang in Urdu with an American accent.

I failed to teach my children the Urdu language. What a mistake! Now they don't know what they are singing. We need to come up with an alternative.

The alternative became controversial. Over the next few years, as more children from the Arab and African American community joined the Sunday school, it became apparent to me that *naats* in Urdu could not be sustained. I broached the idea of English *naats*. I had heard some children at another Sunday school sing an English *naat* to the tune of "I'd like to give the world a home." I got a hold of the lyrics and presented it to the team.

Khalid and me seated with Mummy and Daddy at my wedding. Standing are Auntie Hameeda, Uncle Rehman, and Aba Jee.

My engagement without the fiancé, and with Auntie Hameeda and Rehana.

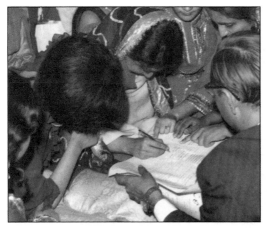

Uncle (my appointed guardian for the marriage ceremony) asks, and I sign the *nikah* form.

Khalid signs the *nikah* form. Also shown are Uncle, Uncle Rehman, the *maulvi*, Khalid, and Daddy with our kid brothers.

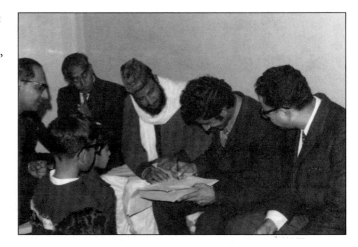

Khalid gains unauthorized access to my bedroom after the *nikah*; my cousin tries to show him my face, a friend pushes my head down, and Tallat protests at the breach of protocol.

His shoe taken by Neena, Khalid
negotiates the buy-back price.

My *mehndi*. Auntie Hameeda applies
mehndi, Mummy looks on, and I try to
peer through the veil.

Khalid and I see each other through the mirror.

Our wedding portrait, taken after the *walima*.

With my classmates at College of Home Economics, standing, fourth from left.

Saqib and Asim at their mommy's graduation in New York.

Director of Compliance and
Managed Care at University
Hospital, Newark.

Asim's *Ameen*, as he recites the closing chapters of the Qur'an.

Sunday school registration day.

Saqib receives Sunday school graduation certificate from Borough President Ralph Lamberti.

Asim receives the Bismillah Award from Boy Scouts of America and Borough President Ralph Lamberti.

The Pakistani *bhangra* dance at the Harmony Day Fair. Asim performs his solo, as Khalid beats to the tune.

Asim offers morning prayers on Mount Sinai in the Sinai peninsula in Egypt. He was doing a semester abroad at the American University at Cairo.

Saqib's *mehndi*. Khalid and I lead the procession, Asim and his friends holding the canopy over him.

Saqib's *mehndi*. Saadia receives a gift of
bangles from me.

Saqib's wedding. Daddy ties the *sehra* garland over his turban. Standing: Khalid, Mummy, Daddy, Arshed, me, Salman, Neena, Aneela, and Asim.

Saqib's *nikah*. Hands held in prayer, the imam is flanked by the fathers, the mothers are seated next to the bride and groom, and the two witnesses are at the back.

Asim's *mehndi*. Saadia and I put *mehndi* on Brinda and Asim.

Asim's wedding *walima*. Mummy gives Brinda her *salami*.

My parents on their third wedding anniversary.

With Daddy in the weeks before he passed away.

Raising funds for autism research.

National Autism Association NY Metro Chapter rings the opening bell at NASDAQ.

Offering Muslim prayer at the 9/11 Unity Walk.

Press conference at City Hall. Interfaith leaders speaking out against hate speech in subway ads.

A *naat* in English!

I tried to rationalize my proposal: we have children from various ethnic backgrounds and not all of them understand Urdu. We need to institutionalize English as our medium . . . be inclusive.

Silence.

I could tell from their looks that they didn't know what to do with me. They tried to reason with me.

What's there to reason about?

I huffed and I puffed and stormed out. Now I preach tolerance. Where was my tolerance when my short fuse would light up each time I heard the voice of dissent?

Years later, when I took a course in change management, I appreciated my folly. This approach does not work: "I want you to change the way you are doing things and do it the way I suggest, because my way makes better sense." If it means change, then it doesn't matter if my way makes more sense. There is an art, a whole industry around managing change. And I thought that waving an English *naat* in front of them would be a moment of enlightenment. I was asking them to give up what defined their identity—language—and had steered the plane into an air pocket.

A Negotiation with God

The Sunday school announced a celebration of Isra Meeraj. In Pakistan, we had never held this function, but I was glad about it—my children will learn something. Saqib was given an assignment: a five-minute speech. He had no reference material. There were no books on this subject, and in the 1980s, there was no Internet. We didn't even have a computer. But I did remember a story that Aba Jee had told me.

"Saqib, do you know why Muslims pray five times a day? Why not six, or four, or just once a day?" I asked.

Of course he didn't know. So I told him the story as I had heard it.

One night, when the Prophet Muhammad is in a deep sleep, the angel Gabriel awakens him. He takes him to a winged horse and they fly into the night, arriving in Jerusalem at Al-Aqsa. Standing there are the prophets Abraham, Jesus, Moses, and others. They pray together. The angel then takes him on a flight to the seven heavens. He sees the angels praying, he meets the prophets again, he sees paradise and hell, and finally, Gabriel takes him to the highest heaven. "I can go no further or my wings will burn," Gabriel says. "You go on ahead." Muhammad proceeds and finds himself in the presence of God Almighty. God does not reveal Himself to him, but they have a conversation. This night journey and meeting with God is referred to as Isra Meeraj. God tells Muhammad that he and his followers should pray fifty times a day. After the conversation is over and Muhammad returns, he meets Moses on the way down. "How did it go?" Moses asks. Muhammad tells him about the fifty prayers.

"They will never be able to pray fifty times a day. Go back and request God to reduce the number," Moses says.

The Prophet Muhammad goes back. God reduces the number to forty. On his way back, he runs into Moses again.

"What did God say?" he asked.

"Forty prayers a day."

"Go back. Your people won't be able to comply. Mine couldn't; yours won't."

Muhammad went back. God reduced the number to thirty. Moses sent him back again. This went on from thirty to twenty to ten, until God said that five prayers was His final number.

"What did God say?" Prophet Moses asked.

"Five prayers a day."

"Go back. Even five will be too much."

"I cannot go back. God said that this was His final number. I am also too embarrassed to go back again."

So five it was. And five it has remained.

I loved this story when I first heard it, and I loved telling it to Saqib. Of course, he was fascinated. Aren't you? He called his teacher, ran the facts by him, and got his speech ready. When Saqib stood at the lectern and spoke, I thought of Aba Jee. The story he told me, I told my son, and now Saqib was telling it to the world of Muslims on Staten Island.

Twenty years later, when I narrated this story to a group of Jewish students at the Abraham Herschel School in Manhattan, one of the students raised his hand.

"Does that mean that God made a mistake?"

Stumped.

Back home, I pulled out my reference material.

God doesn't make mistakes. He is the All-Knowing, All-Wise. So what was His wisdom in setting the bar high and then lowering it?

I can come up with a number of explanations, but I don't dare put it out there, for I cannot speak for God. All I can say is: only God knows.

Look Back in Pride

It wasn't enough that our children were learning the theology and rituals; they needed to feel confident as Muslims, and that meant pride in their heritage. Someone came up with the idea of a Muslim History Fair. Again, we had never done a fair like that in Pakistan. Children put on a play, "The Golden Glory," highlighting the achievements of prominent Muslim leaders, scientists, and inventors, choreographed with spotlights and music. Posters and models illustrated the works of Avicenna in medicine, advances in algebra made by Omar Khayyam, architectural marvels, and contributions in astronomy, science, and chemistry. I was responsible for putting together a panel of judges for the contest. As I took the judges to each display, I was humbled by the collective knowledge of these children.

I didn't know all this. What went through their minds when they created the poster depicting the role of Muslim scholars in translating ancient Greek texts and bringing the ideas of Aristotle, Socrates, and Plato to Europe? Were they tickled when they learned that it was Muslims who introduced the concept of "zero" in mathematics? And how did they feel when they learned that it was Ibn Firnas, an engineer of Andalusia, who in the ninth century constructed a flying machine, becoming the world's first aviator?

My Feelings Were Mixed with Pride, Sadness, and Hope

It's not enough to look back in pride. What good is the golden age of Islam if we are back in the Bronze Age? What took us back? And please, let's not blame colonialism. Only the weak were colonized. But we can use our glorious history as a springboard for the future. I hope that is what our children take away from the experience.

Mother's Day: American or Islamic?

History Fair coincided with Mother's Day. A week before the event, Imam gave a lecture on this topic, making the point that this American holiday reflects the spirit of Islam. I believe he was addressing the skeptics in the congregation who considered American culture to be at odds with Islamic practices. Many immigrants fear that by embracing the culture of their adopted country, they are scraping away the defining contours of their heritage. He related a well-known story of the Prophet Muhammad, one that Aba Jee had told me.

A man came to the Prophet and said, "O Messenger of God! Who among the people is the most worthy of my good companionship?" The Prophet said, "Your mother." The man said, "Then who?" The Prophet said, "Then your mother." The man further asked, "Then who?" The Prophet said, "Then your mother." The man asked again, "Then who?" The Prophet said, "Then your father."

In another story, someone asked the Prophet, "Where do you find Paradise?" The Prophet said, "Paradise is at the feet of your mother."

Imam recited a verse from the Qur'an that urges respect for parents, stressing that the mother carries the child with hardship, and gives birth with hardship, and nurtures the child during the nursing period.

Can we somehow combine Mother's Day with the History Fair? Sort of Americanize the event. Our children would love it.

Khalid came up with an idea: let's raffle a prize for the mothers.

Raffle? Is that halal? Gambling is forbidden in Islam.

I called Imam. By now, I had a direct line to him. He gave the go-ahead, explaining that as long as no money changed hands, it was OK. So we pulled a name out of a box and made Mrs. Siddique a happy mom. Mother's Day had been Islamicized.

Deaths and Burials

My friend's husband died of a heart attack. The community came together, handling the arrangements like clockwork. The grieving widow and her children, who had no family around, found comfort in the arms of the community. If something happened to my husband, at least I will be among people who care. Then a doctor's wife died, and we had to face up to the fact that we needed a long-term plan to handle burials. The issue was the practice of burying the body facing Mecca. If the alignment of rows in a cemetery faced a different direction, there was a problem. The widower doctor made an arrangement with the Rosehill cemetery in Linden, New Jersey, where the management agreed to parcel out a section for Muslim burial. As long as all the graves in that section faced in one direction, it wouldn't look out of sync. Khalid and I purchased a plot for us. Bathing and preparing the body was the other issue. In Pakistan, the body was prepared in the house. Only women can bathe and prepare a woman's body, and likewise for men. Viewing was at home, and from there, straight to the graveyard. We had to adjust in accordance with the laws of the land. Khalid spoke to a friendly director of a funeral home, who agreed to allow us to use his facilities for bathing and preparing the body ourselves. Then my friend died. In Pakistan, professional women bathers prepared the body. Here I found myself handling the preparations. As she lay dying, I drove to the shopping mall and purchased white fabric for the shroud. The next morning I called the local mosque from my office in Brooklyn to ask for written instructions on preparing the body. They sent a woman, who met me in the hospital lobby and handed me a booklet with instructions and illustrations. The day she died, in the basement of the funeral home, we bathed and prepared my friend for burial. She had to be buried the same day. No embalming.

Our Media

In June 1985, we launched our first newsletter. In Pakistan, mosques did not issue newsletters. We called it *Al-Majlis* (the place of gatherings). A newsletter meant that we had a mailing list—a community; and it meant we had something newsworthy to report. It was Khalid's idea (you are not surprised). He procured desktop publishing software for our first computer, an Apple 2e, asked Saqib to design the format and layout, and assigned me to provide Saqib with the content. My thirteen-year-old son spent six hours creating the first newsletter. He created a banner with palm trees and a crescent on the left, and a dome with two minarets on the right. He put in clip-art graphics and inserted photocopies of black-and-white photos of the history fair. He made a Children's Corner and an Islamic crossword puzzle. For one year, he developed these bimonthly newsletters while I helped with editing. It grew in size and scope, and eventually I took over the task of layout as it was taking too much of his time. I loved creating it, and when people called to say, "I just got the newsletter; it is so good," I tried to down-play my elation. Parents loved to see their children's photos, their son mentioned in the Good News column, and children smiled seeing their article published. Al-Majlis was connecting people with the mosque and with one another. Every time someone said, "I didn't know . . . until I read it in the newsletter," I beamed with a sense of accomplishment.

Community building had lit a spark in our lives, and Khalid and I got swept away by the zeal. We were consumed, and our time after work-ing hours was devoted to the project. Khalid was looking beyond the mosque. He also wanted a community center for other-than-religious activities, a cultural center where our teens could hang out, where we would hold weddings and funerals, even sports. Great idea, people said, but let's first develop the mosque. We did build the mosque, but we never built the community center, not in Staten Island, and not at Park51.

19.

Moon Sighting

As a hybrid of Islamic practices evolved, I continued to have my clashes with tradition.

New York. Circa 1980s

I had my first run-in with moon sighting. I mentioned earlier that the Islamic calendar is based on the lunar cycle. The beginning of a new month is subject to moon sighting. Since Eid falls on the first day of the month after Ramadan, you won't know when Eid is until just the day before, when the moon is sighted. In a Muslim country, no problem. As soon as the moon is sighted, the national holiday is announced for the next day and the country goes into a holiday mood. Try doing that in the US. The next day children may have an exam; the doctor may have patients booked. . . . So what did we do? We'd pray that Eid fell on a weekend. When I first came to the US and there was only one Islamic Center—on Riverside Drive—I would call the center weeks before to confirm the date for Eid, and Khalid would take the day off accordingly. I was pleased that this center was forward-looking and had fixed the date for Eid well ahead of time. But that did not last. No sooner did we get the Sunday school and mosque activity going than the leadership of the mosque announced that Eid day would be subject to moon sighting. I pleaded my case with one of the leaders.

"We should fix the day—the Islamic Center in Manhattan does that. How else can we take the day off? I cannot call my boss the morning of

Eid and tell him that I won't be in because it's a religious holiday. He'll say, 'You are telling me now?' Khalid has patients scheduled. He cannot not show up. Our children have school—they need to let their teachers know."

He explained to me that if he fixes the day, and the moon is not sighted, the community would have missed a day of obligatory fasting. I argued: why not fix it for a day later so we fast an extra day to be on the safe side. He told me that if Eid is indeed a day early, and we are fasting on Eid, that would be a misdeed because only Satan fasts on Eid.

"Can't we follow the findings of the observatory? They predict when the new moon will be visible."

The new moon has to be seen with the naked eye, he said.

"When will we know if the moon has been sighted?" I asked.

He explained that it could be anytime from sundown on the East Coast to sundown on the West Coast, as the crescent has to be sighted anywhere on the landmass of the continental United States.

"But that could be as late as midnight in New York? And how will we be notified?" I asked.

He patiently explained that we should prepare to fast the next day, and if the moon is sighted, calls will go out to the community.

So we may get a call at midnight telling us that Eid is on for the next morning.

He was a learned man. I respected him and appreciated his patience. I was not well-read in theology and was relying on my sense of logic, which was getting me nowhere. I had no choice but to go along. Khalid was the only one who saw eye-to-eye with me—or at least, the only one who had the courage to express his position.

What am I going to say to my boss, my colleagues, and my children's teacher? That maybe I will come in to work, or maybe I won't, and I won't know until the night before that I have a religious holiday the next day? As it is, people's impression about Islam is colored by the "terrorism" lingo on TV. And I thought I could brighten the image of Islam. So much for that! What are my children going to think?

I argued in absentia.

I understand that they are going by the book and believe that devi-ating from what is ordained is a violation. But I don't believe that our religion is so antiquated that it cannot be reinterpreted to make it rel-evant to the times. I don't believe that God intended to make our reli-gion archaic, rigid, and difficult so that it is rendered unpractical. The basic idea is to follow the lunar calendar; it doesn't matter what tools we use to determine the new moon. In the days of the Prophet, the only tool was the naked eye. Now we have the observatory. The Qur'an states how to determine prayer times based on the length of the shadow and the shades of the sky. None of the mosque leaders walk outside every afternoon and measure the length of their shadow. They follow the prayer timetable based on predicted times, down to the last minute. How is that different from predicting when the crescent will be visible on the horizon?

And then one day, I lost my temper. It was the twenty-ninth of Rama-dan. The moon had not been sighted. Midnight came and went. No word, so we followed protocol and got up the next morning at 4:00 a.m. to have *suhoor* and begin our fast. I had just finished *suhoor* when the phone rang. It was a friend of mine.

"Stop eating *suhoor.* The moon has been sighted. It's Eid. See you at Eid prayers in the morning."

"What!" I raised my voice. "You're telling us now! At four in the morning! What kind of an organization are we running?"

"It wasn't my decision."

I had just shot the carrier pigeon, yet I couldn't bring myself to apol-ogize. After I hung up, I continued.

"You know why we have a problem?" I looked at Khalid. "It's because no one speaks up. They just go along. It's the absence of outrage. See how calmly she is calling everyone at four in the morning, telling them to switch gears, as if it is no big deal. Did no one ask the question, Why are we finding out at 4:00 a.m.?"

That morning, the mosque was full. People were coming in, smil-ing, calm, not looking bothered. I sat among them, battling my frus-tration. *Am I the only one upset?* After prayers, after the greeting and eating, I turned to a close friend of mine, more for validation, telling her how upset I was at the late notification.

She gave me a serene look, and said, "Why would that upset you?"

Maybe the problem is with me.

It got worse. I called my friend in New Jersey to wish her *Eid Mubarak.* This was her response: "Eid is tomorrow. Did you celebrate it today?" By the end of the day, it had become apparent that Eid was being celebrated on two different days throughout the US.

It got worse. The following year, mosques in Manhattan celebrated Eid one day, and mosques in Brooklyn the other day. It's the same moon, isn't it?

It got worse. The year after, one mosque in Staten Island had Eid one day while the other mosque had it the next day. Same borough, same moon.

Each mosque claimed that they had it right.

What do I say to my children? What do my children say to their friends?

And here is the bitter frosting on the Eid cake: At work, I took the day off for Eid. My secretary, also a Muslim, took the next day off for Eid. The third day, our colleagues asked, "Don't you both have the same religion?"

I refuse to be embarrassed, but I hold our religious leaders responsible for causing embarrassment and for dividing the Muslim community. Aha! Doesn't the Qur'an stress that the Muslim ummah should stay united? Where is that in the moon-sighting equation?

Circa 2000s

I wasn't the only one fixated on fixing the moon date. Apparently, over the last two decades, some Muslims had undertaken a scientific experiment with the naval observatory, the hypothesis being whether the sighting of the crescent can be predicted based on astronomical calculations. Predictions were made, tested, and tracked over the years. The result: you bet! Several leading Muslim organizations in the US announced they would recognize astronomical calculations for the new moon. *Yeah!* They have since been publishing the dates on their website months in advance. Khalid read me the news, and I raised my hands with an *Alhamdulillah.* A graduation for Muslims in America! Khalid and I now follow their calendar. Not all mosques or organizations embraced this principle, so today you will have half the people in New York City celebrating Eid one day, the other half on the other day. Alternate-side parking is suspended for three days, and the Empire State Building lights up for three days as well—a work-around.

It's not quite over though. Last year, on the first day of Ramadan, I called my granddaughter Laila to say *Ramadan Mubarak.*

"I am fasting," she proudly announced. I asked to speak to Saqib.

"How was your fast today?" I asked.

"I am not fasting."

"Are you OK?" I presumed that my observant son was sick.

"I am OK. But my mosque said that Ramadan starts tomorrow."

"Then why is Laila fasting today?"

Saqib tried to explain that Saadia, my daughter-in-law, had heard that Ramadan starts today and decided to fast. He didn't know what her plan was; he didn't tell her what his plan was; and so, there you have it.

What?!

"When you were missing at *suhoor,* didn't anyone notice?"

More explanations. Saqib doesn't wake up for *suhoor* because, like all surgeons, he has to be in the OR early in the morning. He came home late last night when everyone was sleeping and didn't connect, and for some reason, each of them thought that they were both on the same moon.

"Saqib! You cannot allow this to happen. It's bad enough that Muslims are divided across mosques, but for a family under one roof to be observing different dates is not acceptable. Think of your children. How do you explain it to them?"

"You're right. I should have communicated better."

It never happened again. But it did happen once. And once is one too many.

Eid a School Holiday in New York

I heard talk that the Muslim leaders—particularly the young ones— were lobbying for Eid to be a school holiday.

Are they serious? How can the school system designate the Eid holiday when we can't agree on setting a date?

On March 4, 2015, Mayor Bill DeBlasio announced that New York City schools would be closed for Eid. He even announced the date of school closure. Who had his staff consulted on setting the date? Who cares! Will this compel the mosques to set a date?

I am beginning to like the pattern in my prayer rug.

20.

Tradition versus Women's Rights

And now, the moment you have been waiting for: the tormenting issue of women's rights. Why should my experience be any different!

1986
I decided to run for office. Not a political office, as in the school board—although it did get political—but to be a member of the executive board of the mosque. I believed I was qualified and had earned my way. A year earlier, the chairman of the board had appointed me as the chairman of the women's auxiliary. He gave me a free hand in defining my role. I was invited to all board meetings as a guest to give my report. I organized ladies' functions and family events, participated in planning meetings, and mobilized the ladies to take an active role. As editor of the newsletter, I connected community members with the mosque. I had actively fundraised. Recently, Khalid and I had performed the hajj, an experience that strengthened my spiritual connection with the mosque. Therefore, when the board announced that elections would be held for the executive board, I threw my hat in the ring. I consulted Khalid and spoke with some of the key leaders of the mosque and got their support. One of the leaders proposed my name on the slate.

All hell broke loose.

Reason: I am a woman.

Reason: a woman cannot be on the board of a mosque. She cannot serve in any official capacity in a mosque.

Reason: men and women should not work shoulder-to-shoulder in a mosque.

Doesn't my service count? Which authority has ruled that a woman is to be excluded? If the teacher and spiritual leader say it is permissible, what is the basis for overruling him?

My candidacy became a referendum on the status of a woman in the mosque. The leadership of the mosque was divided, and in the community lines were drawn. When I went to the mosque the following Sunday, one of the men approached me. This is how I recall the conversation:

"You should withdraw your name," he said.

"Because I am a woman?"

"Yes."

"When I worked for the mosque all these years, I didn't hear anyone object to my being a woman. Why now?"

"You can work unofficially. But you cannot hold a title."

"I already hold two titles. I am chairman of the woman's auxiliary and editor of the newsletter."

"That is different."

"How is that different?"

"You cannot be seated at the table with men."

"She has been at the same table every month at board meetings." Khalid had walked up.

"That was a mistake."

What!

"Brother, let me tell you something." An African American member of the board had walked up. "Women have fought in wars—the Prophet's wife Aisha led troops in battle. So much of the *Hadith* comes from Aisha. Women actively participated in decisions made in mosques in the Prophet's lifetime. . . ." He continued to make more points, much of which I don't remember.

"Sister Sabeeha, this is how it is going to be. Whenever you have anything to say, tell it to Khalid, and he will convey it to us."

Now it is coming to that.

"I am not backing down." I looked him square in the face.

He turned his back and, taking quick steps, walked away.

I felt people averting their gaze. Some women chose to sit away from me; others huddled around me to convey, "We are with you."

Khalid and I talked about it that evening and agreed that backing out was not an option. If I pulled out, it would send the wrong signal. People will say, "Once she realized that a woman has no place in a mosque, she withdrew." And that would shut the door on women.

"Win or lose, you will have made your point and set a precedent to stand up for your beliefs and not be cowed by those who use religion to intimidate," Khalid said.

Khalid got on the phone and called members of the board. After the first call, he hung up and relayed the conversation.

"He says," quoting the board member, "'We cannot allow the ultra-conservatives to set the wrong precedent. Tell Sabeeha that not only does she have my support, I would like to be the one to nominate her. I will clear my calendar and be there.'"

Next call.

"He says," quoting the other board member, "'My wife is very concerned and feels strongly that we cannot afford to lose this one. We don't want our daughter's rights curtailed.'"

Third call.

"He says, 'This is ridiculous! If we let these mullahs prevail, they will destroy the mosque. I am campaigning for Sabeeha.'"

These were the they-will-support-me-no-matter-what board members. The tone shifted when Khalid called the we-support-her-but-wish-she-wouldn't-run members. The opposition had already gotten to them.

"He says, 'Sabeeha has done a lot of good work, and of course she deserves to be on the board, but wouldn't it be better if she did not run? It is dividing the community.'"

And then there were those who said, "Yes, of course," and no more. Those were the ones who voted nay.

In that moment, that evening, my prospects looked good.

"You should call some of your friends," Khalid said.

I feel awkward doing that. My friends know me, know my work. I trust them to use their judgment. I don't like tooting my own horn.

I had to push myself to pick up the phone. I made two calls and was jolted into the hard truth of politics.

The first call was to a dear friend. After pledging her support, the whole women's rights stuff, she laid it out for me. The opposition had already called her—and it was a woman who had made the call.

"Sabeeha, you think the men don't want you there. Well, let me tell you. It's the women who don't want you."

Women?

"Sabeeha, after I gave her my argument on women's rights, she backed off from that argument and attacked you personally. But know that I am here for you, you have my vote, and you have my husband's vote."

Why are the women against me? I have had good relationships with all of them. We have worked well together. Wouldn't they want to see a woman on the board? What is going on?

The next call was worse.

Another close friend, someone whom I looked up to as an older sister, gave me a dressing down.

"People have been calling me," she said. "They are dead set against you. No one is arguing about the great job you have done. It's your image that is the problem."

"My image?"

I still recall her words: "You are Americanized. I am too—more Americanized than you. Nothing wrong with that, until one decides to be a representative of a mosque. The two don't go hand in hand. You cannot be Americanized and be a mosque person. I am not saying that it is right, but it is the reality. If you want support as a mosque-ish person, then you have to look like one. You don't cover your hair, and you dress American, and those who oppose you are using that against you. I have told these people off and said that my husband and I are behind you, but I am just letting you know what's going on."

I felt my cheeks burn. The dress comment stung.

I am not backing down. Definitely not now. I will fight this.

Election day came. The mosque had standing room only, was noisy, and on that October evening, it felt cramped, stuffy, crowded, and chilly. I saw people I had never seen and never saw again. I knew then what the outcome would be. My supporters were there. One of my friends, so sick with multiple sclerosis that she could barely stand, walked in, walked up to the opposition, and made a statement. The men made speeches after nominating me, put forth arguments in my favor, and, when the votes were counted, I had lost big time. But something grim and ominous had happened. Several key members on the board who had supported me were de-elected. Those who had stood for the rights of women had taken a fall. I looked across the room at them, somber and quiet, handling it with dignity, and felt guilty. My friends surrounded me, outraged, not at the outcome but the circumstance that led to it.

My children were there. As we sat in the car, Asim, my eleven-year-old, reached out from the back seat and put his hand on my shoulder. "Mummy, I am sorry."

Khalid and I had strategized when the controversy first started on how to address this with our children. We did not want to draw them into the wrangling of adults, yet they saw and heard what was going on. They respected the leaders of the mosque, and we wanted to preserve that relationship. On the other hand, they had to understand that women had a place, and their mother was fighting to uphold those rights. It was painful to see my children exposed to controversies within the Muslim community, just when we were getting them to feel pride in their flock.

The phone rang all evening. Khalid's friends were incensed. Many who were inactive in the mosque pledged to get active and roll back this wave of conservatism.

That was almost three decades ago. I can see clearly now. Given a chance, would I run again, in 1986? NO. It was premature. You can tell that I was also naïve. My PR skills were nonexistent, nor had I placed any value on them. Benazir Bhutto, when she ran for president of Pakistan, did two things. She got herself an arranged husband, and she donned a white *dupatta* over her head. Image. If you cannot yield to a required image, then don't run for office. But above all, I question my intent. Why did

I aspire to be a board member in the first place? Recognition? Ego? If that was so, then God humbled me. I could have carried on the work without the title. And that is what I did over the next several years—just carried on, keeping a low profile.

A year ago—in late 2014, my Jewish friend Lenny called me. "Sabeeha, it's in the news. The mosque in Long Island has elected a woman to be the president of the mosque. I thought of you."

In August 2015, the Islamic Society of North America (ISNA), one of the largest Muslim organizations in the US, launched a campaign for the inclusive, women-friendly *masjid* (mosque), stating "we call upon all *masjids* to ensure that . . . women actively participate in the decision-making process of the *masjid*, best realized by having women on the governing bodies of *masjids*."

21.

My Brand of Islam

1987

We never went back to being the same. The controversy over women's roles had forced the hands of the conservatives and split the community, and the issue was no longer that of women but rather: what brand of Islam does the mosque represent? I worried.

What form of Islam will be taught to our children? Will boys and girls be segregated in the classrooms? Will they be told that music is forbidden? What will they be taught about how Muslims relate to non-Muslims? Is tolerance being preached or are they encouraging a stick-to-your-own-kind-and-you-will-remain-pure mentality? What will be the role of women? Will they be relegated to meal planning or be allowed to teach? Teach preschool girls only or older boys as well?

Until recently, I had been grateful that we had a mosque and someone was teaching my children. The election and women's issue elevated our level of awareness about the content of what was being taught. I started paying close attention. So did the other parents.

"Do you know what the teacher told the children in class today?" one of my friends called and asked me. "He said, 'You should not waste your time listening to Noor Jehan's songs.'" Noor Jehan was a very popular Pakistani singer.

It has started. My children are being told that music is forbidden. What next? How do we stop this?

Another friend called. "Guess what happened in class today. The children were segregated. Boys on the left, girls on the right."

Now I have no problem with self-segregation. We ladies did it all the time at parties. Our children do it with school, boys clustering with boys, girls with girls. As long as that is by choice, fine. But I had a problem with imposed segregation, particularly among grade-school children.

What next?

Nail polish. Yes, nail polish. A woman pointed to my nails, said you cannot perform ablution if you have nail polish. Why not? Because the water has to touch the nails, and nail polish is a barrier. Let me see if I get this straight: I cannot have a conversation with God because I have nail polish on my nails?

Khalid started speaking up. Each time we ran against what we felt was contrary to what we wanted our children to learn, Khalid would speak up. On the advice of my friends, I became silent. I was told that if I spoke up, the conversation would deflect from the "what" to the "whom." "Keep a low profile," I was urged. What they were really saying was: you have made enough trouble, now lay off until the dust settles. The dust never settled. Khalid was given a gag order: he was not an authority on religion and therefore should back off from making pronouncements. Khalid pushed back. Lines were drawn and the community split into two factions: the ultraconservatives and the progressives.

That label—ultraconservative—was my bias. I should have said, "their-way-of-thinking-ers" and "our-way-of-thinking-ers." We agreed on nothing. It was like gridlock in Congress. Eventually, both camps parted ways. It was a sad outcome. Muslims, who should stay united, had broken up so early in the stages of community building. The "Us" was much smaller in number, had no teachers and no space, but we had our spiritual leader and we had our ideology. Now it was up to us to give our children the brand of Islam that we wanted—one that preached tolerance and inclusivity and was unencumbered by cultural baggage from the old country. We were taking charge.

I said that we had no teachers. We sat around the table, seven of us, and looked at one another. There was only one answer.

Us.

We had to become teachers.

"I'll take the preschoolers," I raised my hand and said. The beginning class was all I was equipped for. "I will teach them the Arabic alphabet and basic Islamic studies."

"I will teach Islamic history," said Khalid. Another easy one. "I want children to be proud of their history."

The others, well versed in Islam, took the classes in Islamic studies, and Imam took the adult classes. We had a faculty of seven.

An interior decorator once told me that it is a decorator's nirvana to start with an empty space rather than work with existing furniture. An architect once told me, "Give me new construction, and I will hand it to you in six months. Ask me to renovate, and it will take a year and cost you more." Sitting around that table, that is how we all felt. We were starting with an empty school and furnishing it with the curriculum of our choice, one that focused on the spirit and values of Islam: God consciousness, spirituality, tolerance, inclusiveness, dignity, compassion, equality, and social justice. Whereas I knew little about Islamic theology, I knew what kind of Muslims I wanted my children to be, and I was going to build this Sunday school to make my kind of Muslims out of them. So help me Allah.

Allah did help us. According to the sayings of the Prophet Muhammad, God says to us, "Take one step toward Me, and I will take ten steps toward you." The first step was space. Khalid spoke to the CEO of Bayley Seton Hospital, and he handed us a cottage on hospital grounds—rent-free. Furniture? St. Vincent's Hospital decided to replace its classroom chairs and donated the used chairs to us. Saqib rounded up his friends, and in a friend's station wagon, we drove to Pergament, carted the blackboards, made donor stops at friends, and picked up rugs, folding tables, chairs, and sofas; by Saturday evening, the school was set up. Sunday morning, our faculty welcomed the students. We were ready.

Will we even have a congregation? Will we even have students, other than our own children? Will we have to rebuild a community as well?

Remember *Field of Dreams*? "If you build it, they will come." I will amend that to say—not so modestly, "If you build it right (for them), they will come." One of the faculty members stressed from the beginning, "We have to establish a first-rate school. If we have a solid school with a well-defined curriculum, people will come, and we will have a community for our children." She was right.

The day school opened, classes were full. But what proved her right was what happened the following year. On the first day of school, as I pulled up into the parking lot, I was besieged by families lined up outside the door—Pakistani, Indian, African, Egyptian, African American . . . so many children. Sitting at the registration desk, I looked up at one of the mothers and said, "We don't have teachers for so many children."

"I will teach," she said. And the lovely Mona, an Egyptian American, outlined her credentials and joined the faculty. Two of the Egyptian fathers, standing by, offered to teach. On the first day of school, our faculty doubled, and we had more students than we had dreamed off. Allah had taken many steps toward us.

An unintended consequence of the furor over the women's issue was that it galvanized the moderates. Families who had been on the periphery in terms of their level of participation in the mosque became active. So incensed were they by what they saw happening, and what they saw coming, that they felt they owed it to get involved to turn the tide.

Yet another unplanned consequence: Khalid and I had to educate ourselves—Islamically, that is. We mail-ordered books from Kazi Publication and got down to teacher-training ourselves.

And yet another consequence: we became custodians of the Sunday school. Every Sunday morning, we would get to the school an hour before opening, carrying our vacuum cleaner, and clean up the classrooms and bathrooms. *I want Saqib and Asim to see what it takes.* At the stroke of the hour, classes would start, and Khalid, the other teachers, and I would ferry out to the classrooms. Imam held adult classes in the living room, and everyone gathered around him on the rug. In the afternoon, young adults would join his class. During break, the ladies would set up refreshments in the living room, and the school would come alive with chatter and laughter. At the end of the school day, we would clean up again and lock up. We came to school charged with anticipation, going over checklists, and drove back with an "Aaah!"

In time we would go on to establish a summer camp for children— all the fun stuff and all in a Muslim setting. We did field trips; made museum visits; held picnics; had parent-teacher conferences; organized a library with books indexed by the Boy Scouts of America as Saqib's Eagle project; hosted *Taraweeh* prayers in Ramadan; and went all out on Eid festivities.

Saqib was fifteen, Asim twelve. These were their formative years in Islamic education, and they got the best of what was available. They also got the best of both worlds—the Pakistani values of hospitality, respect for elders, respect for authority, family values, politeness, modesty, and restraint; and the American values of discipline, punctuality, patience (waiting in line), tolerance, pluralism, embracing diversity, diligence, civic mindedness, and the work ethic. Our brand of Islam was taking shape, and I was threading my prayer rug in red, white, and blue, blending in harmony with the green.

22.

Abraham's Sacrifice

We even Americanized the festival of Eid-ul-Adha.

Summer of 1988

"Where are the poor?"

It was the Muslim festival of Eid-ul-Adha, and we had a challenge. How do we distribute meat to the poor?

"I just send the money to Pakistan and ask my parents to sacrifice the lamb for us. It is so easy to distribute meat over there," one of my friends said. "There is so much poverty in Pakistan. Some eat meat only once a year, on Eid."

"It is time we start thinking local," Khalid said to me. "There is a halal meat butcher on Staten Island. Perhaps the butcher can help us distribute the meat to the poor."

I could feel the gears in his head turning.

"How?" I asked. "How do we find 'the poor'?"

"I will figure something out."

I am sure you will.

So Khalid started his research. Mind you, this was 1988—there was no Google. He had to let his fingers do the walking. Sure enough, one day Khalid came home and said, "It's all worked out. Families will place their lamb orders with Bahri Halal Meat and pick up their two-thirds portion. Project Hospitality, which runs a soup kitchen for the homeless, will pick up the one-third portion for the poor. And

I have called the press. They will be there when the meat is picked up."

"You called the press!"

"Most people believe that Muslims are a bunch of terrorists. I want people to see that Muslims are giving to the community."

I love him.

The day after Eid, Reverend Terry Troia, director of Project Hospitality, drove up to Bahri Halal meat and lugged six hundred pounds of lamb meat to her soup kitchen. Her parting comment was: for once, the homeless will be served meat. The next day there was a spread in the *Staten Island Advance*, the local newspaper, with a photo of the doctor, the butcher, and the soup kitchen gal. And thus began a partnership between Project Hospitality and the Muslim community of Staten Island. As the Muslim community grew, Project Hospitality was the institution that enabled us to practice one of the core pillars of our faith—charitable giving. Terry came year after year, carrying sheep loads of meat—a hands-on servant of God. And as the lines at the soup kitchen grew longer, no one was turned away.

So what about the one-third portion of the meat that has to be distributed to family and friends? Some families preferred to donate that portion to the poor as well, partly for charitable purposes, and partly because it made practical sense. I decided to go by the book. Picture this: Khalid brings two-thirds of the lamb meat into our kitchen. I freeze our one-third portion. The children and I take the remaining one-third, pack it into a dozen freezer bags, and load it in our car. Saqib, who has his driver's license by now, drives Asim and me to our Muslim friends' houses. Asim rings the doorbell. An auntie answers.

"*Eid Mubarak*," we all chime. "Here is some meat for you," and we hand her the pouch. Her husband and children have gathered behind her in the hallway.

"Oh, thank you. Won't you come in?"

"No, thanks. We have meat to deliver. Another time," and we drive off to our next stop. It takes all evening to make the meat drops. I choose not to include my dear neighbors. It would have been too shocking for them. Wouldn't you be shocked if your neighbor's son rang your doorbell, and instead of saying, "Trick or treat," handed you a pouch of raw meat?

Later that evening, our doorbell rang.

"*Eid Mubarak.* Here is some meat for you."

By nighttime, my freezer had filled up with a two-thirds equivalent.

Was this the intent of the family portion?

For the next two months, guess what my answer was each time my children asked, "Mummy, what's for dinner?"

I was back to examining the pattern in my prayer rug. What if I gave away all the meat in charity? What if we didn't do the sacrificial lamb at all, and just gave money in charity?

23.

Grounded in Roots

Now that I had made the distinction between culture and religion, focusing on rebranding religion, I shifted gears back to culture.

New York. 1980s

OK, so I have the religion track pretty much under control for my children. But what about Pakistani culture—their heritage, traditions, language, music, and history—the nonreligious stuff that makes life so colorful? Their cultural clock is ticking. They are Americans, no matter what. But if we don't make a deliberate, strategic effort, they will never know what they missed and will be a reminder to me of everything Khalid and I have failed to pass down to them. Religion is on auto-Islam; let's get the cultural track going. Like with everything else, let's start with stories.

Mummy and Daddy were visiting us.

"Tell them about my birth, what my childhood was like," I asked Mummy.

Saqib and Asim sat around on the rug, legs crossed, their chins resting in their palms. I have heard Mummy tell this story so many times. Now I tell this story to my granddaughter.

Once Upon a Time, I Was a Little Girl

. . . growing up in a far-off land, in a newborn nation that had just been christened Pakistan. Mummy's name was Farrukh, and Daddy's was Kazim. Mummy was expecting me when Daddy, a lieutenant in the army, got transferred to England for a five-year course. She stayed back with my grandparents, which was the custom—ladies came home to their mother for their delivery. Daadee Amma joined them to await the big day. I was born in the comfort of their home, delivered by Daadee Amma. This was in the middle ages of the twentieth century, and babies were born at home in Pakistan.

Mummy tells me that I was the most beautiful newborn. Perfect skin, no blemishes, gorgeous baby-pink coloring, and a well-defined nose, a hallmark of beauty. My grandmothers proceeded to spoil me, and Mummy got all the pampering that a just-delivered mom receives in Pakistan. By the time I was eight months old, and ready to fly out to England, I was thoroughly spoiled. And although Mummy never admitted it, so was she. She had been so pampered that she never got around to mothering. Think about it! An untrained mom and a spoiled baby get onto a seaplane making multiple overnight refueling stops until they finally get to England three days later. Till she passed away in 2014, Mummy would tell the story of that unforgettable journey—and the torture I put her through. My husband, my children, my grandchildren, they all have heard it. My favorite anecdote of that journey is when she ran out of clean diapers on the plane and an older woman took charge, washing them and hanging them to dry along the perimeter of the cabin, despite my embarrassed mother's protests. "Baby in plane," the woman said authoritatively when passengers dared to make a wry face about the wet diapers fluttering in their faces.

Soon after we landed in England, our British landlady took charge of unspoiling me. An older woman, she told Mummy to just "be quiet and listen to me."

Daddy tells me that on Sundays they would send me to church with the neighborhood girls. Now remember, this was a Muslim family living in England. One would think that they would be worried about their daughter's religious identity. But as Daddy explained to me when I became a mother, they wanted to instill in me respect of a place of worship. It was in church that I learned to sit quietly, bow my head, and behave myself. How about that!

I am told that I was the darling of the neighborhood families and the Pakistani-army clan—more so, I believe, because I was the first-born in that batch of families, and because I was just so well-behaved. Mummy would doll me up in oh-so-stylish home-sewn dresses, curl my tresses into ringlets, and see to it that I had impeccable manners. At four, I was a perfect lady, and the aunties and uncles adored me.

When I returned to Pakistan at age five, I spoke only English. Hearing Urdu being spoken all around me sent me into shock, and I went mute. I was fascinated by flies and would chase them around the house, upset when the servants swatted them. Lizards on the walls were a joy to behold. Goats and donkeys on the streets! Life was one huge zoo! Somewhere along the line I lost my British accent, and any memory of my time in England was now the preserve of family albums and stories my parents told.

Pakistan was emerging from the bonds of colonialism and having its own identity crisis. It was a nation founded on the platform of "a homeland for the Muslims of British India." Religion had a prominent place in people's lives, yet the middle and upper classes also held on to the legacy of the British, taking pride in being Anglicized. The military, in particular, maintained British traditions, and our lifestyle reflected that—discipline, punctuality, order, and respect for authority. English was the official language, and the ability to converse fluently in English was the norm. My parents tried to find the right balance in integrating Muslim values into a British lifestyle. I believe they did that well. Daddy was always dressed in a blazer and necktie when not in uniform. Mummy was exquisite in her attire, and they were very proper in their etiquette—formal, very British.

But their family values were conservative, more so than most families in our circle of friends. I was not allowed to sleep over at friends' houses. I was always chaperoned. I was driving at age fifteen but never alone, and when at nineteen I played the role of Amanda Wingfield in *The Glass Menagerie* in college and Pakistan TV wanted to film it in their studio, Daddy allowed it on one condition: he would be present during the taping. I was the only student whose parent watched over the taping—I stood out among my peers, but I also knew that it wasn't that they didn't trust me. These were the rules my family lived by. I still remember the stern look on Daddy's face when he came home one day and found me serving tea to a male visitor who had dropped by to see him. He called me into the adjoining room and said, "You will never go in the presence of a male visitor unless I am present or unless his wife is present. Not your mother, not your grandmother. Is that clear?" Very clear. I was fifteen, and I understood; he was safeguarding my reputation.

Jedi Mamoon, my uncle who was in his twenties, sat me down one evening and gave me a talk on "protecting your reputation among the guys." A young man, he had taken notice of how boys talked about girls, what traits in a young lady won their respect, and which ones they dissed. I had no idea. The nuances—how to converse without crossing the line—is what I may not have figured out on my own. I listened, feeling awkward but also absorbing it. I took his advice seriously. I now had more than instincts to rely on.

Daddy had a beautiful voice and loved music. Often when we entertained, Daddy would sing for his guests. I was seven when Mummy started teaching me to sing. She would write the lyrics and ask me to sing to her. Daddy taught me to sing Doris Day's *"Que Sera, Sera* (Whatever Will Be, Will Be)." Daddy would sit me down with my sister Neena and have us listen to songs on the radio and sing along in a chorus. I can't say that I enjoyed it—I would rather have played outside—but we were trained to be obedient. When family visited, singing sessions were held in the drawing room, and the children had to sit and sing. When visitors came, I was asked to sing for them. It was only when I entered my teens that I began to enjoy music. My talent as a singer was recognized, and soon I was being asked to sing at school events. By this time I had graduated from the convent and gone into a public high school.

In college, I was hailed for my singing. I entered girls-only student contests, winning first prize, and my parents beamed with pride. But it stopped there. When I was approached by the local TV station and asked to perform, the answer was NO. Girls from respectable families did not sing in public, and most certainly were NOT professional singers. And that was that!

My granddaughter Laila has my music genes. Listen to her sing "Let It Go," from the movie *Frozen*.

I was in my teens when Pakistan and India went to war, and I tasted the threat of enemy invasion and promised myself never to lay eyes on an Indian. Life has taught me otherwise.

This was the sixties. There was segregation of the sexes for unmarried women and men. However, it was considered appropriate for married people to mingle, within certain limits. I was a city girl, and that was the city culture.

I left home for the first time to go to the College of Home Economics in Lahore for my baccalaureate degree. Daddy took me, and on the train, gave me a piece of advice. "You are going to be on your own for the next four years. Remember that the only restrictions that apply to you are the ones you impose on yourself. We have done our part in defining the boundaries. Now it is up to you." In that moment I realized that Daddy was placing his trust in me, and with it the weight of responsibility. I made a promise to honor that trust.

I kept that promise. I fiercely guarded my reputation as a "nice girl." I was fifteen, very young, on my own, and there were temptations galore. But Daddy had trusted his daughter to uphold the family reputation, and I wasn't going to let him down. My clean reputation won me many marriage proposals.

Once Upon a Time, Again
"What about you, Daddy?" Saqib asked Khalid.

"Daada Jan will tell you," he said, referring to his father, who was visiting us.

And my father-in-law would tell the story of his lost roots. His parents had perished in the great earthquake of Quetta in 1935, and a wealthy lawyer took him and his brother in. He never found his parents' family. He had always wanted to be a doctor, but circumstances got in the way, and he promised himself that he would raise his sons to be doctors. He married within his adopted extended family. As a stationmaster in the railways, he had a modest income, and with a family of eight children, making ends meet was a challenge. My mother-in-law was well educated, talented, and wise, and she knew how to stretch the rupee. The gateway to their future was clear: their sons had to become doctors. Doctor sons would bring economic prosperity to the family, raise their stature in society, and open the door for suitable husbands for their daughters. Keeping their eyes on the prize, they both put all their energies, resources, and planning into the education of their children. They had two mottos: one: study, study, and no play; and two: don't make friends. *Don't make friends! How can a child not have friends?!* Because, my father-in-law explained to me, friends are a distraction. If they want to play, they have seven siblings to play with; I wanted them under my roof, under my eye, and to keep them studying. After they finished their homework, he would make up home-homework for them and make them do it; and when they finished, mother would make up more homework for them and watch over them as they did it. When that was finished, father would ask Khalid to write a speech and then make him stand in the doorway and deliver that speech to passersby. Notwithstanding the rigorous study routine, these were happy children, despite what popular understanding might lead you to expect. I saw the high esteem they held their parents in, the utmost respect the siblings have for one another. And they are wholesome, regular, typical, adults. As for their career choice, they were not given a choice. They were told that they had to become doctors, and that was it. Three of the four sons became doctors; and all four daughters married well. The sons took over the financial responsibility of the family, their socioeconomic status rose, and my father-in-law would proudly say, "I have two factories in America," referring to his two older sons, both doctors.

Now my father-in-law turns to me and says, "Bia, I have some advice for you. I have no problem with you working, but if it gets in the way of your children's education, then you should not work. And second, don't let your children make friends."

So I humored him. For as long as he was visiting, I changed my routine. I would walk in the house after work and call out, "Children, Mummy's home. Have you done your homework?" I'd poke my head in the living room, "*Salaam.* Let me check their homework, and then I will be with you." I would do just that, and once the homework was under control, I would attend to my in-laws and to dinner. My father-in-law was the happiest man in the world. Every time someone came to visit, he would say, "Bia is the best. Do you know what is the first thing she does when she comes home from work?" One day, Saqib's friend from the neighborhood came to play. My father-in-law reserved judgment until he saw the little boy's mother show up in our backyard. She looked over to see what her son was doing, waved at me, made some small talk, hung around for a few minutes, and left. My father-in-law looked at me and said, "Her son will become a doctor."

Khalid and I made a pact when Auntie Hameeda came to visit us. Asim was four months old. "Bia, my mother is not used to seeing men working in the kitchen. It won't sit well with her if she sees me doing kitchen work." I told him not to worry. As long as Auntie Hameeda was here, my kitchen would be a no-man zone. And that is how we kept it whenever she visited. I wonder if my children noticed. If that was a double-life thing, I gladly embraced it.

Seeing Is Understanding

I didn't want my boys to look upon Pakistani culture as foreign, strange, and out-of-synch with time. Of course, they could not have the same appreciation that I have, but I wanted them to understand and respect the culture, perhaps adopt some of its beauty. Stories can only take you so far, and I didn't want them to have the next best thing to being there. I wanted them to be there—to directly experience the squeeze of an embrace, the warmth in conversational exchange, the deference given to family elders, the chatter in an extended family household, the sound of the *adhan*. I wanted them to watch my mother prepare for my father's arrival from the office—put away her sewing, fix her hair, freshen up her makeup. On one of our visits to Pakistan, when Saqib was five, I asked him, "So what do you like about Pakistan?"

"Two things," he said with conviction. "Lots of relatives, and lots of animals."

I had never missed the animals, so relieved was I to see the streets of New York free of the clutter of cows and donkeys and the whiff of dung, and I couldn't understand why the Central Park horse carriages were such a novelty. Seeing Pakistan through the eyes of my children, I wondered if that is what it had been for me when I returned from England.

"Would you like to spend the summer in Pakistan this year, when we go for hajj?" I asked Saqib and Asim, when they were thirteen and eleven.

"Yippee!"

They left with my parents and flew back by themselves. After that, my goal was to get them to Pakistan every summer. Sometimes we would take them and return back to work, leaving them behind, and sometimes they would go by themselves. In those years, they played and bonded with their cousins; reveled in stories told by their grandparents; listened to Pakistani music; delighted in the performance of a monkey dance and snake charmer; felt stricken at the sight of maimed children begging on the street; were puzzled seeing the eunuchs singing at the front gate; went scurrying for their prayer rugs at the sound of the *adhan*; chased the goats in the street; took donkey rides; sat with Mummy as she took inventory of the laundry delivered by the *dhobi*; watched Aurangzeb bargain for vegetables; kept Razia company in the kitchen as she boiled the milk just delivered by the milkman; and smiled shyly every time a visitor said, "Look how big you got." Something must have stirred in them, because when Saqib got accepted into medical school at SUNY Syracuse, he announced, "I want to take a year off."

"And do what?"

"I want to go to Pakistan."

"Why? Why do you want to waste a year?"

"I want to go back to my roots." He had tears in his eyes. "I will work there. It's not a waste—what's a year in a lifetime? The medical school has agreed to defer my admission."

He wants to go back to his roots. My dear, dear child. Of course you should go.

The Association of Physicians of Pakistani Descent of North America runs a public health nongovernmental organization (NGO) in Pakistan. Khalid, a life member of the organization, put Saqib in touch with them. He was accepted into the program, run from their office in Rawalpindi, and off he went. He stayed with Mummy and Daddy and spent a year conducting health interview surveys in one hundred and forty villages all over Pakistan. I had never set foot in a village, and now Saqib was seeing Pakistan as I had never seen it. He navigated the dirt roads on crowded buses, slept outdoors on the roped *charpoi* with no bedding, and to quench his thirst drank fistfuls of water from the village pond. Yikes! As he sat outdoors on a *charpoi* on the clay floor conducting interviews, surrounded by village men and women sitting on the floor with arms wrapped around their bent knees, people so poor they couldn't afford to feed themselves would serve him tea. He was moved by their hospitality, the look of sincerity in their eyes, their nods of appreciation, and their quiet acceptance of fate. He wrote to me that on one of the bus rides, he sat next to an old man who asked him, "How much money does your father make?" Saqib was to learn that, from the Pakistani perspective, asking your salary is a standard get-to-know question. Which reminds me: when my father-in-law was visiting, and friends came to visit us to pay their respects to him, he would ask Khalid.

"What does he do for a living?"

"He is a doctor."

"How much property do they have?"

"How am I supposed to know?"

"You mean you didn't ask?"

"Of course I didn't ask. You don't ask these questions."

"Why not? Don't you want to know?"

"No. I don't want to know."

"Why not?"

"Because it's personal."

"No, it isn't. OK, I'll ask them."

"*No.* Promise me you won't."

Three years later, Asim made a post-graduation announcement. You guessed it. He had been accepted to the University of Michigan, School of Law, got a one-year deferment, and went off to pursue human rights in Pakistan. Nawaz Sharif was now prime minister, and here at home Bill Clinton had been elected for a second term. He worked with Asma Jahangir, a human rights lawyer, and pursued prison and child labor reform. Interviewing prisoners in the bowels of the jails, holding hands across the world to protest child labor stirred in him the yearning for public service. He wrote to me from there, "I don't want to go behind corporate walls. I don't want to forget these faces."

The world has changed. Today if a young man said to his parents, "I want to go spend a year in Pakistan," they are likely to tie him down and take away his passport.

Culturally Correct

One evening, in 1988, I called my friends: "Come over this evening for a cup of tea. We want to share an idea with you." Three families came, and over a cup of a blend of Earl Grey and Lipton tea—my concoction—we put forth the idea: How about creating a Pakistani cultural association? An organization apart from and independent of the mosque. It's not enough for our children to know the history of Pakistan—we want them to speak about it. It's not enough for our children to be somewhat familiar with the music—we want them to sing it. It's not enough to clap to the beat of a *luddi* or *khattak* dance; we want them to dance to the beat.

"Let's do it"—a resounding yes.

I pulled out my yellow pad. "President." I pointed to the one of the gentlemen. "Vice president." I pointed to one of the ladies. "Who wants to be secretary?"

"You." The fingers were pointing at me. Khalid was made founder and cochairman with another gentleman, and thus, between us four families, the Pakistani Cultural Association of Staten Island was formed.

Parents cheered when I held music classes in my living room, teaching children Pakistani national songs. Pakistanis cheered when we held the first celebration of Pakistan's Independence Day in August, and our children gave speeches on the history of Pakistan and danced to the tune of *bhangra*. Politicians cheered as they dropped in to pay homage. And the borough of Staten Island cheered when our girls got up on the stage at Harmony Fair in Snug Harbor and performed the *luddi*, and we served *chaat* and *pakoras* at the Pakistan booth. That year, President Zia of Pakistan was killed in a mysterious plane crash, along with the American ambassador. Later that year, Pakistan elected a woman as its prime minister, Benazir Bhutto.

We left Staten Island many years ago, but the cultural association lives on. What didn't happen, though, is that our children's generation did not take up the torch. It was my dream that they would carry on what we had started for them, and the culture would live through the generations. They moved away, life happened, and when they got organized, it was to form professional organizations around their heritage or to get involved in faith-based activities. Asim cofounded the Muslim Bar Association of New York. Saqib was county commissioner of Boy Scouts in New Jersey. They have cut across national boundaries and created a network of professionals with a shared history and culture, in an American context, driven by civic consciousness. Daddy used to say, "My daughter is a major improvement over me." I now say that about our children.

Taking Staten Island to Pakistan

Do my children still go back? Saqib was there for a family wedding in 2007. The last time Asim was there was when Daddy passed away in 2010. He had wanted to be by his bedside, say his farewell, and lay him to rest. Daddy couldn't hold on and slipped away hours before Asim landed. Asim kneeled by his gravesite and wept, and I stood behind him, my heart weeping. I go every year, but I haven't pushed my children. It's not safe, as you all know. I am a product of that culture, so bombs notwithstanding, I go, but I don't want to put my children in harm's way. Each time I go, they say, "Mom, it's not safe," and I say, "I have to see my parents." Now it's my relatives. My mother yearned to hold Asim's daughter, Asha. Each time she saw Sofia, Saqib's youngest, on Skype, she wanted to reach out and poke her lovely chin, but the computer screen was the closest she got. On one of my visits, as

I was leaving for New York, she gave me a pair of gold bracelets for Brinda, Asim's wife. "I was hoping to give them to her when she came to Pakistan, but I don't know if she will come in my lifetime, so take these for her." Mummy died two years later.

PART FIVE

An American Muslim in New York

24.

An Arranged Marriage for My Sons?

I didn't arrange Saqib's marriage. I engineered it.

It is the desire of every Muslim parent that his or her child marries within the faith. As our children entered their teens, our Pakistani one-dish party conversations graduated from *Tell me that recipe again* to *I hope our children don't marry an American.* Did I just offend you? Let me explain: the term "American" in this context meant "out of faith" primarily and "non-Pakistani/non-Indian" secondarily. For first-generation immigrants in the late 1980s, the mere idea of their children marrying outside those boundaries was enough to land them in the trauma ward of a psych hospital (Khalid tells me that there is no such ward). OK, I just exaggerated, but you get the picture.

If you were a butterfly on the wall at the parties, this is the chatter you heard:

"My son has to marry a Pakistani girl, not even Indian—she has to be Pakistani."

"I'd die if he married a *gori*," referring to white, American female.

"Look at the bright side. Your grandchildren will be white."

"It's not funny."

"I think we should just bring a boy or girl from Pakistan."

"I have already picked a girl from Pakistan for my son."

"Bringing a girl from Pakistan may work; but I doubt if importing a boy is a good idea. Men from a patriarchal society will not adjust to a wife from a liberal culture."

"They should marry a Pakistani who grew up in America. They will have more in common—same music, same lingo."

"No, no. It's better if they marry someone from Pakistan. This way, they will maintain the culture. And they will keep going back to visit their in-laws and stay connected with Pakistan."

"I don't care if my son-in-law is Pakistani or Indian or Egyptian or African, as long as he is a Muslim."

"No, no, no. What are you talking! He has to be of our culture. How else will the two families get along? I want to be able to call up my son-in-law's mother and talk in Urdu. Stop saying things like that. I don't want our children to hear it."

"Did you hear Asma's son is marrying a Latino?"

"And Dr. Khan is marrying an American."

"Oh, dear! This is not a good example for our children."

Why were we even having this conversation? Because Islam prohibits dating, and in Pakistani culture it was a huge no-no. A girl and a boy cannot be alone unless they are married, the idea being that one thing leads to the other, and things can get out of hand. So how does one find a spouse? In Pakistan, parents arrange it. But this is America. Children raised here, no matter how much you shelter them, will not agree to the prospect of seeing the first glimpse of their spouse by looking into the mirror on their wedding day. What then lies between arranged marriages and dating?

Chaperone

Mummy and Daddy, who had been visiting from Pakistan and were listening to this conversation, gave me a piece of advice.

"Don't consider the idea of a daughter-in-law from Pakistan. Your children should marry a girl who was raised here, in America. Cultural compatibility is important," said Daddy.

Makes sense to me. Thank you, Mummy and Daddy. I never would have come up with that thought on my own. I better start working on it now. I am noticing that at home parties, the teen girls and boys have started self-segregating and barely talk to one another. I have to find a way to redraw the boundaries. If these boys and girls put up walls between themselves when among Pakistanis, how will they ever find a spouse?

I talked to Khalid. He advised that as long as they are together in groups, it is OK for them to mingle.

That's it! I will arrange teen activities for them, chaperoned of course—beyond the Sunday school, beyond the home parties, and beyond the watchful eyes of the aunties.

My first attempt? I got an F. I formed a teen group. They were to pick an activity and place and find a mother to escort them. For the first trip, they picked me as the escort; we went to the Statue of Liberty and had a great time. For the next trip—well, there was no next trip. No more escorts. No mother was available to go hang out with a bunch of teenagers.

I think I took the wrong approach. I should have first worked on the parents, coaxed them, implored them, wooed them, brought them on board, and then organized the teen group. If I try, try again . . .

My second attempt? An F minus—in bold red. I had sat down with one of my friends and presented the idea. First, the preamble: we want our children to marry among Muslims. . . . They can't date. . . . We want to make sure that they are comfortable with one another, make friends, and when the time comes, who knows . . . ? Then my brilliant solution: so what if we try to bring them together in a chaperoned environment . . . and as long as there is a mother hovering in the background, it will keep things in check.

"Sabeeha, that is not a good idea. I will not allow my daughter to be part of this."

"Why not?"

"Because it will hurt her reputation."

Excuse me!

"It's chaperoned."

"It doesn't matter. Other women will point fingers at my daughter and say, 'She was out with the boys.' If they are then seen talking to each other at parties, women will gossip about my daughter. I won't have it."

"They talk to boys in school, don't they? They will talk to boys in college. If you keep them apart from Muslim boys, guess what!"

"Sabeeha, you don't have a daughter, so you don't understand."

I don't understand! I don't understand why she doesn't understand that she is locking her daughter out of future prospects, and locking our sons out of their prospects. How does she envision finding a suitable boy? Does she really believe that her daughter will agree to an arranged marriage? And what if she does? How many young men out there would be agreeable to an arranged marriage? Perhaps a few, but it's a small pool to fish from. But I do understand. I understand that she is afraid, but isn't she being shortsighted? I now understand why there were no escorts. I bet no mother wants to be perceived as facilitating interaction between girls and boys. Does she think that I am being too Americanized and paving the way for my boys at the expense of the girls? Goodness!

Well, I just have to take my "boy-gets to-know-girl" project outside of our tight-knit community to a more distant, loosely knit group, with minimal auntie effect.

I was beginning to see Khalid's wisdom in having a community center for our children. That forum would have given them the space to be with friends and make friends.

My third attempt? An A+. Boy met girl, boy married girl, boy and girl have three beautiful children, and boy and girl are going through the usual joys and challenges of life. Now that I have given away the ending, let me tell you the story.

A Marriage Engineered

The loosely knit group I found was APPNA, the Pakistani physicians' group. Whereas its primary purpose was to promote continuing medical education, its annual conferences quickly morphed into a venue for family socializing and eventually branched into matchmaking. The conference was the venue where we reconnected with our friends—friends from medical school in Pakistan and friends we made during our residency years who had moved across the continent to establish their practices. If you had walked into the lobby of the Hyatt Hotel in Washington, DC, on a July 4 weekend, you would have been met by an air of elegance—no, not in the hotel décor but in the graceful array of Pakistani ladies in their colorful *shalwar kameez,* chatting in clusters in a buzz of Urdu, rushing with open arms to welcome an old friend, while men in well-tailored suits greeted colleagues with a warm embrace and little Pakistani boys and girls rushed out of elevators, looking for their lost mothers. Forget about the scientific session—come join the party for a sold-out banquet and savor the sounds of music as Abida Parveen, a mystic singer, performs with her head swaying to the beat of the Sufi music.

The association formed a children's group first and then, as children grew up, added a teen group, a young adults' group, and a young professionals' group. Youngsters would hang out together, under the watchful eyes of supervising parents. As children entered graduate school, the conference became a fertile ground for matchmaking. Another group was added to the association: singles' group.

I was in heaven.

So many girls!

I'd drag my boys, now undergrad students at Haverford College, to events and introduce them to friends who had daughters.

I hope their daughter will walk up and then the two shall meet.

I'd let them loose, hoping they would team up, make friends.

They are still young, but for now I just want them to get comfortable having Pakistani girls as just friends.

Then I hit the jackpot! It was 1996, and the four of us had just returned from the Olympics in Atlanta. By now, Saqib was in medical school at SUNY Syracuse and Asim was a senior in college.

"Saqib and Asim, I want you to go to Detroit to the APPNA conference next week," I announced.

"Why?" Saqib asked. "We just got back from Atlanta."

"Because I want you to go find a wife."

"Mom!"

"And why do I have to go?" asked Asim.

"Because I want you to make sure Saqib doesn't just hang out with the boys." I have to explain: Saqib is the quiet one and is likely to stick to his old chums and not venture to get to know anyone, which makes cutting through the boy-girl divide a little harder. Asim makes friends when crossing the street. If anyone can help Saqib find a girl, it will be Asim.

"Asim, you make sure that Saqib gets to meet some nice girls. And at the banquet, see to it that you both sit at a table where girls are also seated. Don't just cluster up on the boys-only table." I was making my goal and strategy very clear.

Asim smiled; Saqib tried not to smile.

"Why aren't *you* coming?" Asim asked.

"We can't afford another trip. Besides, I have used up my vacation."

So I put them on a plane, and off they flew. Sure enough, at the banquet they sat at a table with boys and girls. From across the table, Saqib met Saadia. They exchanged emails. A year later they were engaged, and in 1998, while he was still in medical school, they were married.

YES!

Backtrack: I had picked the boys up from the airport after their trip to Detroit. Driving home, I asked, "So, meet any friends?"

"Yes." Saqib knew exactly what I was getting at.

"Made any new friends?" I tried to be subtle.

"Ummm! Maybe."

Back off. Either he did or he didn't.

A few weeks later, they went back to college, and neither of them had said anything.

I'll try again next year.

Thanksgiving came, and the boys were coming home. I had planned a trip to Pakistan on the Tuesday before Thanksgiving to beat the high-season airfare in early December and was flying alone. I was at work when the phone rang.

"Mom." It was Saqib. He never calls me at work.

"Is everything all right?"

"Yes. You see, I am coming home Tuesday morning, and I was planning to drive you to the airport that evening, but, you see, (pause), there is this girl. . . ."

Breathe, keep breathing . . . girl . . . Muslim girl?

"You see, she has invited me to a Pakistani cultural event in New Jersey Tuesday evening, but I had planned to take you to the airport. . . ."

"GO," I must have shouted.

"But I wanted to see you off at the airport."

"Go. It's OK. Don't worry about it. Asim and Daddy will take me. Go, go."

"You are sure?"

"Yes, yes. Positive."

Dear, dear Saqib. He called me at work. There will be so many Pakistani girls there. . . . Maybe he will meet someone nice . . . maybe this Pakistani girl who invited him?

Saqib came and put on a suit. (*Good sign; he is trying to look his best.*) He did look so handsome, and hopeful Mommy waved as he walked down the kitchen steps to the garage.

I flew off to Pakistan. And that was that.

Saqib and Asim were back again for the winter holidays. Returning from work, I pulled into the garage and was walking up the stairs to the kitchen, when I saw Khalid waiting for me at the landing. He had heard the whirring of the automatic garage door. He followed me into the bedroom and closed the door.

"Bia," he almost whispered with a smile.

"What is it?"

"The phone rang a few minutes ago, and a girl asked to speak to Saqib. Her name is Saadia." Khalid's smile had widened.

A Muslim name! YES!

"Saqib is on the phone right now, upstairs. Now don't say anything when he comes down."

"I won't."

I quickly changed, came into the kitchen—Saqib was still upstairs—I got an onion out of the fridge and sliced it for the *daal tarka*—Saqib was still upstairs. Rather than my usual "Dinner is ready," I decided not to interrupt his call, put the *daal* on low heat, and joined Khalid in the family room. I picked up the *Staten Island Advance*, the local paper. *Oh, I can't concentrate. Maybe I can pretend to be reading when Saqib comes down.* After five long minutes, Saqib came hopping down the stairs. *Was that a leap of joy in this stride? Is that a flush on his face?*

"Assalam Alaikum," he said. "I didn't know you were home."

"*Wa Alaikum Assalam.* I got home just a few minutes ago."

Just sound matter of fact and stop staring at him.

"How was your day?" I asked, looking back at the paper.

"Fine." The usual Saqib response.

"Anything new?"

"No." The usual Saqib response.

"Ready for dinner?"

"Sure."

And that was that.

The next evening, coming home from work, there was Khalid again, waiting for me at the landing. He was smiling. He followed me to the bedroom and closed the door.

"Saqib just spoke to me. About the girl."

I sat down on the bed.

From the look on Khalid's face, it looks good.

"Her name is Saadia. He met her at the APPNA event in Detroit."

I giggled.

"She is a medical student. Her parents are both doctors from Pakistan, and they live in New Jersey. He says that she is a devout Muslim, and he likes her."

I wanted to get down on my knees and thank God. A Muslim girl. And he likes her. My dear Saqib likes a girl.

That evening Saqib talked to me. They had met at the APPNA banquet; they had sat at the same table. Saqib mentioned a book on Islam that he had written, she expressed an interest, he offered to mail it to her, and they exchanged emails. Then began the email courtship, without the phone calls. She lived in Trenton, New Jersey, and was going to the UMDNJ–Coopers College of Osteopathy. He was in Syracuse, New York. Over email, they chatted about his book. Then she invited him to the pre-Thanksgiving cultural event, their second meeting, and that is when they hit it off. I learned later that the same evening, Saadia had pointed Saqib out to her mother, "See that boy—he is the one I was telling you about."

"I like him." Her mother had quickly formed an impression, from a distance.

They graduated from emails to phone calls.

"How tall is she?" I asked.

"Five seven"

Nice height. How did he know that?

"I am meeting her tonight for dinner," Saqib told me. "I guess I will go up and change."

I looked at Khalid.

He looked at me.

A silent exchange.

They can't date. It's not allowed.

"Khalid, I have to talk to Saqib right now. He knows the boundaries, but if he is going out to see a girl, I have to remind him of the rules. But this is awkward—he is an adult, and I don't want to insult him by telling him what he already knows."

"I know," said Khalid.

After going back and forth in my mind, I decided to put my parental duties first.

"I am going to go up and talk to him. I will just say this, 'Saqib, just make sure that you meet her in a public place." Implied: don't be alone with her.

I started to walk up the stairs. I was barely halfway up, when I saw Asim walking briskly over to Saqib's room, carrying a change of clothes.

"Saqib, what time are we leaving?" Asim was asking Saqib.

I made a U-turn and walked down the stairs.

"Khalid, he is taking his brother with him. Isn't that sweet!" I cooed.

Dear God. Thank you, thank you, and thank you. Thank you for making my boys turn out right.

Khalid and I were having dinner when the boys walked down, dressed semi-casual, looking handsome both of them, and we waved them a happy good-bye.

"Khalid, when we got married, did we ever think that this is how it would work out for our children? Saqib on a semi-date with his brother for a chaperone."

"We are bringing them up in a different world. They are good boys," he said.

Next morning, over breakfast, I couldn't help myself.

"So, how was dinner?"

"Fine." The usual Saqib response.

"There were so many of us," Asim said.

"What do you mean 'so many'? It wasn't just the three of you?"

"All Saadia's siblings were there. There were six of us." Now Saqib was talking.

"That was a very good idea," I said.

"It was her mother's idea," said Saqib.

That's my kind of mother. Hmmm! She made sure her daughter wasn't alone with a boy and sent all three siblings with her, and they all came.

"Saqib, I would like to meet her family."

"Sure. I'll ask Saadia."

"If you're going to be seeing her often, we would like her parent's permission—implied permission." I said.

Then, turning to Khalid, I said, "I want her parents to know that we were all in this together and were taking responsibility for our son seeing their daughter."

"Saadia is OK with the parents meeting," Saqib informed me a few hours later.

I called Saadia's mother. But before I did that, Khalid and I did our due diligence—Google hadn't hit the web, so Khalid and I looked up the APPNA Member Directory and found her parents' names, noting that the mother was a graduate of Dow Medical College in Karachi and her father had graduated from Nishtar Medical College in Multan, the same as Khalid. The two dads were from the same town. How about that! He was a nephrologist, and she was a pediatrician. From the dates of graduation, it was apparent that they were just a little older than us. Then I picked up the phone. A woman answered. This is how I recall the conversation:

"*Assalam Alaikum.*"

"*Wa Alaikum Assalam.*"

"Is this Mrs. Raza?" I asked in Urdu.

"*Jee.*"

"This is Sabeeha Rehman, Saqib's mother."

"*Jee.* How are you?"

"Fine, thank you. Our children have met, and my husband and I would like very much to meet you. May I invite you to our house for dinner?"

"We would like you to come over," she countered, which was the response I expected. It is the boy's parents who walk the extra mile and go to the girl's family's house in the pre-engagement phase—a Pakistani custom to honor the girl.

"Of course."

"I will discuss it with my husband and call you back." Another appropriate response. I was getting to like this lady.

Sure enough, she called back the same day, and we set a date and time.

I picked up a cake from Alfonso Bakery on Victory Boulevard, and the four of us drove down to Trenton, New Jersey. Saqib had noted the directions—this was pre-GPS days—and was navigating. We drove by the river and turned the car into a residential community, going uphill into a quiet tree-lined street, with houses set far back and long driveways. Khalid, in a blue blazer and khaki pants, looking handsome, rang the doorbell. A gentleman opened the door—wearing a blazer and dress pants.

"*Assalam Alaikum,* please come in," a pleasant welcome by who I gathered was Saadia's father.

We entered the foyer and were immediately surrounded by three pretty girls in *shalwar kameez*, a good-looking teenage boy, and a tall, elegant woman with light brown hair shaped in light waves ending just above her shoulders and wearing a rust-colored outfit. The elegant woman, the mother, greeted me with a hug and a kiss on both cheeks, and the girls chirped. I looked around.

Which one of these girls is mine?

Elegant woman brought us into the living room and the pretty girls clustered around me. I looked from one to the other to the third. *How*

do I ask, *"Which one of you is Saadia?" without seeming too inquisitive.*
The pretty girls started chatting with me, while elegant woman went
into the kitchen.

"Are you Saadia?" I asked pretty girl who was talking to me.

"No. This is Saadia." She pointed to pretty girl next to her. *She is the*
prettiest. I shouldn't stare. I don't want her to feel that I am sizing her up.

We fell into an easy conversation, and the room filled with chatter. Saadia, tall, light-skinned, oval eyes, light brown hair falling just
below her shoulders, had two deep dimples in both cheeks and a smile
that would make you smile. *I'll take her.* Elegant lady had laid out
an elegant dinner, with fine linen and silver-plated serving dishes. I
had carefully picked a 3:00 p.m. time to avoid imposing lunch or dinner on them, but she served dinner anyhow, home-cooked—biryani,
kebabs. . . . She had laid out a feast. Elegant lady, whom I will now
call by her name, Mahmooda, sat down next to me on a dining chair
against the wall, and we chatted while the young ones sat around the
kitchen table, their laughter making me feel charmed. I listened to
her intently. I wanted to get to know the mother who raised the girl.
I didn't have to check out Saadia; that was up to Saqib. As we chatted,
I expected Mahmooda to ask me stuff, as in the usual get-to-know
questions: "Where in Pakistan are you from? How long have you lived
in Staten Island?" My job, Khalid's work, our boys—the normal questions that Pakistani women ask, delicately probing whether the family
is a good fit for their daughter. She asked me nothing—as in nothing.
I have to tell you that this was highly unusual for a Pakistani lady, and
that was enough to impress me. Of course, I didn't make any inquiries
of her either—it's just not my style. Mahmooda was beginning to look
more and more like my kind of mother. "My children stay at the dorm
during the week, and on Fridays they all come home." *Wow! She has*
managed to keep a tight control over the girls. And look at them, all
relishing one another's company, laughter in the kitchen, so cohesive. I
looked at my watch. *Is it evening prayer time?*

"Do you have to say your prayers?" Mahmooda asked.

"Please." *How did she guess?*

"Let's go."

In minutes, the entire party of ten was in the basement, prayer rugs were laid out, and we all stood up for prayer.

When we left, I spoke to Saqib in the car.

"I like the mother. A woman like her must have raised her child right. And I like the family. You have to decide about the girl."

Next week Mahmooda called and invited us for their daughter's engagement party. Not Saadia, but the younger daughter. After I left the party, as we were getting in the car, I said to Saqib, "You can tell about people from the company they keep. I liked their friends. I am OK with this match, if you are OK with it." Quiet Saqib said nothing, but inside the moonlit car, I could feel him smile.

Khalid and I decided that we would not say anything to our family and friends about Saqib's interest in this girl—not yet. She is someone's daughter, and we have to safeguard her reputation as we would if she were our own. Notwithstanding that they are not dating and they are always chaperoned, a mere whiff of her name being associated with Saqib when they are not yet engaged might lead to gossip, and that would not be fair to her or to her family. "The first time anyone hears Saadia's name will be when she is introduced as Saqib's fiancée." I was firm on that. I was reminded of the mother who objected to teen activities. See how protective I am of my maybe-daughter-in-law-to-be, while that was her daughter she was protecting.

Spring break, Saqib was back and drove down to New Jersey with Asim, to meet up with Saadia and her siblings. While he was out, I had a talk with Khalid. Clearly, he likes the girl. It has to be mutual, and with all three of her siblings chaperoning her, clearly the family is OK with it as well. So what are we waiting for? Let's have a talk with Saqib, and if he is serious, we should get them engaged.

That night, sitting around dinner in the kitchen, Khalid and I had a talk with Saqib. This is how I recall the conversation:

"If you like Saadia, then it's time you get engaged. It's not fair to her to drag things out. Do you want to marry her?" I asked.

"Yes, I do."

"Are you sure?"

"Yes."

"Then speak to her. If she is agreeable, we will ask her parents for her hand in marriage."

Asim was listening but did not inject his opinion. He was deferring to Saqib.

Next morning at breakfast, Saqib made the announcement. He had called Saadia the night before and asked her to marry him.

Awww! My spoon stopped halfway, hanging in the air. *Don't ask. Let him have his private moment to himself.* He was smiling.

"She is going to tell her parents." Saqib was smiling.

"She said 'yes'?" I asked.

"She did."

Awww! Don't cry. Just say a prayer.

I put down my spoon, pushed back the chair, walked around the table, and put my arms around him.

"Khalid, you, as the elder of the family, should make the call to Saadia's father and ask if we can come see them tomorrow. Saqib, let's go buy the engagement ring. Today we get the ring, tomorrow we propose to her parents, and if they say yes . . ."

"What do you mean 'if'?" said Saqib.

"I mean parents like to think things over."

"What is there to think about?"

"OK. When they say yes, we will ask them if we can come the next day with our families for a formal engagement—the ring and all the trimmings."

"I want to give her the ring now."

"Look. I understand that this is the American way, but in Pakistani culture, engagement is a family affair. Your uncles, aunts, and cousins have to be present when you give her the ring. They love you; your big day is their big day. Remember, this is the first engagement in this generation in our family. No one is going to want to miss it. You want their prayers and blessings. Besides, not including them will be disrespectful."

Always the one to do the right thing, Saqib acquiesced. Khalid picked up the wall phone, and the three of us sitting at the kitchen table watched and listened as he made the call to Dr. Raza.

"If you are available tomorrow evening, we would like to come and propose for Saadia's hand in marriage for Saqib."

We sat and watched Khalid nod into the phone.

"Seven p.m.?" He looked at me. I nodded. "Yes, we will be there. And please, it's a workday, so don't worry about dinner. Please."

"Now, before we go ring shopping, we have to inform our parents and the family," I told Saqib.

It was 9:00 p.m. in Pakistan when I called Mummy and Daddy.

"I have good news for you. Saqib has found a girl."

Mummy squealed. "Tell us," Daddy said, ecstatic.

Khalid called his father. Auntie Hameeda had passed away two years earlier. *She would have liked Saadia.*

With their blessings, we called our brothers in New York. More squealing, more "Tell me more." Phones were put on speaker, cousins were shrieking, and voices crying out, "*Mubarak!*" were coming off the airwaves. Saqib was beaming.

"We are going this evening to propose. Put a hold on your calendars for an engagement on Saturday. I will confirm."

"Let's go ring shopping."

When the four of us finally picked out the ring and the jeweler priced it, Saqib was taken aback. "That much!" Being a medical student with no income, he had never gone diamond shopping. Neither had his mother, for that matter. And this was a small diamond—nothing fancy—a medical student–size diamond. I could tell that he was feeling bad that his parents were spending all that money. "Saqib, we have put aside money for your wedding. Don't worry about it." On the way home, he kept opening the box and looking at the ring.

We rehearsed our script on our way to Saadia's.

"Daddy, as the elder, will propose to Saadia's parents." I looked back at the children in the back seat—I shouldn't say "children," but they are my children. "After Daddy, Mummy will propose, sort of like seconding the motion."

"And then I will propose," said Saqib.

"No. You are not supposed to propose to the parents. This is a parent-to-parent thing."

"But I want to propose."

"You have already proposed to her."

"I still want to propose to her parents. I know what I want to say to them."

"That's fine, you can do that," said Khalid.

"And then I will propose," said Asim.

"You?!" I asked. *This is not the script I had envisioned.*

"Yes. Me."

Just go along with it.

All six of them greeted us at the entrance. It was Friday, and the children were home for the weekend.

"I want everyone to come in the living room," Khalid announced.

We all took our seats on the sofas. Khalid began.

"We are here to ask for Saadia's hand in marriage for Saqib," he said, addressing Mahmooda and Dr. Raza.

My turn: "We love your daughter." *Don't get weepy.*

Mahmooda smiled.

Saqib's turn: "I would like to say something," he said, addressing her parents.

"You are an American boy, so sure." Mahmooda helped him along.

"Saadia is a wonderful person"—his voice trembled—"and I would be honored if you accepted me as your son-in-law."

He did OK. Nervous, but OK.

"And now I would like to say something," said Asim, smiling and looking around.

Laughter.

Asim turned to Saadia, "Saadia, will you be my sister-in-law?"

Laughter. Actually, he said *bhabi*, sister-in-law in Urdu.

"Yes." Saadia nodded, smiling.

She is not supposed to do that. She just preempted her parents. I guess I keep forgetting that our children are American.

We all turned toward Saadia's parents. Mahmooda spoke, looking at Khalid and me.

"We hope Saadia will be the daughter you always wanted," she said with a smile.

That means YES.

I jumped out of my seat, walked over to her, and gave her a hug. "*Mubarak.*"

Then over to Saadia, another hug. *Mubarak.*

The dads embraced, hugs all around, and *mubarak* in the air.

"I have a request of you," I asked Mahmooda and Dr. Raza. "We would like to come tomorrow with our families for an engagement ceremony."

"But it is too soon. I have a commitment tomorrow, and there is not enough time to prepare." Mahmooda was not ready for this.

"It's just family. Please don't prepare anything. We will come just for an hour, at any time outside of your commitment."

"How many people?" A reasonable question.

"Just my brother, Salman; Khalid's brother Arshed, his wife, and two children; Khalid's brother Najeeb, his wife, and two children; and us. That's all." *Right, that's all.*

Poor Mahmooda. She is the perfect hostess, goes all out to welcome her guests, and now I was pushing for a next-day engagement.

"OK." She was so agreeable.

I quickly got on the phone, called all three brothers. "*Mubarak*, Saadia's parents said yes, and the engagement is tomorrow. I will confirm the time."

Mahmooda canceled her other plans, and when we all walked into the house the next day, we were greeted with rose petals, the sounds of Urdu music, golden balloons, and the chirping of Saadia's friends, who had all gathered on short notice to watch Saqib slip on the ring. Khalid's sister-in-law Aneela had prepared all the trimmings: a Qur'an wrapped in green silk and gold ribbon and a hand-decorated basket laden with *ladoo*. We all took our seats, and then Saadia was brought in, dressed in a deep blue tie-dyed *shalwar kameez,* looking lovely. That morning I had taken out my wedding outfit and had brought the *dupatta* with me. I draped the red *dupatta* over her head and placed the Qur'an in her lap. Khalid said a prayer, and as Asim stood behind Saqib and everyone looked on, Saqib slipped the ring on her finger. *Mubarak.* I took the basket of *ladoo,* took a pinch of it, and fed it to

Saadia, then Saqib; Khalid repeated the ceremony, and then everyone in our party took turns.

Throughout the evening, I noticed Saadia lift her hand and look at her ring. Saqib was smiling. Everyone was smiling.

I printed engagement announcement cards, had *ladoo* gift wrapped, and delivered them to all our friends on Staten Island.

Still being chaperoned, they decided to get married the following year. We supported the idea and had a traditional Pakistani wedding. Mummy brought all the wedding outfits from Pakistan, and our families joined us from all over the US and from Pakistan. I decided to give Saadia two sets from my wedding jewelry, and two I put away for Asim's wife.

In many ways, the wedding was part Pakistani, part American, part Egyptian, part improvisation, and part Islamic. Saqib's aunties hosted pre-wedding *dholak* parties—musical evenings—and Saadia's parents hosted the *mehndi* party—that's Pakistani. Saqib's cousins from New York and Pakistan gathered at our home and practiced every day until they had the group dances choreographed to perfection. At the *mehndi,* when the cousins entered, clicking shimmering sticks to the beat and dancing in unison, their flowing *shalwar kameez* glittering, people's faces lit up. The boys all wore white *shalwar kameez* with colorful scarfs, and Asim, as he danced away, was the happiest, after Saqib, of course. Musical evenings have evolved from being strictly "girls only" and just singing to unisex and dancing—that is the new Pakistani. On the wedding day, the groom's party gathered in our house, and we held the *sehra bandi,* a ceremony in which an elder of the family ties a *sehra,* a headdress with strings of roses, on the groom's turban, draping it over his face—a veil of flowers—that's Pakistani. Daddy did the honors, assisted by my brother Salman and Khalid's brother Arshed. Assembled guests walked up one by one and placed a cash gift in Saqib's lap—that's Pakistani. Saqib wore a white *sherwani,* a long coat-like garment, with a turban—that's Pakistani. As the party departed for the wedding, his sisters, in this case, his female cousins, blocked his way to the car, asking for a ransom of sorts—that's Pakistani. All his *sehra bandi* earnings—gone. At the Marriot in Princeton, as our cars pulled up, the bride's family greeted us with garlands—that's Pakistani. The DJ announced our party, with Mummy and Daddy leading the party and Khalid and I escorting the veiled Saqib to the stage—that's American. Once seated, Khalid removed the *sehra*, allowing him to see without having to squint through the strings of roses. Saadia wore a red shimmering *gharara* with a glittering *dupatta* draping over her head—that's Pakistani. She carried a bouquet of flowers—that's American. As Saqib stood up to receive her, he looked like a Mughal prince. She took her seat next to Saqib, on the sofa—that's American. The imam, an Egyptian, who performed the *nikah*, asked them to sit on seats across from one another, explaining that an unmarried couple cannot be seated together—that's Islamic. He asked both parents to come up to the stage and take a seat next to their children and asked the dads, in their capacity as guardians of the children, to sit together and hold hands—that's Egyptian. The marriage ceremony was performed in the presence of all the guests, with the bride and groom in the same room—that's wholly Islamic and American. When asked if she accepted Saqib as her husband, Saadia flashed the loveliest smile and said yes—that's Islamic and American. Saadia did not sit with her head lowered or eyes downcast; she socialized, looked oh-so-happy—that's Islamic and American. Saqib received *salami*—cash gifts from the bride's family—that's Pakistani. Saadia's sisters and friends took away Saqib's shoe—the *joota chupai*—and demanded ransom—that's Pakistani. At *rukhsati,* when the parents bid farewell to the bride, we held the Qur'an over her head and escorted her to the waiting car— that's Pakistani. She turned back and threw the bouquet into the outstretched hands of squealing girls—that's American. She did not cry when leaving but sat in the car and, with a big smile, waved—that's American. The following week, we hosted the *walima*—the post-wedding reception given by the groom's family—that's Islamic and Pakistani. The highlight of the evening was Asim's "Ode to Saqib." It was sheer entertainment, packed with humor and a young man's love for his brother. Hugs, kisses, embraces, tears, laughter, prayers— that's anyone and everywhere.

"Now don't go around showing wedding pictures to everybody," Mummy cautioned me.

"Why not?" I was already looking forward to doing just that.

"You have to protect them from *nazar*." She meant the evil eye.

Now, I am not superstitious, but something about the tone of her voice resonated with me, and I listened. *No harm being careful.* I removed the photos from my pocketbook.

Saudi Arabia

Soon after Saqib's marriage, the ground starting shifting beneath my feet. It was Khalid. He was getting restless and wanted to get out of private practice and explore something new. He was in his mid-fifties and, yes, going through a midlife crisis. Opportunities came up in Connecticut, in Cleveland, and I accompanied him on job interviews. Then came a big one: Saudi Arabia.

No!

It's enough that I have to consider relocating from the house I thought I would spend the rest of my life in; now we are talking about moving overseas? To Saudi Arabia, of all places? I can't leave my children. I don't want to give up my place in the driver's seat. And I definitely don't want to go through another identity crisis. And Asim is still not married. I can't just leave him and go off. No!

More than me, it was Mummy who opposed it. "This is our second home. This is where we come every year. This is everyone's second home—a place for the family to get together. You are the elders—you cannot just leave!"

"It's their life," Daddy said.

Let Khalid look into it. I am sure he will turn it down.

"I will take you to Paris every weekend." Khalid was not backing down.

Paris!

"They want me to come for a month to do a locum, for both sides to try it out."

Let him go. When he is there, he will see for himself and turn it down.

Khalid called from Saudi Arabia. "They want you to come here for a week. They will pay for your airfare."

I shouldn't fight him. I will go and together we will decide that this place is not good for us.

One look at Khalid's face—standing at the receiving line at Riyadh airport, and I knew. By the end of the week, *I* was sold. This was an American-style hospital, with an American staff, with American accreditation, with American standards and policies, and with a Saudi staff that loved Americans. Blink and you could be in a hospital in America, only this was newer, shinier, state-of-the art, and a city in itself with parks, waterfalls, shopping center, bank, swimming pool, and restaurants—like an oasis. I was wooed, dined, toured, and offered a job as an administrator. The chairman's wife, an American, took me out to lunch, dazzled me, and with every question I asked—"But what about driving? But what about missing my family? But what about having to wear the *abaya*?[2]—she presented herself as the answer: "This is what I do. . . ."

I suppose if it's just for two years, it won't be so bad. Like an adventure of sorts.

I may even like the change. Khalid wants this. He has always supported me in my endeavors, always stood by me, always promoted me. I cannot stand in his way and make him unhappy. What kind of a life would that be?

I had one big misgiving, though.

"Khalid, Asim is not married. I would like to have settled him before taking off."

"Asim is an adult. He is going to find his own way. You can't run his life for him," he answered.

We left, went for two years, and stayed for six.

He Did It His Way

"I am telling you now. I am going to do my wedding my way," Asim kept announcing throughout Saqib's wedding ceremonies.

He wasn't kidding.

If you have seen *Fiddler on the Roof,* you will know where I am going with this. I was able to cajole my firstborn, from start to the

---

2 Black cloak worn over clothing.

wedding, but my baby wanted to do it his way. No sooner was Saqib married off than I shifted my attention to Asim, my handsome, charming, sensitive, compassionate, affectionate, warm, and loveable son and now law student at the University of Michigan. I was dragging him to APPNA events. I was calling close friends: "Can you suggest a nice girl for Asim?" Then I'd get them to meet by sending him to young adult forums, which were becoming more and more focused on meeting a match. Nothing materialized. Asim knew what he wanted and hadn't found her yet.

And then he found her. Brinda and he practically came up together—they had known each other in college, she at Bryn Mawr and he at Haverford, neighbor colleges. "She is perfect," he emailed us when we were in Saudi. Of Bengali origin, her parents, doctoral scientists at the National Institutes of Health, had migrated from India. An only child, she was of the Hindu faith, the seventh generation of Brahmins. Brahmins, as you may know, are of the highest Hindu caste, principally priests or teachers.

Now I will pause. I was relieved that Asim had found the girl of his dreams. But the out-of-faith circumstance gave me pause. I wondered how we would manage the issue of religion and worried. Would she be able to adjust to the lifestyle of a devout Muslim family? How would her parents feel about their daughter marrying a Muslim? What about the children? I was sure that Asim had thought this through and knew that they had talked about the issues, but I worried. I sought the counsel of my parents, my family, and friends who were in an interfaith marriage.

I remember the first time we met Brinda. Khalid and Asim picked her up from the Staten Island Ferry and drove her to our home. Petite, her dark hair framing her face, Brinda sat on the sofa beside Asim, and I took a place on the floor cushion, facing them. Leaning against the floor-to-ceiling windows overlooking the valley, with the sun warming my back, this was my most comfortable seat. Brinda chatted easily in a soft, gentle voice, unhurried, and, unlike many of her generation, at a refreshing pace that was not a mile-a-second. Her face radiated a serene glow—a Pakistani would call it *noor*, or light. She did not try to impress and displayed no affectation. Any auntie would take one look at her and tell that she was cultured and well bred.

Asim and Brinda approached the issue of religion as two mature adults. Brinda decided to explore Islam and study it and, in the process, started making Muslim friends to see if this was a community she could relate to. Asim held her hand through this journey, and we all did what we could to be there for her. In those months, which turned into years, I grew to respect Brinda. She was not rushing herself; she wanted to know what she was getting into; she wanted to understand, and make up her own mind, in her own time, on her own terms.

She is going to need a lot of support. God please guide me to guide her.

At first I gave her books to read, but then Mummy cautioned me. "Don't overwhelm her with books. You need to spend time with Brinda and help her get to experience what life in a Muslim household is like. Have her come and stay with you, let her see how you interact with Saadia. Be loving toward her. Your conduct is the best example of your faith." I was grateful that my parents were still around to impart their wisdom. I needed that guiding hand.

Brinda would chat comfortably about her quest, what she had learned, and her questions about the status of women in Islam. She was open and honest about her issues, and I was grateful that she was seeking answers from me. Then she told me that she had been going to Masjid Al-Farah and listening to Imam Feisal's sermons.

Now if there were one imam I would have picked for Brinda's mentoring, it would have been Imam Feisal. How fortunate was that?!

I had first heard Imam Feisal speak at a wedding several years earlier. He was officiating the wedding of our dear friend's son. A gentleman of Egyptian origin and with a gentle demeanor, he was soft-spoken and charming. Saadia, my daughter-in-law, was awestruck. "He must be a Sufi," she said to me. "I want him to perform my sister's wedding." Next month, when he officiated at her sister's wedding, he took the audience by surprise when he asked the bride to propose to the groom. He was invoking the example of Khadija, Prophet Muhammad's wife, who was his boss and had proposed to him. How empowering is that?! His inclusive and all-embracing approach, and his power to connect with the listeners, gave him celebrity status, and after 9/11 he was in high demand on the interfaith circuit. He was the imam of a small mosque in downtown Manhattan, and the devout young, thirsty for spiritual fulfillment, filled the space. And among them was Brinda.

Thank you, God, for guiding her there.

I was growing fond of Brinda.

I don't want to fall in love with her, not just yet.

Daddy, who visited often, spent much time with Brinda and developed an immense affection for her and often noted her "special qualities" to me. He and Brinda became close during those years. She was loving toward him, and he got to see what she brought out in Asim.

Brinda asked if we could meet her parents. Khalid, Asim, and I drove down to Maryland to meet them. On the drive, Asim lectured us on how to conduct ourselves.

Has he forgotten that we raised him?

Her parents welcomed us into their home with a warm greeting, a hearty handshake, and a big smile. In the airy, bright room, with walls decked with paintings in vivid colors, I settled into a comfortable posture and felt myself relax. We talked about anything from travel, art, music, books, food, to Erica Cain in *All My Children*. Asim and Brinda exchanged smiles as the parents got into soap operas, our voices getting high-pitched over Erica's meanderings. Our mutual interests kept us engaged and happy in one another's company. We had more in common than most couples I have met—even the military background of our families. We definitely "clicked." There was laughter, and Asim and Brinda could have been posing for an ad for Crest toothpaste. They took us out for lunch, and Asim chuckled when we all ended up ordering the same item off the menu—crab cakes. When we came home for dessert, I almost squealed with delight when Brinda's mother brought out a bowl of homemade *rasgullahs*. I hadn't had these cheese balls dipped in crystal-white syrup in years. I gleefully accepted her offer to pack a doggie bag for me. From the sheepish smile on Asim's face, I couldn't tell if he was relieved or embarrassed. I was moved by their demeanor, grace, and hospitality and impressed with their intellect and refined simplicity. They made us feel welcome and at home. On the drive back, I kept thinking about them. Over the years, we have continued to meet, and bond, sharing music and stories. The love for our children brought us together, and now our respect for one another keeps us together.

Three years later, as Asim and Brinda strolled through the courtyard of the Frick Museum in Manhattan, Brinda noticed a bouquet of flowers on the bench. Lying next to the flowers was an envelope, and written on the envelope was "Brinda." In that instant she knew, as Asim went on his knees and asked her to marry him. It had taken him weeks to get permission from the museum management to allow his package to be placed, getting security clearance and whatever. Khalid and I were still in Saudi Arabia, and Asim called to give us the news. I cried.

May Allah bless her with all the joys that marriage can bring. I will love her and cherish her, and hold her dear, dear, dear to my heart.

I called my parents. "This girl will be good for you," Daddy said. How did he know? What was that special quality his wise eyes had detected?

The next day, I told my boss, Dr. Adnan Ezzat, a Saudi doctor. Wearing our white lab coats, we had just sat down at the round table in his office for our standing 8:00 a.m. meeting. He was the executive director, and I was his executive consultant. He stood, his face lighting up. "*Ya Sabeeha*," he said, "you have earned a place in *Jannah*.[3] Allah has showered you with his blessings. This girl is Allah's gift to you, I can tell. . . . My advice to you is: don't watch over her; don't tell her what to do; don't judge her; don't push her to say her prayers, or fast, or read the Qur'an. Just leave her alone. Let her be. She will find her own way in her own time, at her own pace. The hardest part is over. Make the rest easier for her."

Allah's gift to me!

Tears flowed, and I let them. He took his seat, and we pulled out our files and went back to business, as I fumbled for a tissue in my pocket.

---

3 Paradise.

I took his advice. What a relief! I would have driven myself mangoes and bananas if I had allowed myself to be driven by my drive. I would have done exactly what he told me not to do, stressing my daughter-in-law, my son, my husband, and me. Thank you, Dr. Ezzat. When I had prayed to God for guidance, He did guide me. There were no letters from heaven, no dreams, no epiphany, no visions, no voices. He spoke to me through His vessels: my parents, my husband, my friends, and my boss—people whom I would listen to. Thank you, God.

A wedding date was set for May 2007. We decided to return home for good. Our grandchild Omar had been diagnosed with autism, and he wasn't making much improvement. We were needed back home. I also wanted to be around for Brinda.

I flew to Pakistan to order outfits for the wedding. For Brinda, I picked a turquoise *lehnga* studded with silver embroidery for the *walima*, and, of course, a yellow *shalwar kameez* for the *mehndi*. For Asim, I picked the traditional *sherwani* and turban. When the dresses arrived and I showed Brinda the *lehnga*, she went *oooh*, got up, and gave me a delightful tight hug. "I love it!" Some moments of joy one never forgets. I still feel that tight hug.

Brinda made a beautiful and oh-so-happy bride. The *nikah* was performed in a mosque; her parents held a wedding ceremony in Washington, DC, and we hosted the *mehndi* and *walima* reception in New Jersey. Brinda wore her grandmother's red wedding sari at a nondenominational ceremony. As they held hands and looked up at each other, Daddy remarked, "Look at them—love, admiration, and respect." That afternoon, we clustered in her parent's hotel room, and along with her aunts, uncles, and cousins, sang Urdu songs, Daddy surprising them all when he sang a Bengali national song. At the *walima*, with her *dupatta* draped over her hair, she danced the evening away. I took her mother by the hand, led her to the dance floor, and holding hands, we swung our arms to the beat—she in a sari, I in a red *shalwar kameez*. Earlier, after the guests were seated and the family had lined up to make our welcome remarks, I remembered Dr. Ezzat's words: "*Allah's gift.*" Mic in hand, I turned toward Brinda's parents. "Today is the happiest day in my life. . . . Thank you for your gift." Brinda's parents stood up, bent their heads over clasped palms, and nodded in acknowledgment. The room went up in cheers, as I fought back tears. Family from all over the US and Pakistan flew in. It would be Mummy and Daddy's last visit to the United States.

Daddy was right about Brinda. She has been good for me. My respect for her grew into love. I beamed when, three years into their marriage, my sister-in-law said to me, "I pray that everyone in our family gets a daughter-in-law like Brinda."

Brinda knows that. I told her.

I pondered over what my sister-in-law had said. In the initial years of their courtship, I had let the boundaries of tradition cause me much worry. Had I at the time opened my heart to look beyond, below, and above the surface coating of creed, I would have seen what Daddy saw, what Mummy knew, what Dr. Ezzat sensed, and what Asim fell for. They saw what matters. What I first saw as a hurdle was a figment of my perception. Brinda revealed herself to be a blessing, and now even my extended family, my in-laws, were taking note. More musing: when Allah says in the Qur'an that He is All-Knowing, and He knows best what is best for you, believe it. Have faith.

Singles, Matchmaking, Speed Dating

Muslim girls of immigrant families are finding it harder and harder to find a Muslim husband. In the US, that is. They are remaining single longer and longer, and their parents are getting desperate. I hear this tale of woe in almost every family I know. When they are in their twenties, they won't hear of marriage—they are busy getting their careers going and are confident that when the time is right, they will have no trouble finding a match. They brush aside their mother's entreaties to get serious, with a wave of the hand and a "Mom, I'm not ready." By the time they enter their thirties and get serious, reality hits. There aren't many choices. The few who will agree to an arranged marriage learn that most young men won't hear of an arranged match. At this stage they start going to Muslim singles events. Some want to be wooed but are not allowed to date; some want to fall in love, only to learn that the young man wants to have an affair, and she won't cross the line.

Mothers are wringing their hands, cajoling and pushing, calling their friends with a plea: "Please keep an eye out for a young man for my daughter," and spending sleepless nights. As the women start getting close to forty, single men who want children walk past them, reducing their choices to divorced men, possibly with children—not a fresh start a young girl had dreamed for.

Community leaders and female activists are coming up with creative ways to address the issue, ranging from organizing singles events, including speed dating, to professional matchmaking. In my spirit of volunteerism, I too had my brush with one of those.

At one point I got involved in organizing a singles event. Our team went through the contact list and culled out the singles, created a profile, and selected a group based on our criteria of age, profession, interests, etc. The idea was to ensure that we had a compatible group. Invitations were sent out. When the RSVPs came in, we had thirty-five women and fewer than fifteen men or some embarrassing number like that. We salvaged the event the best we could and then did a focus group of sorts. Why were the guys not interested? The guys said: Our parents kept us segregated. We were made to feel that Muslim girls were out of reach, and so we never got to know them. We were also told to call them "sister"—Sister Fatima, Sister Noreen. They called us Brother Imran, Brother Tariq. Don't you see what that does to our psyche? We start looking at one another as brother and sister. We cannot just make a U-turn, show up at a singles event, and socialize with them as potential partners when we have been conditioned to stay away. Islam allows us to marry women of the Book, i.e. Christians and Jews. So if Muslim women stay segregated and there are women of other faiths who are willing to engage in a relationship, why bother when we have other choices?

That said it all. And that is the case at all such events—girls show up in droves, and the boys stay away. Matchmakers have set up shop. Go through their listings and see what you find: all women and just a few men. Muslim boys are marrying out of faith, and the girls are being left out.

Now let me back up a little. I just quoted one of the boys saying, "Islam allows us to marry women of the Book." This has been the general belief for centuries: Muslim men can marry a Christian or Jewish woman, but a Muslim woman cannot marry out of faith. That doctrine is now being reinterpreted, challenged, and reversed among some progressive Muslim scholars, particularly in the United States. Their conclusion is that both sexes can marry people of the Book. Rationale: The Qur'an does not forbid women from marrying men of the Book. It is the mother who raises the child and creates an environment of faith and learning in the home, and according to the principles of Shariah, every woman has a right to have a family, to be a wife and a mother, and it is not fair to deprive her of that right by limiting her choices. On the basis of this rationale, some imams in the US are now performing the *nikah* of Muslim women to Christian or Jewish men. There is resistance to this trend, and it is tearing families apart. When a young girl in our close circle married a Catholic, one of her family members, feeling that this union was not sanctioned in Islam, decided not to attend the wedding. He eventually came around, but more so out of family commitment.

Dear Muslim immigrant parents: Turn the denial dial to the Off position, listen to your children, talk to them, walk with them, and grow with them. Your children are American. Trust them to redraw the boundaries as American Muslims. Recognize that our children will be better Muslims than us, because you have molded them into informed and educated Muslims and have given them the best values of both worlds. Trust them to redefine their identity. Trust them to recast Muslim practices as Americans. You are doing more than changing the direction of your prayer rug—from facing west in Pakistan to facing northeast in America—the picture of your prayer rug has changed.

25.

The Shia-Sunni Schism

My father was a Shia, my mother a Sunni. What does that make me? A Sushi?

I was raised in the Sunni tradition and didn't know that my father was a Shia until I was a teenager. My impression of Shias, shaped by what my friends in school would tell me, was that they were the bad guys. "They beat themselves," they would say.

One day I asked Mummy about it. "Why do Shias beat themselves?"

Mummy explained that it was during the Muslim month of Muharram that Imam Hussein, the Prophet Muhammad's grandson, was killed in the battle of Karbala. Every year in Muharram, Shias commemorate his martyrdom by holding gatherings called *majlis,* where they relate the narrative of the battle and read poetry on the suffering of the imam and his family; processions are led through the streets, and yes, men beat themselves as an expression of grief for the pain of Imam Hussein. "One should not inflict injury on one's body," she told me.

So the Shias are wrong.

Driving me home one day in our red Fiat, Mummy took a different route, explaining that the streets of Raja Bazaar had been closed for the Muharram procession. The next day, someone in school told me that riots had broken out in Raja Bazaar during the procession, and people had been killed. What riots? I asked. Shia-Sunni riots, I was told. There were two Shia girls in my class, and sensing the tension in the air, I held my next question. Why were Shias and Sunnis fighting each other on the streets? I asked Mummy when I got home. She was sitting at her usual place on the verandah overlooking the garden, head bent over her Singer sewing machine.

"Because some crazy person said something crazy to another crazy person, and the whole mob went crazy. When are these people going to learn to be patient and tolerant? Muslims fighting Muslims!" She shook her head, her voice rising in pitch, with her frown making vertical waves on her forehead. "These riots are going to go on until after the tenth of Muharram."

"Why the tenth?" I asked.

"That is the day Imam Hussain was killed. That day, there are more Shia-Sunni riots than any other day. Until then, we stay away from Raja Bazaar." The whirr of the sewing machine signaled that discussion was over.

Mummy still hadn't told me what they were fighting about, and I had homework to do. As I turned to go to my bedroom, she called out, "Head up." My head shot up on cue. I had been growing in height, was towering above my classmates, and, conscious of standing out, I had started hunching my shoulders and lowering my head when walking. I owe my perfect posture to Mummy's relentless commands: "Head up. Sit up straight. Shoulders back."

Once Muharram was over, I forgot all about it. More pressing controversies distracted me. President Ayub Khan was meeting President Kennedy at the White House, and as I looked at the two men on the front page of the *Pakistan Times*, I made my pronouncement: our president was definitely more handsome.

Do Not Say, "Happy New Year"
A year went by, and we were back into Muharram. By the way, Muharram is the first month of the Muslim calendar. Keep this in mind: do not say, "Happy New Year" to a Muslim in Muharram. It's a month of mourning. Daddy would often remark, "I wish our religion was more fun-loving: no music, no dancing, even our new year begins in mourning." Daddy was fun loving and enjoyed making naughty jokes of the faith.

The girls at school were back on the Shia-Sunni topic. I was at the Sir Syed School for Girls in Rawalpindi, on the cusp of puberty, struggling with forbidden curiosity about what a friend had whispered during recess on Facts-of-Life-101 and star-struck by Jackie Kennedy, who, rumor had it, had taken a fancy to the dashing President Ayub Khan when she visited Pakistan. The girls at school seemed to know all about the Shias and the Sunnis—who wronged whom, who could have and didn't, and the verdict: Shias had it wrong. *How do they know all this? How come my parents never talked about this?* Well, Daddy didn't say his prayers or read the Qur'an, so I didn't expect him to get into religious controversies, but Mummy hadn't volunteered any Shia-Sunni information either, nor had Daadee Amma, Daddy's mother, who lived with us.

Can a Shia Love a Sunni?

Another year, another Muharram went by. That year I was visiting Aba Jee and Ami Jan. Not only were my grandparents devout Sunnis, Aba Jee was a religious scholar. He would wake up before dawn, say his pre-dawn prayers in his prayer room/library, and then sit cross-legged on the prayer rug, the Qur'an placed on the *rihal,* the X-shaped foldable bookrest, and study the scripture until the *adhan* rang out for dawn prayers. People often visited him to seek his opinion on religious issues. Muharram had just passed, and the controversy was still lingering in my mind. I remember walking up to Aba Jee, sitting next to him on the rug as he read, and interrupting him: "Aba Jee, what is the conflict between Shias and Sunnis?"

Aba Jee fished for the ribbon in the spine of the book, placed it as a bookmark, and smoothed his palms over his face and beard, taking in the positive energy of the Qur'an. "*Acha.* Let me tell you." And thus began my first introduction to the schism between the two major sects. He told me the story of the dispute of succession that arose after Prophet Muhammad passed away. There were those who believed that the prophet's cousin and son-in-law, Ali, should succeed him and take the mantle of caliph. Another group was of the opinion that his father-in-law and close friend, Abubakr, should be the successor. Abubakr became the first caliph, and that is at the heart of the issue. The mantle was then passed on to Umar, then Uthman, and finally Ali. But the schism never healed, and Muslims were forever divided—the Shia, who believed that succession was a family right, and the Sunnis, who believed that the decision to appoint a caliph rested with the community.

"Who should have been the caliph?" I asked.

"Abubakr." Aba Jee was emphatic. He then gave me a passionate discourse on why he believed that Abubakr was the rightful successor. Having no other frame of reference, I was convinced.

The Sunnis are right. The Shias are wrong. Got it.

"Be careful what you say about Shias," Ami Jan chimed in. "Your father is a Shia."

NO!

That is not possible. My father a Shia! Daddy doesn't beat himself; I have never seen him go to a majlis.

I looked at Aba Jee. He nodded.

They wouldn't say that if it wasn't true. But it can't be! Daddy isn't who he says he is—just a minute—come to think of it, I don't remember Daddy ever saying that he was a Sunni. Mummy never told me he was a Shia. I just assumed . . . Oh, my God.

Aba Jee inched a little closer to me.

Aba Jee and Ami Jan are such devout Sunnis. How did they ever agree to the match?

This is what I remember him telling me: When your father's proposal came for your mother, I turned it down. I would *not* marry my daughter to a Shia. Then your father came to see me. He made me a promise. He promised that the children would be raised Sunni, and he would never let his beliefs as a Shia influence his wife or his children. I trusted your father's word and said yes to the proposal. Your father kept his word.

I pictured Daddy, a young man of twenty, light brown, curly hair, milky white skin, handsome, standing in the presence of this imposing man, making a vow for the woman he loved. *Oh, Daddy! And you never said anything to us. Oh, I hope I never said anything bad about Shias in your presence.*

I retreated to my room and lay on the *charpoi*, looking up at the tiny pale lizards playfully crisscrossing the ceiling, staying close to the walls to avoid being blown off the ceiling by the draft of the ceiling fan. *Daddy must have loved Mummy so deeply.* Daddy had first told my sister Neena and me about their "love marriage" some years ago. I must have been nine, Neena seven. We were visiting family in the city of Lyallpur (now Faisalabad). He was driving around, showing us the school he went to, the field where he played cricket, and then he pointed out a gate of the high school for girls. "And that is where I saw Mummy for the first time." Daddy always referred to her as Mummy. "She was standing outside the gate, holding her school books. She was beautiful. I knew then that this is the girl I wanted to marry." He turned to smile at Mummy in the passenger seat. Mummy had a shy smile on her face, and I felt a bit embarrassed. "A few days later, I saw her again, at our house. She had come to visit my cousin Zakia. I said to her, "I want to marry you," and Mummy said, "I also want to marry you, and so we were married." Mummy was now getting rather uncomfortable at Daddy spilling the beans with his little girls.

He had oversimplified it, of course—it hadn't been as smooth as that. "I went to meet Aba Jee," Daddy had told us, "and I told him that I would join the army as a commissioned officer and be able to support a wife. I then applied, got accepted, and Aba Jee agreed to the marriage." Daddy had smiled as he told us the story. *And he had left out the Shia bit. Dear Daddy.* And what about Aba Jee? This was the 1940s; my grandparents were conservative Sunnis, and Aba Jee was strict. No music, no romantic novels, definitely no movies. Forget about dating; Mummy wore the burqa. How did my grandparents agree to their daughter having a love marriage, to a Shia, no less? Daddy was not wealthy, so it wasn't the money. A student at the Forman Christian College in Lahore, he was not on much of a career path either. Mummy was drop-dead beautiful—quite the eligible maiden. Aba Jee's wise eyes must have seen something in Daddy, and beneath the façade of strictness, his love for his little girl. On the checklist of an eligible bachelor, Daddy didn't stand a chance, yet Aba Jee agreed to the match. Isn't that what love is all about—what parents will do for their children?

I never talked to Daddy about this—the Shia part, that is. I wish I had. I wish I had told him that I saw him as man of his word, a man who gave up part of himself to allow us to grow in a home free of conflict. Isn't that was love is all about?

I did raise it with Mummy. "They are converted Shias," she told me. "For many years, your grandparents' children would die in infancy. Your grandfather went to see a *maulvi*, who advised him that if he became a Shia, his children would live. So your grandfather converted. They then had five children. Seeing that, other members of the family also converted."

I asked her about Daadee Amma, my paternal grandmother. I had never seen her engaged in any of the Shia rituals. "She was born and raised Sunni, so even though she converted, she has kept a middle-line approach," Mummy said.

I think it was more than that. Daadee Amma was a hands-off mother and mother-in-law. She lived with us but never interfered, not in household affairs, comings and goings, and definitely not in matters of religion. Her children would quibble over whom she would stay with—they all wanted her, and each time she said goodbye to go stay with the other son or daughter, her children and grandchildren would start counting the days when she would return. Not getting into the Shia-Sunni rituals was just her way. It made for peace in the family.

I had an awakening in 2008 when I read Reza Aslan's *No god but God*. Of course there was another side to the story: the Shia believe that it was Ali's birthright to succeed the prophet and that the caliphs were to be from among the Prophet's descendants, that Ali was qualified and had the support. They too had their narrative about the events that prevented Ali from becoming caliph. The compelling case that Reza Aslan made gave me something to think about.

So who was right?

Who Cares!

Daddy was filling out admissions forms at our new school. I must have been fifteen. One of the questions on the form asked for the sect. Daddy wrote: none.

"Daddy, you didn't write Sunni," I was quick to point out.

Daddy stopped writing and looked up. "Sects are not important. If you can just focus on the Qur'an, practice its teachings, and do what it instructs you to do, that is what will make you a good Muslim. Fighting over history will not."

Fighting over history. That is what this is all about, isn't it! Who rightfully or wrongfully succeeded the Prophet. Isn't complying with the moral principles in the Qur'an enough of a challenge in itself, rather than to divert one's energies into who, once upon a time, did what to whom?

Daddy's words have stayed with me. I find myself repeating his words each time I hear a Sunni badmouth a Shia. When that doesn't work, I tell them that God says in the Qur'an, "Do not divide yourselves into sects, for it will weaken you." We belong together, brothers and sisters in faith. There are no theological differences between the two sects. It is all about what should or should not have happened in seventh-century Arabia. Who cares!

Get over it.

26.

Don't Ghetto-ize Islam

We had done our in-reach in building a community and making good Muslims, but what about outreach to the non-Muslim community to raise awareness about Islam?

A Challenge from Within

It was not 9/11 that triggered interfaith dialogue. Sure, it accelerated it, but in New York it began way back in the 1970s. Yes indeed! A few—just a few—Muslim community leaders, who had the foresight to envision the concept of building bridges, had started engaging with faith communities, civic leaders, and the media. They faced a challenge—not from churches or synagogues—but from within. How about that! Some Muslim families were not ready for it, did not see the need for it, and some even felt that it would dilute the effort of Muslim-izing our children. The sense was: "Sure, it's a good idea to learn about other faiths, and sure, it's a good idea to raise awareness about Islam, but you know what? I first need to focus on strengthening the faith in my children and keeping them in the fold." Some felt that it was an exercise in futility: "The media have so distorted the image of Islam and left such an indelible impression on the viewers that nothing we can do can change that. Why bother?"

We may not have been ready for the world, but the world was ready for us. The first opening came not from an imam, a priest, or a rabbi—it came from a Boy Scout.

Scout's Honor. The Early 1980s

One evening, Asim came home from a Cub Scout meeting at his den mother's house. "Daddy, Mr. Phalen wants to talk to you," he said. Mr. Phalen, the cub master, explained that the Boy Scouts of America have always had a religion award for Muslim Boy Scouts (*I didn't know that*), but this is the first time they have created one for Cub Scouts, and Asim, if he worked at it, would be the first Cub Scout in America to receive the award—the Bismillah Award. Mr. Phalen was beaming.

The Boy Scouts of America is recognizing the Muslim faith. Mr. Phalen—definitely not a Muslim—is rooting for Asim to seize the prize. This is America!

The award ceremony was held at a banquet in Manhattan, sponsored by IBM. Asim sat at the dais with high-ranking executives from the Boy Scouts and IBM, gave his cute little adorable speech, and walked back to us bejeweled with a medal and accolades. A nice surprise: a proclamation from the borough president of Staten Island and Councilman Vito Fossella. *I know!* This was my first encounter with interfaith whatever and my first awakening to the sense that "they" were open to, willing, and enthusiastic about "us." I was embarrassed that I should even be affected that way. Shouldn't I have given them more credit than that? And what do I mean, "them"? Shouldn't I have given people more credit than that?

Here is my chance to convince the skeptics that there is value in interfaith dialogue. I will tell them, "See what they are doing for us."

A Church Beckons. The Late 1980s

A minister walked into my office one afternoon as I sat shuffling papers, wishing I had a computer. It was the late 1980s, and I was the director of planning at Interfaith Medical Center in Brooklyn. Interfaith. It follows me and finds me. Reverend Peter Nelson was the VP for marketing, and over lunch, we would chat about Islam and Christianity. He and his wife had visited us in our home when I held BBQ parties on our back porch, overlooking the valley.

"My church would like to invite you and Khalid to talk to our congregation about Islam," Peter said.

I looked back at the reverend with surprised reverence.

"I have never done that."

"Yes, you have. You do it every day over lunch."

"But that is different."

"More people need to hear what I am hearing."

"But we have never made a speech on Islam. I am not qualified."

"You and Khalid will do just fine."

"Khalid, wait till you hear what Peter said." I told him the story as I walked up the stairs to the kitchen. "Can you believe it—a church inviting Muslims to tell them about Islam?! Only in America."

"We have to be well prepared," Khalid said.

One would have thought we were preparing for the bar exam. This was before PowerPoint was invented. We were to just stand there and talk, and then take questions. *What should we focus on? What questions will they ask? What if we don't know the answer? What if they ask us, "Do you believe that Jesus was the son of God?" How do we answer that without offending our hosts?*

The meeting was in the basement of the church, and the minister introduced us to a gathering of ethnically mixed families, who gathered around us on folding chairs. I looked at the audience: eager faces, smiling, as if waiting for candy to be distributed or a fairy tale to be told. *They are smiling. They like us. I think we will do OK.* I began: "Islam means 'submission' to the will of God. A Muslim is one who submits."

"Give me more," their looks said.

"There are five pillars in Islam: belief in the one God, prayer five times a day, fasting during Ramadan, charity, and hajj. . . ."

Hands shot up. Why five prayers? Do you go to a mosque five times a day? Can you drink water when you fast? Have you made the hajj? Can you give charity to non-Muslims . . . ?

I am loving this. See how eager they are to learn. Aren't they respectful? Keep those questions coming. Look at Khalid—all animated.

The slotted hour ran overtime. The audience gathered around us after the formal talk with more questions and so many parting words of thanks. "It's the other way around," I told them. "Thank *you* for opening your sacred space to us."

"Bia," Khalid said to me as I sat in the car, closing the door, "they are open-minded, welcoming, and enthusiastic. I wish we were like that. Think of it: all these people that we talked to today now know enough about Islam to discount what they watch on TV."

"In fact, they can become our ambassadors. Now if anyone discredits Islam, they know enough to say, 'That is not true. I know a Muslim family.'"

We both rode home on a high with the intoxication of mutual respect. That night, we had been initiated into interfaith dialogue at the initiative of a church. Khalid and I were now ready to take our show on the road.

A Hospital in Brooklyn Goes Interfaith. The Late 1980s

When Brooklyn Jewish Hospital and St. John's Episcopal Hospital in Brooklyn merged in the early 1980s, my boss quipped, "They are saying the name of the merged hospital will be St. John's Jewish." He was close. They named it Interfaith Medical Center, and in 1986, I went to work for them in their Planning Office. My boss, Ted Jamison, the CEO, an African American (and a Republican, I may say), took a keen interest in my Pakistani background and my Muslim faith. He set the tone for a culture that was inclusive, tolerant, and pluralistic and saw recognition of Muslim staff as the ultimate validation in making the hospital truly interfaith. He assigned the chaplain and Reverend Peter Nelson to work with me on accommodating the spiritual needs of the Muslim staff and patients. The chaplain dedicated a room for *jumma*, the Friday prayers. One of the medical residents—they were mostly Pakistani-Indian—would do the sermon, and a reception was held twice a year on Eid and attended by the CEO and senior management. When Dr. Jamil Khan presented Mr. Jamison with a framed script of the prophet's last sermon, Mr. Jamison, in accepting the gift, announced that if he placed this in his office, only those who visited his office would see it, but if he placed it in the lobby, everyone would see it. And there it was mounted, with an inscription. The program for

Muslim patients took a lot more doing. Reverend Nelson and I went to all the neighborhood mosques in and around the Crown Heights section of Brooklyn, met the imams, and asked them to advise their congregation that, at our hospital, we would provide Muslim chaplaincy services, halal food, prayer space, and female obstetrician services. Our admission intake and IT system was reconfigured to identify Muslim patients, and the dietary department equipped itself accordingly. When we rolled out the program, our first patient was the imam. "I could have gone to any hospital, but I came here because I want to support this program," he told me. I thought of Aba Jee that day. How pleased he would have been. It didn't happen because of me. I was just the instrument. It happened because this is America.

Call of the Rabbi. The 1990s

It was inevitable. Word had gotten out that there is this Muslim doctor and his wife who go around talking about Islam. I bet they prefaced it with "handsome" Muslim doctor. My colleagues always—*always*—remarked when they would first meet Khalid, "You didn't tell us how handsome he is."

So one day, the rabbi called and caught us off-guard.

"My Hebrew school students have never been inside a mosque," he told Khalid.

Uh-oh!

Khalid knew that he would have to get permission from the board. The board was divided between "Great idea, most welcome" and "Why are they interested in seeing a mosque?" *Why can't we get past this distrust?* Khalid pulled out his canned speech on harmony and awareness, and prevailed. That Sunday, we welcomed the synagogue students, mostly high school level, and introduced them to the rituals of prayer. Moved by their presence, a board member approached the rabbi and invited him to come and give a lecture to the Sunday school students. The rabbi accepted. The Jerusalem wall had come down. That spring, the rabbi invited the mosque families to join them for Seder services at the synagogue. "Do you have any dietary restrictions?" he inquired of Khalid. "We don't drink alcohol and don't eat pork."

"Not even wine?"

"Not even wine."

Wasn't that gracious of him to ask!

I had never been to a Seder and as our group of families walked in, I was excited. The rabbi greeted us and introduced us around. After services, as we left the sanctuary, a waiter walked up serving drinks in mini cups. We gestured "No, thanks," assuming it was wine.

"There is no wine being served," the rabbi said, "I had wine removed from all the trays."

That is so nice of him. He didn't have to do that just for us.

Khalid and I lifted the cup and took a sip. The whiff of alcohol hit my nostrils. I looked up at Khalid. We discreetly looked for a place to put away the cup and said nothing. Mistakes happen, and there was no need to embarrass our host. Too late. In a minute, the rabbi was beside us.

"I apologize. I don't know how this happened. I am so sorry. I first had special trays prepared for your group, without the alcohol. Then, not wanting to take a chance, I had it removed from all the trays. I had specific instructions. I am so sorry."

"It's OK. Please don't feel bad." I was feeling so bad for the poor rabbi. He looked mortified.

One of our men walked over, "I finally got a taste of wine," he said with a chuckle. *Thank God he has a sense of humor.* We had mobilized and brought the group to the synagogue and wanted them to leave feeling good about the experience. Too soon. Another turned to me and whispered, "They did it on purpose."

Ohhh! Why feel like that? How I wished we could get past the distrust. The hard rocks in the Jerusalem wall were unyielding. *I understand where this is coming from. But here in this sacred space, please, let's open our hearts.*

I was troubled on the ride home and late into the night. *How can we change perception when suspicion is so deeply entrenched? All it takes is one kitchen chef's error in placing wine cups on a tray to reaffirm, "They are out to hurt us." If the wine episode had not happened, would the skeptics in our group have undergone a conversion—just a mild conversion? Is interfaith dialogue only for the "Let's be friends-ers"?*

Always the voice of reason, Khalid counseled me: "We will continue to do what we have started. Those who are committed to interfaith dialogue will join us, and those who don't see the value in it . . . we are not going to worry about them. Now go to sleep."

Thank you, God, for Khalid. With him by my side, I can always count on a good night's sleep.

A Catholic Hospital Hands over the Mic. 1990s

Every morning, Sister would say a prayer at St. Vincent Medical Center, where Khalid was on staff. The prayer was heard all over the hospital through the public announcement system. One day Khalid came up with one of his many bright ideas.

"I will ask Sister if I can do a Muslim prayer on the PA system. We have a large Muslim staff, so why not have a prayer by a Muslim as well?"

Is he bold, audacious, or what?

I stopped stirring the cumin seeds I had put in hot oil, lay the spatula on the spoon rest, turned around, and gave him a hug. "I love you." The crackle of cumin and whiff of the aroma twirled me back to the frying pan.

The following week, at the precise hour in the morning, a voice boomed over the PA system in the hospital, "This is Dr. Khalid Rehman. In the name of God, the Beneficent, the Merciful . . ."

I wasn't there to hear it, but one of the Muslim doctors on staff told me that he had tears in his eyes. It was a brief fifteen-second prayer, a prayer for patients, the caregivers, the staff, nothing different from what Sister would pray for; but this was a Catholic hospital, and a Muslim was offering the prayer. I too had tears.

"What did you say to Sister?" I asked.

"I just asked for a meeting, told her that I would also like to say a prayer, as we have many Muslims on staff, and she said that would be fine. She took me to the telephone operator's room and told them that I would be saying the prayer."

The next day, as I returned home from work and was walking up the stairs to the kitchen, Khalid was waiting for me at the landing.

"Guess what! Sister wants me to say a prayer every week."

And thus, until Khalid left the hospital many years later, once a week he was the prayer man, and everyone in the hospital would hear the Muslim prayer.

Only in America.

Am I a Christian, a Jew, a Muslim, or All in One?

Have you ever engaged in interfaith dialogue? Watch it! You may get converted. Khalid and I were going through a metamorphosis. My friend Jenny invited us to attend Sabbath services at the B'nai Jeshurun synagogue on the Upper West Side. In 2007, we had moved to Manhattan. The first time we walked in, we were greeted with, "Shabat Shalom, Shalom Aleichem."

"What did he just say?" I asked Khalid. "Did I hear him say what sounded like *Salaam Alaikum*?" *Wow! Do people know that? Even our greetings are similar. Wait till I tell my family in Pakistan.*

Sitting in the pew, reading from the prayer book, Khalid pointed out the text. "See this. Our religions are so similar." And sounding like a broken record: "If I hadn't seen the cover, I'd think I was reading the Qur'an. Honest!" All charged up too, I decided to observe the Sabbath at home the next weekend. God, it was hard! I kept reaching for my phone; and in the end, I just put it away in the other room. Not to sit at my computer for a whole day! Will I survive? By midmorning, I had settled into my chair with a book, and I was not moving. I'd look out the window and see the sailboats drift along in the glistening waters of the East River, wave to the tourists on the Circle Line, and just read. In between, I'd daydream. What luxury! What a smart idea, to have one day when you just rest—rest you mind, your body, and just chill. What discipline, to be able to just rest.

An interfaith music feast was planned, and Reverend K. Karpin offered his space at the Church of St. Paul and St. Andrew, also on the Upper West Side. He opened his office for us to meet, assigned his staff, opened his kitchen and cooked beside us, set up the tables, carried the linen, affixed cables and microphones, and then stood at the dais and offered the opening prayer. All in the spirit of bringing communities together. So Christian! Isn't that what the Qur'an teaches us—building harmony, fostering respect? Maybe I am a Christian at heart. When the music began, I joined the rabbi and the reverend on the dais, and we took turns singing *Allah hu, Allah hu, Allah hu,* the rabbi and reverend sang *Hallelu, Hallelu, Hallelu,* and the audience of Jews, Christians, and Muslims joined in, swaying in "perfect harmony." We have kept the tradition going. Each year we have a theme for the interfaith feast: green feast, peace feast, fall feast. We read from the scriptures—and guess what, they all say the same thing, and why not, isn't it the same God? We have now taken it to a different level: comedy feast. Enough about educating us. Let's have some laughter; let's laugh at ourselves. I took a family member—an airline pilot—who was visiting from Pakistan, to the comedy feast. He was floored. Seeing Muslims making fun of themselves in the presence of Christians, Jews, and Hindus, and vice versa, was like nothing he had ever seen or expected. He had some stories to tell when he went back home.

One evening, after I had finished delivering a lecture on Islam 101 to an interfaith gathering, had done the Q&A, and was now just hanging out, a lady sitting on the side beckoned me. She was in a wheelchair and must have been in her late eighties or thereabouts. I walked over to her. "Can I ask you a question?" she said. *A sensitive question perhaps; one that she didn't want to raise in public.* I pulled over a chair, sat next to her, leaned close, and braced myself. She asked, "Can you tell me where you got your blouse from?"

I didn't convert, but all this exposure to interfaith communities gave me pause. I was seeing how much joy a more open approach could bring, how much peace there was in embracing all. I recall a sermon given by Imam Feisal Abdul Rauf: "God is your audience," he said. *If I could just hang on to that.* "Before you start your prayer, prepare your heart to welcome God, just as you would prepare your house to welcome a guest." *God consciousness.* Conscious that you are alone with God. One day I would work for his organization, The Cordoba Initiative. It opened a door to the beauty in Sufism, the mystical version of Islam, one that was all-inclusive and pluralistic. I believe now that Daddy was a Sufi at heart: open to all, embracing all, with his love for God and for all His creatures. He would have been sitting in the armchair in the sunroom of his house in Pakistan, his freshly pressed striped shirt and necktie looking good on him, his curly hair carefully groomed, sipping coffee, the china clinking each time he placed the cup in the saucer, me across on the divan, light from the windows brightening the walls adorned with framed photos, Mummy's voice somewhere in the background giving instructions to the help, and I would be telling Daddy . . . But Daddy died before I could say to him, "Look what I found!"

A Gift from the Media

It was the media that opened their presses to us. Yes, the media. Khalid is a letter writer. Whenever he sees a problem, be it a missing road sign, a pothole, a biased opinion article in the paper, he picks up the pen—now the keyboard—and sends off a letter. And the *Staten Island Advance*, the local newspaper, would publish his letters—every one of them.

It was May 1988, and Khalid came up with yet another bright idea.

"Bia, I have an idea." Khalid walked into the kitchen one evening as I was heating dinner. "Ramadan is coming, and I think the *Staten Island Advance* should do a story on it." His face was animated as he set the plates on the table.

"Good idea." I put the naan in the oven. "How are you going to go about it?" I sprinkled chopped cilantro over the steaming curry.

"Yeah, Dad. How are you going to go about it?" Saqib had just walked in.

"I will call their Religion Desk and ask them to do a story."

Just like that. Given his success rate, or charm, I bet they will say yes.

On Saturday, May 7, 1988, Staten Islanders opened their newspapers to a half-page spread titled "Island Muslims Fast in Month of Ramadan." It was the photographs, three of them, that caused me to shriek with glee. "Saqib, Asim, come quick. Look. See this."

"Oh, wow!"

We huddled over the paper, reading out, "It's 3:00 a.m. and Dr. Khalid Rehman is having breakfast with his wife and two sons in their

Egbertville home. They must eat before the sun comes up, and they won't eat again until the sun goes down around 7:46 p.m. . . ."

The *Staten Island Advance* staff had listened to Khalid's call, sent a reporter and photographer to the mosque, interviewed attendees, sat through the adult and children's classes, and done a heartwarming write-up, covering all aspects of Ramadan, prayer, and Sunday school. Just like that!

Next morning, Sunday school was buzzing. "My dad's picture was in the paper. . . . Did you see my picture was in the paper?" Monday morning, as Khalid walked through the hallways of the hospital, the staff kept stopping him. "We read the Ramadan article. . . . So you can't eat or drink all day? What would be an appropriate greeting? Should we say, 'Happy Ramadan'? Good luck with your mosque building."

I think we are making a dent in the image that "Muslims are terrorists." Thank you, Staten Island Advance, *for advancing that cause. Thank you, America.*

On Saturday, December 24, 1988, the *Staten Island Advance* ran a story, "Muslims Also Celebrate Christmas." It was Christmas Eve, and Staten Islanders were reading, "According to Dr. Khalid Rehman . . . Prophet Isa (Jesus) is one of the most revered prophets for Muslims." Khalid had quoted the nineteenth chapter of the Holy Qur'an, titled Mariam, detailing the miraculous birth of Jesus.

Monday morning, hospital staff was commenting, "We had no idea that the Qur'an mentions the birth of Jesus."

"You see"—I looked over the dining table at Saqib and Asim—"knowing is understanding; understanding is unifying. It's up to us to raise awareness. Actually, I take that back. It is our responsibility to raise awareness. How else will anyone know? We can't blame people for misunderstanding us if we don't take the initiative to educate. See what a difference just an article has made!"

They saw. They saw that it took effort, but they also saw a lot more, as their father plugged away, and the conservative community of Staten Island kept opening its doors.

Another bold idea.

"I am going to ask the *Staten Island Advance* if I can start writing a regular column on Islam. I have made an appointment with their religion editor."

Just like that.

Khalid proposed; the *Advance* agreed. On Saturday, May 11, 1991, the first in a monthly series of "Islam" was launched. Over the next seven years, Khalid wrote on prayer, moon sighting, women and equality, sects, adoption, abortion, interest on loans, family relationships, birth, death, commonalities with other faiths—but my favorite is the piece he wrote when we sent Asim off to college.

A Muslim Father Offers Some Advice to His Child
Going to College Can Be a Test of One's Faith
By Dr. Khalid L. Rehman
Advance Correspondent
Staten Island Advance. Saturday, September 2, 1995

My dear child! I know that you have grown, become a young adult and are leaving home to live by yourself at college but please allow me to refer to you as my child.

When you were younger, I and your mother worked very hard to give you the best education, moral values and spiritual guidance.

Whereas all that knowledge is surely tucked away in the memory cells, I feel the need to remind you of the do's and don'ts expected of a young adult Muslim.

New college life will bring independence, freedom and new challenges. The parental pressure and scrutiny will be replaced with peer pressure. . . .

The human being is a social animal and needs friends and company. When you are with others, remember to treat them with dignity and respect. You don't have to be a stiff, but your manners, conduct and language have to be becoming to a Muslim, someone who knows that God is always there and that we as humans are His viceroys and hence have to be dignified and pious.

I have always reminded you to be gentle and soft-spoken and avoid cursing, foul language and angry outbursts.

Do remember that your faith, Islam, prohibits sex outside of marriage. Don't be alone with a member of the opposite sex in a social environment. This may lead to intimacy and a conduct, which is not permitted for unmarried people. You may go to the movies and concerts together, but always in a group, as you have done in the past.

Your teachers deserve the same level of respect that your parents do, if not more. Every adult who is your senior in age commands respect, and the younger ones, your love and affection.

All human beings are equal and a creation of the same God. Remember the last sermon of the Prophet Muhammad (peace be upon him), in which he said that Arabs and non-Arabs, black and white, rich and poor are all equal, and only those who are pious and God-conscious are superior in the eyes of God.

Be good to your neighbor and continue to give to charity.

Keep up your five daily prayers. These take only a few minutes, but provide an opportunity to wash up, set aside the worldly things for the few minutes, and commune with your creator.

Take the time to thank Him for all the blessings, ask forgiveness for transgressions you may have committed and pray for success in this world and in the world hereafter. Do remember us, your family and friends, in your prayers.

The month of Ramadan, which is the month of fasting, will soon be here. Remember your obligations to fast from sunrise to sunset every day, and be generous and charitable.

Alcohol and other similar intoxicants are prohibited. The argument that one or two drinks do not make you drunk is a fallacy. Your ability to distinguish between the permissible and the forbidden is chipped away with each drink. One may end up socially disgraced and harmful to the others. Say, "No, thank you" as you always have.

If Halal meat is available, it would be preferred. Otherwise, you may partake of the Jewish kosher meat. Pork and pork products are forbidden.

To uphold the values of your family and the dictates of your faith may appear to be difficult, but then as a young Muslim student, you must set an example and be a role model.

You may be surprised to know how many of your friends, Muslim or non-Muslim, also subscribe to the same ethical and moral values. Stay within the group whose members reinforce each other's strong moral character.

You are a grown-up person now and, although not answerable to me, you surely have to settle the score with your Creator, as we all have to do for our individual conduct. Your mother joins me in praying for your good health, happiness and prosperity.

Beautiful, isn't it!

And why should television be left behind? *Island in the Sun* was a local program broadcast by the local TV station. Someone spoke to someone, and the moderator of the program, Joe Madory, called Khalid. He wanted to hold a panel on Muslims on Staten Island and asked if we could recommend panelists. Khalid contacted the chaplain of the correctional facility and a scholar of Egyptian descent. As we went live, sitting around the table with Joe were two Pakistani Americans, an African American, and an Egyptian American, three men and a woman. That's the face of Islam. Viewers called in. Most questions were directed at me. I guess the callers wanted to know if I was for real, or did I sound oppressed. Not fair, but I couldn't help sticking that in. One of the questions asked still bothers me: do you believe that now that the bogeyman of Russia is gone that the next big conflict America will face will be with the Muslims?

The light of the answering machine was blinking away when we came home. Message 1: "You did great." Message 2: "You were wonderful." Message 3: . . . *Why did he ask that question? Muslims, the next bogeyman! Muslim women are being raped in Bosnia, thousands massacred in Srebrenica, millions of Palestinians displaced. But I suppose that is irrelevant. Does he speak for himself, or is this a widely held perception? Can a splintered, fractious, multinational people of faith, divided along national and sectarian lines, be a threat to the United States? Of course not, but then why this perceived threat? You know what! Khalid and I cannot control what Muslims do around the world, but at least here at home, in America, thanks to a liberal media and freedom of speech, we have the opportunity to persuade the average American on Main Street, USA, that we are regular people, like them. Like Joe the bus driver, Jack the cashier, or Janice the hairdresser. We share the same dreams: a house with a backyard; the same aspirations: my son, the doctor; the same fears: I hope it is not cancer; the same yearnings: I wish Mom were here.*

The Bogeyman Strikes

And then it happened. The towers fell and the world was never the same again. The horror, the loss, the grief, and the pain consumed us. The Bogeyman had struck and taken us all down with him. Islamophobia reared its ugly head, and Muslims found themselves encircled by lions. They ran for cover: women uncovered their hair, men shaved their beards, children refused to go to school, the ten-year-old Osama became Sam, Mohammad became Mo, and Salman became Sal. An eerie silence stunned the Muslim community. And then America opened its heart: priests, ministers, and rabbis started calling the imams: "Come talk to us. . . . Come pray with us. . . . Break bread with us." Thus began the transition of the Muslim community in the USA from being inward-focused to reaching out. Reaching out, beyond the comfort zones of their tight communities, extending invitations, exposing themselves, and making friends. It took a tragedy of humongous proportion to come out from behind the veil. And they knew that their work had only just begun.

27.

Flashpoints

Ask any Muslim in America, "What was the turning point in your life?" and they will say: 9/11. True. But flashpoints occurred even before the century turned, and these were major turning points in my quest for religious understanding and the redefining of my identity as an American Muslim.

Rushdie Affair. February 1989
Muslims lost the battle, but they won the war.

They wanted the book banned, and they lost on that one. It was a battle they could not have won. They should have known that. This is America—the land of free speech. Did they really think they could get Viking Press to take the book off the shelves! But, and here is the "but": it got something going. They got organized. Oh sure, Muslim organizations existed long before Imam Khomeini put a price on Rushdie's head, but they were doing their own thing. There was little integration. The Rushdie affair pulled them together, and the image of Muslims praying in the streets of New York, taking a break from the street protest, got many a spine tingling. How many of us who saw that image felt a surge of gratitude? Only in America; only in America can one pray freely on the streets of New York—not just pray but have the police protect you while you pray! In this land, we have a voice. If we don't like what we read, we can speak up. We can give the faith a face, and we can raise a banner and be seen across the screens from sea to shining sea.

I was among those who believed that the book should be banned. Don't panic. My children made me change my mind. Exhale. At first, I was outraged: he wrote what?! How dare anyone say something so disrespectful about the Prophet and his wives! That's terrible! At weekend parties, the voice was unanimous—the book should be banned. But at work, in the cafeteria over lunch, Reverend Nelson peered at me over his round spectacles, pursed his lips, and said, "You want a book banned just because you don't like what it says?"

"Yes," I said, my pitch rising, "because if you allow such books to be published, people will say anything they want to about the Prophet."

"So? It's freedom of speech."

"Well, freedom of speech should have its limits. You don't abuse your rights and insult others."

"What are you afraid of?" he asked.

"People will believe it."

"So exercise your right and speak up. Tell the world it's not true. Tell them why."

"Oh! So now I am supposed to write a book that no one will publish." I could feel my argument weakening. "How would you feel if someone said something like that about Jesus Christ?"

He tapped my hand with his finger and in a serene voice said, "I'd say, 'What's your problem?'"

Stumped.

Now why can't I be that way? Calm. Indifferent. Is it insecurity?

By that time, others had joined us at the table and no one was taking my side. I kept arguing because I didn't want to lose the argument, and the harder I pushed, the weaker I felt. I argued in absentia driving all the way home. I should have said . . . And if they said . . . I would say. . . . *They just don't understand. How can they? It's a matter of faith, of reverence.*

I was still fighting my confusion when I got home.

We discussed this over dinner. I don't recall the exact conversation, but I do remember asking my children what they thought about the whole controversy and listening to them in awe.

"It's offensive, but it's freedom of speech," my sixteen-year-old said without batting an eye. He didn't even pause. Asim, my fourteen-year-old, nodded. I listened to them voice their take on it, and I must have stopped eating. I must have looked at them with the eyes of a child. My babies were now teaching Mommy, and Mommy was listening. In those moments, I felt my confusion unravel.

Time to retire. Hand religion over to your children. They are ready.

"I have an idea." I looked across the table at Saqib. "I want you to organize a youth panel discussion on this issue. We will hold it in the mosque. You children select the participants, the format, the content, the publicity, and Khalid, you get the approval."

Parents need to hear what their children are thinking, and like me, learn from them.

Then came Khomeini's fatwa, and Khalid got a call from the press, the *Staten Island Advance*. They wanted a statement. It was printed the next day: he found the passages in the book to be offensive and disrespectful toward the Prophet and his wife but opposed Imam Khomeini's fatwa that Rushdie be put to death. That evening, after dinner, our phone started ringing. "Well said," said one. "I wish you hadn't said that," said another.

On March 12, 1989, five high school students, two girls and three boys, faced the congregation in the mosque. Every inch was taken, men and boys sitting on the wall-to-wall prayer rug in the front rows, women and girls at the back. I know! Saqib took his position at the lectern, the tapestry of the *Kaaba* adorning the wall behind, and introduced the panelists. I held my breath. I had taken a risk and wasn't sure how this would roll out—a charged issue had split the community, and what had I done? Handed the mic to a bunch of teenagers. I listened as each of them analyzed a particular aspect of the controversy and then took questions from the audience. I watched our children speak dispassionately, with compassion, keeping emotions at bay, with chip-less and baggage-free shoulders. The audience, split bitterly over the banning, exercised restraint and acted like adults—benevolent adults. Someone asked the question: do you agree with Khomeini's fatwa? The children's response: for every allegation, there is due process. Evidence has to be introduced—in this case the evidence is the book—expert testimony is required, the law has to be examined and upheld. . . . The congregation took it all in.

Do they see what I see? Our children are reshaping Islam in an American context. These are the Muslims of tomorrow. Get to know them.

That was the moment when I saw the emergence of an American Muslim identity. I saw our children reshaping Islam in an American setting, one that was Islamic in its values and American in its ethos.

Gulf War. August 1990

"The problem is with your creed."

Reverend Nelson looked down at me, towering over my desk.

"No, it isn't!" I fought back with hollow words, my face feeling hot.

He was referring to jihad, now a bad word, synonymous with holy war and violence.

"Jihad means to struggle, the inner struggle against oneself, a spiritual striving. It's the politicians and media who have labeled it as holy war."

"Muslims waging violence are calling it jihad. They are quoting the Qur'an."

"Well, they are wrong."

"Are they?"

Stumped and speechless, with nothing more than blind faith and utterly lacking in knowledge, all I could say was, "It isn't true." He stood looking at me, silent, waiting for me to come up with something more than "It isn't true."

"Islam was spread by the sword," Dr. Goldstein, a doctor who must be fifteen years my senior and a dear colleague, remarked over lunch.

"No, it wasn't!" I almost shouted.

"She is so naïve." He shook his head, as the others around the table gave me a sympathetic look.

You know what my problem is? I am ignorant. Totally, hopelessly ignorant. I cannot come up with a single quotation from the Qur'an to refute his argument. It isn't enough to believe and have the faith. It was enough in Pakistan, where no one challenged the faith. Here one has to be equipped with knowledge. How else are we going to stand up to the onslaught, set the record straight, or educate?

The drive home was a one-woman planning session. By the time I pulled into the garage, I had it mapped out.

"Khalid, I am going to get myself an education," I said to him as I walked up the steps, through the kitchen, into the bedroom. He followed me.

"Law school?" he teased.

"Islamic school. I have a plan. I am going to home-school myself. I start tonight."

"You can teach me as you go along." Khalid smiled. "What brought this about?"

After dinner, I settled in the den in my gray corduroy armchair by the fireplace, surrounded by family photos on the burlap walls in dusty rose, and started my study of the Qur'an. The Qur'an was revealed in Arabic and has been translated into hundreds of languages, by hundreds of translators. I could read Arabic but could not understand it. Go figure. I studied the translation in English, then in Urdu, then in English again. I studied the translation of Abd'Allah Yusuf Ali, Maulani Maudoodi, Pickthall . . . every translation on my bookshelf. I went through the catalogue of Kazi Publications and ordered the *Hadith*, sayings and deeds of the Prophet, books on jihad, Islam, and democracy, the Prophet's biography, and women in Islam, and I read them all. I searched for answers in the sacred text. Much of what I read, I forgot. Some of it I retained. In Pakistan, we used to—people still do—recite the Qur'an in Arabic and walk away feeling good and understanding nothing. And now, here I was, with copies lying around on the coffee table, neon-orange Post-it notes sticking out, highlighting over the text, and handwritten notes in margins. A visitor remarked, "You are writing on the Qur'an!" implying that I had desecrated the holy text. *I don't think God will be offended if I highlight his text. At least I am getting something out of it. Isn't that the whole idea?* I was on a treasure hunt, scratching, digging, uncovering, and finding jewels. "Look what I found!" I would call out to Khalid sitting upstairs at his computer, "It says right here in the Qur'an about jihad:

Permission [to fight] is given to those against whom war is being wrongfully waged—and, verily, God has indeed the power to succor them: those who have been driven out from their homelands against all right for no other reason than their saying, "Our Sustainer is God!" For, if God had not enabled people to defend themselves against one another, [all] monasteries and churches and synagogues and mosques—in [all of] which God's name is abundantly extolled—would surely have been destroyed [ere now]. And God will most certainly succor him who succors His cause: for, verily, God is most powerful, almighty.[4]

"You see. It's self-defense." I had my answer, and I had the reference.

I had to share my find. I did go back to Reverend Nelson, this time armed with my newly discovered quotes from the text. Intrigued, he started an interfaith dialogue at the hospital. Over lunch, once a week, Muslims, Jews, Christians, and Hindus would talk—just talk, about what was troubling us in the world of religion, and of course, it was always related to jihad. Having read a few books, I considered myself an authority, and you should have heard me speak—such confidence, such an I-know-it-all air. On March 11, 1991, *Time* magazine published my letter, "Defining Jihad."

Women! The question I had been waiting for cropped up. Did I think I could dodge it? No discourse on Islam is complete without women's rights. It doesn't matter what the forum is or who the speaker is—it always becomes the central question. Issues were also being raised from within: Is a woman impure when she is menstruating? Can she touch the Qur'an? Recite the sacred text? Fast? Pray? Come to the mosque? Perform hajj? What are the boundaries in that state, if any?

Back to the books. This was the early 1990s. No online Qur'an or *Hadith*, no Google, no e-Qur'an. It was hard copy all the way. I was going to study, study, and study until I had absorbed everything I could get my hands on. I was going to tap into the best minds. I started going to seminars, picking up books from the vendor exhibits, and cornering the speakers. I had a goal: I wanted to get to a point where, if any-

---

4 Qur'an 22:39–40.

one told me what a woman could not do, I could say, "Show me the reference," and could hold an informed debate on whether this was cut-and-dry or had ten shades of green. I discovered translator's bias. Often, when reading a verse of the Qur'an, I'd stop and wonder about it, reach out for another translation, and find that it had been translated differently, sometimes to the extent that it changed the meaning. I could now tell which translator had a women bias, who was conservative, who saw God as One to be feared, and who saw Him as One to be loved. I knew which translator's version to reach out to satisfy my bias. By the mid-2000s, I had settled on *The Message of the Qur'an*, by Muhammad Asad. Get a copy. His commentary is beautiful. But until then, I was waking up to the fact that the only way to understand the message of the Qur'an is to study it in the language in which it was revealed—in Arabic. I decided to study Arabic. And I did. For five years I studied classical Arabic. But I was unable to master this beautiful, complex language, and today, I still study the Qur'an in the English. It's just easier.

So what about women? I found jewels studded in the holy text. How is this for starters: Let's go back to the beginning. Eve was not made from Adam's rib. She was stand-alone. *Yeah!* There is more: Eve did not tempt Adam. God held both Adam and Eve equally accountable for their transgression, they both received equal penance, and they were both forgiven at the same time.[5] The birth of a daughter is a gift from God and a blessing. It is evil to grieve over the birth of a daughter.[6] She has a right to an education. The Prophet Muhammad advised that people seek religious knowledge from his wife Aisha, who is a major contributor to the *Hadith*. In his last sermon, he said, "No man has superiority over a woman." A woman has the right to bear witness, and a woman's testimony can invalidate a man's testimony, e.g. if a man accuses his wife of being unchaste, and she denies it, his case is thrown out. In financial transactions, two male witnesses or one male and two females witnesses are required (I am still struggling with that).

---

5 Qur'an 7:19–25.

6 Qur'an 16:58–59.

And guess what: a woman retains her maiden name after marriage. It states explicitly in the Qur'an to call them by their father's name.[7] It's about identity and lineage. In Pakistan, influenced by British colonialism, women took their husband's name. Sabeeha Akbar became Sabeeha Rehman. Too late, I will have to change all my citizenship papers, degrees, social security, passport. . . . Forget it. Here is the fun stuff: women are entitled to a gift from their husband on marriage—the dowry. It is written into the marriage contract. It is hers to keep.[8] Speaking of which, her consent is an absolute requirement for the marriage. So many cultures have taken away that God-given right. She has the right to dissolve the marriage by petitioning the court. Whereas custody of children hasn't been specified in the Qur'an, jurists have ruled that the children remain with the mother up to a certain age, after which the arrangements are to be worked out with mutual consent. Widows and divorcees are free to remarry.[9]

And now the big one: polygamy. I actually knew someone who had two wives. One of Khalid's neighbor's in Multan, a wealthy man, was married without children. They were guests at our wedding. Months later I heard that he had taken a second wife. Why? Because he wanted children. We were scandalized. On my first visit back to Pakistan, my mother-in-law took me to visit them. I was curious: *What are the living arrangements? Do the wives talk to each another? How is the husband handling this?* I was sad: *Poor first wife.* I was angry: *How dare he do this to her! If you didn't have children, accept it as God's will and move on.* I was feeling downright awkward: *What is the protocol? Who do I greet first? Will I offend one wife if I talk to the other? Do I compliment the chef not knowing who stirred the pot?* As fate would have it, the new wife bore him no children. And a few years later, the first wife found herself pregnant, giving birth to a boy. The new wife remained childless. God has His ways. The baby boy is now a young man, and Khalid is in touch with him.

---

7 Qur'an 33:5.

8 Qur'an 4:4.

9 Qur'an 2:228, 234.

Getting back to the theology of polygamy. This is what I under-stand: It's contextual. During war, many women were widowed and many young girls were orphaned. It was in the context of orphans that God ordained:

> And if you have reason to fear that you might not act equitably toward orphans, then marry from among [other] women such as are lawful to you—[even] two, or three, or four; but if you have reason to fear that you might not be able to treat them with equal fairness, then [only] one—or [from among] those whom you rightfully possess. This will make it more likely that you will not deviate from the right course.[10]

There you go—polygamy is permissible but restricted. "As regards the permission to marry more than one wife (up to the maximum of four), it is so restricted by the condition, 'if you have reason to fear that you might not be able to treat them with equal fairness, then [marry only] one,' as to make plural marriages possible only in quite exceptional cases and under exceptional circumstances. . . ."[11] Having said that, I don't care what the exceptional circumstances may be, I will never ever want Khalid to have a second wife (not that he is contemplating it—I think).

Women have the right to own property and a right to inherit—a right given to them fourteen hundred years ago, a right that women in the West got only in the last hundred years or so. Much in the Qur'an is allegorical, but some principles are clearly specified, down to the last digit. The laws of inheritance are one of those, lest there be any dispute. Check it out.[12]

Should I go on with the women's rights business, or have you had enough? OK, very quickly. The highest status is accorded to the

---

10 Qur'an 4:3..

11 *The Message of the Qur'an*, translated and explained by Muhammad Asad (London: The Book Foundation, 2008), chapter 4, note 4, 118.

12 Qur'an: 4:7, 11–12.

mother.[13] If anyone launches a charge against chaste women and cannot produce four witnesses, they are to be flogged with eighty stripes and their evidence is never to be admitted in court again.[14] If she commits an offense, her penalty is no less or more than a man's.[15] Did you know that Prophet Muhammad's wife Khadija was a businesswoman? That the Prophet's wife Aisha led the troops in battle? That in the early years of the Islamic caliphate, women attended congregational prayers in mosques, participated in educational forums in mosques, learned and taught religion? And they were not veiled.

Let's talk about "impurity." Here is what I found: the Qur'an places only one restriction during the menstrual cycle: no marital relations.[16] That is *it*. As for all the other restrictions—I question the decree imposed by jurists, by male jurists speaking for women, from a male lens. I don't believe that the All-Loving, All-Hearing God would close the doors on women for seven days, month after month, throughout their reproductive life. I don't believe that God, who speaks to women in the Qur'an, and tells them to pray and fast to achieve God consciousness, would deny them equal opportunity, and I don't believe that only a male Muslim can be a full Muslim. Forgive me God, if I have erred.

OK, enough about women.

In those early years of my quest—the 1990s—I came to believe that I had all the answers. After all, consider all the studying I had done. I eagerly volunteered to teach, to speak, to lead group discussions, and I reveled in my newfound knowledge. I felt like an authority, and I had done it all by myself. I loved my faith. I still do, but the years have humbled me, and I am aware of how much I don't know.

There was an unintended consequence to my pursuit. I was reading the chapter of Light, Surah Nur. After reading this passage, I stopped using makeup:

---

13 Qur'an 31:14.

14 Qur'an 24:4.

15 Qur'an 24:2; 5:38.

16 Qur'an 2:222.

And tell the believing women to lower their gaze and to be mindful of their chastity, and not to display their charms [in public] beyond what is apparent thereof . . .[17]

I remember closing the Qur'an—I must have bookmarked it, letting it rest in my lap, and pondered over this verse: ". . . not to display their charms beyond what is apparent thereof"! So that would mean that applying makeup is enhancing "what is apparent thereof." I picked up another copy of the Qur'an, by a different translator, then another. No luck—I was not getting an out. I read the commentary, looking for loopholes, absorbing the import. *How does a woman display her charms? Flowing hair, lipstick, mascara, revealing clothing, what else?* I made a mental list of my charms and all the ways in which I display them. *It's about display, about modesty in one's appearance and demeanor. But I adorn myself for me; it makes me feel good when I look good. What is wrong with that? Nothing, other than: Why do I have to depend on red lipstick to feel good? I should have more confidence than that. Right? Right. But I cannot give up makeup. I have used makeup since the day I got married.* I had ten shades of red lipstick jutting out on my dresser, two shades of blush on, and tiny boxes of eye shadow in multiple colors, mascara. . . . I never left home without my face made up. *I can't give it up. I would look pale and not as pretty. I'd be unattractive. Aha! There you go. So you want to be attractive! To whom? Gotcha!* I put the Qur'an on the coffee table, stood up, and walked up the stairs to the computer room. Khalid was typing away, probably another article for the *Staten Island Advance*.

"Khalid, I want to talk to you about something."

He looked up, stopped typing, and swiveled his chair around. I kept standing.

"How would you feel if I stopped wearing makeup?"

"Where did that come from?" he asked with a loving smile.

"I was reading Surah Nur in the Qur'an, and it says that women should not display their charms in public."

---

17 Qur'an: 24:31

Khalid kept smiling, as if to say, "Go on."

"It also says that this restriction does not apply when I am in the presence of my husband, brother, father, etc. So I will still use makeup at home. And charm you," I said with a giggle.

Khalid stood up, opened his arms, and gave me a hug. "Whatever pleases you."

"Thanks." Khalid had always liked to see me in makeup.

I went back down, and Khalid went back to typing. A few minutes later, he came down. "Bia, that means you won't wear makeup when you go to the hospital dinner-dances." I nodded.

The next morning, I applied some moisturizer, a little blush-on, and no lipstick or eye shadow. *Let me go easy on myself and get used to it little by little.* I got through the day without anyone saying anything at work or me feeling any different. The next morning, I put away the blush-on and went scrub-faced to work. No one recoiled from my plain face. The most I got was, "Are you not well, you look pale?" and I said, "I'm fine. I just stopped using makeup."

"Allergies?"

"No." *Don't hesitate. It's OK.* "You see, uh, I was reading the Qur'an, and, uh, it had an effect, and . . . well . . ."

"Oh, sure! You look great just the same."

When I came home from work, I'd wash up, walk over to my dresser, and apply color on my lips, and blush on my cheeks. Khalid was tickled. It went on for a few years, this makeup-for-your-husband's-eyes-only, until I ran out of lipstick and blush-on. I never went shopping for them again.

Mummy was upset. At every special occasion, she'd say, "Just a little lipstick won't hurt," but I was stubborn. How I wish I had put on some color, just to make her happy. My cousins in Pakistan were aghast. "She is becoming too religious. Where does it say in the Qur'an that you cannot use makeup?"

Then I donned the *hijab*—the headscarf. Well, not quite. Let's say that I became a part-time *hijabi.* Soon after tossing out Revlon and Maybelline, I decided to tie my hair in a bun—no more display of curly, thick, glossy black hair. Be modest, I commanded myself. I was getting comfortable in my no-frills, no-fuss appearance, and covering my hair was more of a natural progression than religious conviction. Whereas I wasn't convinced that the *hijab* was a religious requirement—though many would argue otherwise—it felt right. By cloaking myself in another layer of modesty, I was assuring myself that I could do it. I could resist the temptation to have my hair adorn my face. "I will take it a step at a time," I told Khalid. "Let me start with the *hijab* off-hours, build up my confidence before I start wearing the head covering at work." By now I had changed jobs and was the director of managed care at University Hospital–University of Medicine and Dentistry of New Jersey (UMDNJ). I tried to picture myself: a high-profile executive in a business suit with a calf-length skirt at the boardroom, in a *hijab. I will feel out of place. My colleagues may view me with a different eye. They may feel that I don't fit in. Maybe I should wait a little. First get used to wearing it outside of work.*

Coward!

"Don't be a hypocrite," a friend advised me. "If you want to wear the *hijab*, wear it full-time. Otherwise, forget about it."

It was Saqib's wedding. Mummy asked, "Go to the parlor and get your hair done."

"Why would I do that? My hair will be covered with the *dupatta*."

"It's your son's wedding! For once, don't you want to look nice?"

"I will look just fine."

Mummy shook her head in exasperation, looking visibly distressed. I wish I had humored her. I don't know what I was trying to prove to myself.

In the end, I cast it off—I couldn't handle the conflict inside me. Maybe one day I will put it on again. Who knows how I will evolve into my eighties. It's a shifting relationship.

Meanwhile, a postscript: Whereas I see the headscarf as a cultural expression of Islam, I have utmost respect for women in the US who, compelled by religious conviction, have chosen to don the headscarf, particularly the teenagers. They have made a choice and exercised that choice. It is part of their identity and a reminder of their faith. Who doesn't want to style their hair, try the latest look, have highlights, perms, and the like? Isn't vanity one of the most powerful feminine traits? Sorry, feminists. Who wants to stand out, be different and apart, and in the post 9/11 era, no less? Wouldn't it be easier to just blend in? It's a huge leap of courage, and my scarf's off to them.

Another postscript: I have finally reconciled the "how people should dress" issue. Note: I didn't say women. The principle applies to both sexes, and it's all about modesty. With the intent of not attracting unwarranted attention—as in sexual attention—the boundaries of modesty are defined differently in various cultures. A Muslim girl walking down Fifth Avenue in a blouse and jeans is not going to make heads turn. It's kosher. Show cleavage and watch the crescent of the Muslim eyebrows arch. Now, if I walked through the bazaars of Rawalpindi in blouse and jeans, men would stare. In Saudi Arabia, the loosest fitting attire won't fly unless you are cloaked in an *abaya*. As for men, they dress modestly for the most part. I mean, what is immodest about a shirt and pants, or *shalwar kameez*, or the ankle-length Arab *thobe*?

One fine evening I decided to quit singing. Singing was food for my soul, and the sound of music is what I lived with and lived for. I was taking the edict of "Do not display their charms beyond what is apparent thereof" to another level. I decided that I would sing but not in the presence of men. I was interpreting singing in mixed company to be an act that is beyond the boundaries. "Why?" asked my brother-in-law. "Because a woman's seductive voice should not be heard by men." He blushed and said nothing. Daddy had been quiet until now. He had let me experiment with my news ways—until I made this pronouncement. "I was OK with no makeup, I was OK with the *hijab*, but to give up singing, I feel as if my life has been cut short." My friend scolded me, "Have you no regard for your parents' feelings?! What has gotten into you?" Unmoved by guilt, I dug my heels in. A friend had invited the renowned Pakistani poet, Ahmed Faraz, to her house for an evening in poetry recital. The Pakistani community flocked to the gathering. Someone told him that I used to sing one of his *ghazals*, "*Rangish he sahi.*" They asked me to honor him by singing his *ghazal*. I remained silent. Many pressed on. I didn't budge. Then Ahmed Faraz, the celebrity, addressed me and requested me to sing his *ghazal*. I looked down at my hands in my lap, silent. I had made a decision on principle, and I was not going to be pressured, celebrity or no celebrity.

Something had indeed gotten into me. He has since passed on, and I am back to singing. If only! I had broken out of the cocoon on a cruise to Alaska, organized by the Pakistani physicians association. At an evening of beautiful music, I was overcome by the euphoria of the sounds and lyrics, and when someone asked me to come on down and sing, I walked to the stage, took the mic, and sang away. My friend Kausar, sitting in the front row, rushed up to the deck and sent Daddy a text, across the oceans, "Bia is singing again." I suppose you eventually swing back. You cannot get too far away from yourself.

I continue to study and give talks at interfaith gatherings. I have gravitated to the middle, more to the left, inching into the realm of spirituality, am less stubborn, more open, less sure of myself, and more at ease.

First World Trade Center Bombing. February 1993

Sitting at my office desk, I burst into tears. A truck bomb had detonated below the South Tower, six people had died, the perpetrators were Muslim, and the media was bashing my faith and bashing all Muslims. Monique, my secretary, also a Muslim, was shaking her head. "When a Christian does something, no one blames their faith. When a Muslim does it, they blame us all." My Jewish colleague Helene came into my office. "I am sorry this is happening. Is there anything I can do?" I badly needed sympathy and was grateful. *Someone understands how we feel.* I picked up the phone and called my Jewish friend Lenny, also a hospital administrator and an Orthodox Jew. "What should we do?" I asked. We had a shared history. They had been dealing with anti-Semitism for forever and had mastered the skill of pushing back and making allies. He would be able to guide me. "Let me talk to a few people and get back to you," he said. Comforted that someone had my back (I was taking this personally), I was able to clear my head and concentrate on work. Lenny did get back to me. He had gotten something going, a dialogue and a statement. A Muslim in distress had reached out to a Jew and the Jewish community was backing the Muslims.

My family and friends in Pakistan know of Lenny. I tell this story whenever I hear them say, "The Jews are our enemies." Over the years, as each event piled upon the other—9/11, the Danish cartoons, the Boston Marathon, ISIS, *Charlie Hebdo*—the list of Lennys has grown, lining up behind us, never again wanting to see a faith community persecuted.

Oklahoma Bombing. April 1995

I answered the office phone. Monique, my secretary, was at the other end. "An office building in Oklahoma has been bombed, people have been killed, and they are saying the Nation of Islam did it."

"Oh, my God! That's awful! But I don't believe the Nation of Islam would do that. That is not their modus operandi."

"I know. But that is what they are saying. Why are they so quick to jump on Muslims?"

When the name Timothy McVeigh was announced, all I could say was, "Thank God, it wasn't a Muslim."

"Is that how your mother relates to it?" Asim's friend's mother was outraged.

Khalid's Muslim colleague stopped him in the hallway of the hospital. "Thank God it wasn't a Muslim," he said. "Can you imagine all the Muslim-bashing that would have taken place on TV?"

Was it wrong to feel that way? People lost their lives. And I feel relief that it wasn't a Muslim!

The worst was yet to come.

28.

And Then Nothing Was the Same
September 11, 2001

I am angry. I am angry with the crazy, fanatic killers who have set us back beyond square one. All those years of interfaith work, gone up in smoke. What have the perpetrators done to us?! All those efforts to build mosques, Muslim community centers, raising the profile of Islam, getting our children to feel comfortable and confident as Muslims, all smothered in the rubble of the towers.

At the time, we were living in Saudi Arabia and working at King Feisal Hospital. I was in Mecca, performing *umrah*, the lesser pilgrimage, when the towers fell. Were my children alive? Asim's office was in downtown Manhattan, and he often had meetings at the World Trade Center. Phone lines were down. How I prayed, going around and around the Kaaba, praying, "Dear God, please, please, please let my children be alive. Please don't let any harm have come to them." I called again—no answer from Asim's phone. Dear God, please let them be alive. I called again—no answer from Saqib's phone. Hours later I got through to Khalid's sister-in-law, Aneela. "Everyone is fine," was the first thing she said. "I have spoken to Asim. Both your children are fine." I wanted to get on a plane and hold my children in a hug, just feel them, alive, warm, and wriggling out of my arms. All flights had been canceled. The next few days I remained numb. And then they identified the perpetrators: Muslims, most of them Saudis.

Emails flooded in from across the ocean assuring me, e-comforting me. Bob offering to house my children until the anti-Muslim sentiment subsided, Robin promising to push back on Islamophobia, and all of them asking, "What is the reaction of the Saudis?"

Asim was walking back after Friday prayers when the crowd shouted, "Go back to where you came from." At the workplace, the Saudis extended their support. "Is your family OK? Are you OK? Take time off if you want to." Psychological counselors were appointed, the restriction on using the Internet for personal reasons during working hours was lifted, and employees were told that if they wanted to break their contract and return home, there would be no penalties. The Saudis were angry and believed that Al-Qaeda, an organization that is committed to dislodging the Saudi royal family, had framed them by using Saudi men to carry out the attack, putting a Saudi face on the terrorists.

I came home to a world that had changed forever. The face of Muslims had changed. *Hijabs* were off, beards shaved. There wasn't anyone I know on Staten Island who didn't know someone who perished. A neighbor, a friend, a patient . . . Khalid and I took the Staten Island ferry to Manhattan, and when the Manhattan skyline came into view, I burst into tears. We walked to Ground Zero, the charred framework still standing, papers with burnt edges stuck in the road signs.

Whether it was at the supermarket, the bank, or the shopping mall, I wondered if people looked at me as "one of them." A Muslim friend of mine posted an "I love America" sticker on her car, another hung the American flag outside her house, yet another, who always wore the *shalwar kameez,* was now wearing pants. Fear. I worried— worried about the future of Muslims in the US. Will Islamophobia chip away at their self-esteem? Will their civil rights be safeguarded? Will they feel alien in their own homeland? Is my house bugged? Is my phone tapped? Emails? I was hearing horror stories of people being swept away into detention centers, getting into hot water with the authorities because someone's email said, "The party was a blast." BLAST.

In the 2004 presidential election, shaken by George W. Bush's policies on civil rights, I walked into the American embassy in Saudi Arabia and cast my vote for John Kerry. I, a registered Republican, had switched parties.

A personal crisis brought me back home to New York for good. Our grandson Omar was diagnosed with autism. It was time to come home. I left my career to start the New York Metro Chapter of the National Autism Association. But I was yearning to do whatever it took to reverse the damage done to Muslims by the perpetrators of 9/11. I needed to find and associate myself with a Muslim organization that was committed to a robust interfaith outreach. How do I search for one?

Once again, I was reminded that when you take one step toward God, He takes ten steps toward you. One day, I received a package in the mail. It was a book, *The Faith Club,* sent to me by Dr. Faroque Khan, a friend and interfaith activist on Long Island. The book, coauthored by Ranya Idliby, Suzanne Oliver, and Priscilla Warner, weaves the stories of three women, a Muslim, Christian, and Jew, who, post-9/11, wrestle with their issues about and try to understand one another's faith. I came to a chapter where Ranya, a secular Muslim, talks about her encounter with a Muslim cleric, Imam Feisal Abdul Rauf, and his wife Daisy Khan and how moved she was by their approach to the faith and commitment to interfaith work. I had known about them, had been following their work, and now, reading about them from Ranya's eyes, I knew where I was headed.

I wrote to Faroque, "Can you connect me with Daisy?" Daisy was his niece. "You will see her at the wedding next week; Imam Feisal is conducting the ceremony." I cornered Daisy at the wedding, and we pulled two chairs aside and talked. Her brown hair framing her face, she chatted passionately about her work. After 9/11, she and the imam had decided to shift their work from in-reach to outreach, from inculcating Sufism in the Muslim community to doing interfaith work. As people walked around sipping ginger ale, greeting one another and pausing to pick up a piece of chicken tikka, Daisy was charming me. I listened as she told me that no matter where she and the imam go to give a talk on Islam, there are three questions that continue to come up: One, why aren't the moderate Muslims speaking out against extremism? Two, why do you treat your women so badly? Three, is there an example of an Islamic state that is faithful to the principles of Islamic governance?

She and the imam had responded by putting three programs in place. One was the Muslim Leaders of Tomorrow, a global network of young Muslims who would be nurtured and groomed to amplify the voices of moderation. The other was WISE, the Women's Islamic Initiative in Spirituality and Equality, a global network of Muslim women who would advance the causes of women within the tradition. The third was a research project led by Imam Feisal in collaboration with scholars from around the world that describes the elements of an Islamic state and provides an index system to rate how each state complies with the objectives of safeguarding the rights and liberties of the people. That wasn't all. She was also engaged in promoting Islamic values through culture and arts and was on the media circuit. I was sold.

Two months later, I was at a desk in her office as their director of interfaith programs. My first assignment was to give a talk at the Sabbath services at the Brotherhood Synagogue—my first speech since 9/11, and I wanted to be prepared. The gracious rabbi, whom I met for a prep session, advised me on what the audience was looking for, Daisy coached me on what questions to expect, and Dr. Faroque sent me a list of questions and answers. I took a deep breath and walked up to the lectern. After the services ended, the rabbi invited Khalid and me to open the door to the ark. Teary-eyed, I almost stumbled. In the basement, after nibbling on refreshments and chatting with the congregation, we gathered for a Q&A. There were no firework questions; everyone was welcoming and warm. A woman walked up to me and said, "I am confused. Now I am confused." She was shaking her head, and she looked confused. Later I told Khalid, "I am so encouraged by her confusion. Confusion is the beginning of a new beginning."

DETAINED

Saqib, my older son, is detained each time he enters the country—a consequence of having the same name as a terrorist. They run a check and let him go. Meanwhile, his family is pacing in the waiting area, and he, tired after a long transatlantic flight, now has to undergo scrutiny as a potential terrorist. He has tried everything to clear his name and is told that he has only two options: one, stop traveling, and two, change his name. I have spoken to a Homeland Security official I met at a roundtable meeting, who told me that there is nothing anyone can do. Every measure has a risk of fraud associated with it. Short of biometrics, there is no fail-safe way. He advised that Saqib carry a letter with him, issued by the State Department. Saqib got the letter and carries it with him. He still gets detained. "This letter is fine, but we still have to go through our process." I am scared for him. I am scared that one day, some foul-up in the databases . . . I don't even want to think about it.

It gets worse.

Eight-Year-Old with Autism on Terror List: Detained at Airport. January 27, 2010

Omar, my eight-year-old grandson, was detained. Omar has autism. They were getting on a flight to go to Disney World when Omar got taken aside at the airport and was placed in a holding area. I was at the office when I got a text from Saadia, my daughter-in-law. "Omar has been detained. They say his name is on the no-fly list of terrorists."

What the . . .

"Can't they see that he is eight years old?" I texted.

"They say that they know that he couldn't be a terrorist, but they have to follow procedure."

"Which is what?"

"They have to put his name in the database, and if no match, he will be cleared."

"How long will it take?"

"A few hours. We will definitely miss our flight."

"Where are you?"

"In a holding area. All four of us." The four being the parents and two children.

"Hang in there. I am calling the press."

I was president of the National Autism Association New York Metro Chapter and had contacts in the media. I got going and got the word out in my autism network, which was huge. The *Age of Autism* immediately posted the news on-line, "Eight-Year-Old with Autism on Terror List:

Detained At Airport." The *New York Times* demurred—they had done a similar story recently and were not interested. I called the *Huffington Post*.

Another text from Saadia.

"He is hungry, and they won't let any one of us out to bring him something to eat. He is stimming." Stimming is when a person with autism engages in self-stimulatory repetitive behavior such as hand flapping, rocking, pacing.

My grandson with autism, a little eight-year-old, hungry, stimming, and detained. Has our nation gone crazy? Let's just set aside that he is only eight. Don't they know that Omar Rehman is as ubiquitous a name among Muslims as John Smith and David Cohen are among Christians and Jews? God help the Omar Rehmans of America. I called my assemblyman. "He is an eight years old with autism, and they are treating him like a terrorist!" The assemblyman was a New Yorker; the airport was in Philadelphia. I got a lot of sympathy, but no one could help me.

A text from Saadia: "They have cleared him. The terrorist is in his twenties; no match."

Duh!

My dear little grandson, and I couldn't do a thing to help him. I made a lot of noise, continued to make noise, autism moms backed me up, and the autism community made a big splash over it, but we couldn't make a dent in the system. Omar is now fourteen, a handsome young boy with a sprouting mustache. What is going to happen the next time he gets on a plane? I hold my breath. And pray.

Each event had jolted me in a new way, opening windows of awareness, and closing many doors. Some set us back, some propelled us forward; some hit us hard till we could stand it no more, some brought friends to our doorsteps; some caused us to splinter from within, and others made us feel that we didn't belong.

But I am hopeful. This is America. If there is a place in the universe where there is a sparkle of hope for Muslims to restore their image, recover their integrity, and make their voices heard, it is here, in America. But we have to earn that right and work at it. Let's get started—mend the damage done to Muslims by Muslims, and confront extremism and Islamophobia.

29.

Extremism and Islamophobia
Viewed from the Eyes of a Muslim

I Hope It's Not a Muslim

A terrorist attack takes place and how do I react? *I hope it's not a Muslim.* Does that make me less compassionate toward the victims? I carry that guilt. Do I run for cover each time the perpetrator's Muslim identity is revealed? I do. Am I angry with the perpetrators? Of course I am. They are killing innocent people, tarnishing the image of Islam, and giving the Islamophobes just the ammunition they need to paint all Muslims in one broad stroke. It is painful to see my revered faith associated with murder, over and over again, in voices that are getting louder and louder. The acts of a few are hurting us all. Each time an incident takes place, I have to sit and watch talk-show hosts bash us again and again. Well, I don't have to, but you cannot get away from it. Islamic terrorists . . . Muslim terrorists . . . Islamic jihadists . . . all evoking images of terror. Ask anyone on the street: what image does Islam evoke? At times I feel Muslim fatigue.

God states in the Qur'an:

> Because of this did We ordain unto the Children of Israel that if any one slays a human being—unless it be [in punishment] for murder or for spreading corruption on earth—it shall be as though he had slain all mankind: whereas if anyone saves a life, it shall be as though he had saved the lives of all mankind. . . .[18]

---

18 Qur'an 5:32.

Is There a Double Standard?

Why is it that when a Christian, Jew, Buddhist, or Hindu commits a murder, we don't hear mention of their religious affiliation, but when the perpetrator is a Muslim, his religion makes news? Let's face it. It is because these people invoke Islam to justify their deeds. They quote the Qur'an out of context, and those who don't know believe it.

Did I just talk you out of believing that there is no double standard? That is not what I meant. I believe that there *is* a double standard. How many of you heard the story of the Muslim Ring of Peace around the synagogue in Oslo, Norway? Or of Muslim students in Pakistan forming a human shield to ensure that their Hindu friends could celebrate the festival of Holi in peace? Isn't this newsworthy?

Is there a double standard in freedom of speech? I watched Daisy Khan being interviewed on PBS *Newshour* in the aftermath of the killings in the Charlie Hebdo case. When asked if there was a double standard, Daisy responded: "Muslims here in the United States complain that there is a double standard for them. They don't enjoy free speech. If they criticize their government, they are seen as unpatriotic. If they criticize the policies of Israel or question them, they are called anti-Semites, and if they call for examining the root causes of terrorism, they are seen as aiding and abetting. So there is a sense that free speech is not for Muslims, and it's only to be enjoyed by Westerners."

Blame

So who can I blame?

The media? For sensationalizing it?

No. They are reporters, and they will report it as they see it, and they see it through the lens of their understanding.

The Islamophobes? No. They don't know better. Their mindset is a consequence of centuries of conditioning.

Ourselves? And by that I mean "us Muslims"? Yes. Because we haven't done enough to make our faith known. We are afraid to wear our religion on our sleeves, lest we be discriminated against, and take comfort in believing that "religion is a private matter." Well, guess what? Religion is all over the TV monitors, the radio talk shows—so get out of the closet. Some of us wallow in self-pity: "Why us?" Some of us retreat into our fold, exhibiting fear: "They are out to get us." Some of us just give up without trying: "It's no use." A few, who believe in interfaith work, are carrying the burden: giving lectures, writing books and op-eds, accepting invitations from hostile TV talk-show hosts—just to have the chance to put in a word.

It's a huge burden for a few to carry for the whole world of us. My message to my Muslim readers: open your doors. It's not enough to say, "My imam knows your priest." Get to the grassroots level, and let yourselves be known as the Muslim next door. I don't mean to suggest that you walk around with a slogan on your tee shirt, "I am a Muslim, Don't Panic," or a bumper sticker on your car, "Muslim Driver on Board." Invite your Catholic neighbor for *iftar* in your home—not in a catering hall. Fast on Yom Kippur and join your Jewish colleague over dinner. Tell the story of the Prophet Muhammad's exodus over a Passover Seder. Go to the Holi festival with your Hindu neighbor and immerse yourself in color. Take delight in watching your children decorate their friend's Christmas tree. Tell the story of Mary in the Qur'an over Christmas dinner. Start an interfaith book club, interfaith scripture group, movie club, poetry club, and watch the magic work.

Get to be known and love thy neighbor.

Why Aren't the Moderate Muslims Speaking Out?

A bomb goes off. Innocent lives are lost. An Islamic group claims responsibility.

Muslim-bashing commences.

Us: I condemn the bombing; and: Don't blame Muslims for the acts of a few.

Them: Why aren't the moderate Muslims speaking out?

Us: Excuse me, but what did I just do?

Them: It's not enough.

Us: What *is* enough?

Them: Get the media involved. Show them that most Muslims are not like that. Show them that you are law-abiding citizens like most others. They will air it.

Us: We did get the media involved. They turned us down. We issued press releases, begged the newspapers to publish our statements, wrote op-eds, contacted TV reporters. No luck. Muslims being portrayed as regular John Smith kind of people does not make for a good story. On the sensational index, it's minus zero.

Them: Post statements on your websites. That is in your control.

Us: We did. Every Muslim organization in the US posted a statement condemning the attack, referencing the Qur'an.

Them: Maybe it wasn't strong enough.

Us: I will send you the links. Tell me how to make it stronger.

This dialogue is repeated every time ISIS strikes, every time there is a cartoon-inspired killing or a video-inspired killing. Each time, Muslim leaders and organizations rush to condemn the attack and watch as they are blamed for not condemning it. We do raise our voices, but we are not heard.

So what do we do?

Well, Muslim leaders, think tanks, and NGOs across the nation and across the world are devising creative strategies to amplify the voices of the moderates, through education, skill development, and harnessing the power of networking. Imam Feisal Abdul Rauf conceived and is promoting the concept of the Global Movement of Moderates and is starting an imam training program. The Zaytuna College in California, co-founded by Hamza Yusuf, is the first Muslim liberal arts college that aims to revive Islam's educational and intellectual legacy and to popularize traditional learning among Western Muslims. Asim recently moderated a two-day workshop at Harvard, *Representing American Muslims: Broadening the Conversation*, where Muslim activists, artists, scholars, and advocates deliberated on strategies for Muslim engagement in public service, the art of storytelling, creative outreach, and more. You don't have to look beyond Twitter to see the buzz going. These are just a few of many examples.

The extremists use Islam as the weapon to justify killing. We have to use Islam to un-justify the killing. It's the only weapon that will work. Fighting them with a secular argument is not going to cut it. Nothing stirs passions as fervently as religion; nothing is as potent as religion;

and nothing will move you or stop you as well as religious conviction. Harness that sentiment. Use religion as the basis for condemning the murders, for fostering tolerance, and for building harmony. Use the Qur'anic text to take away from the extremists what they took away from us.

When the Next Cartoon Appears

When I was a little girl, Aba Jee would tell a bedtime story to Neena and me.

Once upon a time, long ago, in the desert of a far-off land, the Prophet Muhammad was walking to the mosque to say his prayers. He walked by a house. In that house lived a lady who didn't like the Prophet. In fact, she didn't believe that he was a messenger of God. She threw garbage at him. The next day when he walked by her house, she again threw garbage at him. This went on for many days. The Prophet didn't get angry with her and just quietly walked on. One day, as he walked by her house, the lady wasn't there. She wasn't there the next day either. He asked around and learned that she was sick. The Prophet felt bad for her and went to visit her. He told her that he would pray that she get well soon and asked her if he could do anything to help her. The lady was so touched by the Prophet's kindness that she came to believe that he was indeed a messenger of God and became a Muslim.

Aba Jee would go on to tell us that the Prophet, through his conduct, set the example for compassion, mercy, tolerance, and patience during adversity.

I now tell this story to my granddaughter Laila. When I am tucking her in, her curly hair tangled over the pillow, she will look up with dreamy eyes. "Daadee, can you tell me a bedtime story?" She is too young to know the term "compassion" or "mercy," but she knows the feeling. "You see, Laila, if someone is mean to you, try not to get upset. Be nice to them."

"If I am nice to people, Allah will love me?" Her eyes start drooping.

"Yes, sweetie. He already does," and I kiss her goodnight.

If the woman had sketched his caricature or cartoon instead, would the Prophet Muhammad have acted differently?

A Place of Hope

On the shores of Chautauqua Lake, in southwestern New York State, a community comes alive each summer. Chautauqua Institution is my version of heaven on earth. Each summer it hosts fascinating interfaith dialogues, cultural events, and educational lectures. Founded by Methodists in the late nineteenth century, it is ecumenical in spirit. In a serene and picturesque setting, its beautiful grounds are home to houses of Christian and Jewish denominations. Keen to have a Muslim presence, they have been inviting prominent Muslim speakers and clergy, including Imam Feisal A. Rauf, and sponsoring Muslim cultural events, and they hope one day to have a Muslim denominational house. It is a place for a meeting of the hearts and minds of people of all faiths, from communities all across the US, a place for thought to flourish and for nourishment of the soul. Each morning, at the 8:00 a.m. devotional hour, people will start moving toward the Hall of Philosophy, a Parthenon-like outdoor hall atop the hill, overlooking the lake. They take their seats as Imam Feisal takes his place at the podium for the daily sermon on Sufism and Rumi. His talk leads into *zhikr*—remembrance of God, a collection of sounds to awaken the soul and make it stand before the Creator. The audience—men, women, Christians, Jews, Hindus, and Muslims, join him in the chant: *Allah, Allah, Allah.* For fifteen minutes, they sway, eyes closed, chanting the name of God, unveiling the soul. The next morning, they are back. Later one afternoon, a clergyman sitting next to Khalid and me related his spiritual experience during the *zhikr* led by Imam Feisal. "I always yearned for that spiritual connection with God. Today, during the chant, I finally experienced it." This is just one of many ways in which the Chautauqua community has opened its arms to us. It is a microcosm of what America is all about. This is a place where I see hope, and a place where we can showcase Islam in the twenty-first century.

30.

Upgrading Islam into the Twenty-First Century

I see many practices as being outdated, where the solutions are before our eyes if we can muster the courage to embrace them.

The ritual of moon sighting is one, where the most important Muslim holiday is announced only after one sights the new moon with the naked eye. As movements have sprung up to eclipse moon sighting with moon forecasting, and with impetus from such breakthroughs as New York City's mayor designating dates for Muslim holidays, there is a crescent of hope—hope that the Muslim *ummah*, or community, will come together as it was meant to. Meanwhile, it's a free-for-all. You believe in sighting the moon? Fine. Scan the horizon and stay up in case someone, somewhere on the West coast might call at 1:00 a.m., saying, "I sighted the crescent. Eid Mubarak." You want to have a neatly packaged, pre-planned day off for Eid? You have that option too. Only in America.

What about rituals dating back fourteen hundred years that cannot be replicated on Manhattan Island, such as sacrificing a lamb to honor Abraham? Are there work-arounds? For now, everything goes. I doubt if anyone is slaughtering a lamb in his or her backyard, though. A call will go out to Mom in the old country: "Can you sacrifice a lamb for me? I will send you the money." Go to the website of Muslim charitable organizations, and chances are you will find a Donate button for Qurbani. Click Here, enter credit card #, the money goes to the designated country, a lamb is sacrificed, and meat is distributed to the needy. Then there are the slaughterhouses where families will place the order.

Animal lovers: I also see a shift. Families in the US and in Pakistan are opting for charity in cash versus meat. Last Eid, when I called my sister Neena in Pakistan, she told me that this year she did not sacrifice a lamb. "It's no longer practical," she told me. "I don't have the household help—someone who can go to the bazaar, select, purchase, and bring home the lamb— and I don't have the space to house it. Due to power outages, meat goes bad in the freezer, and the needy are now asking for cash instead, because they don't have the capacity to store meat." Some families in the US are beginning to take that view. I am no authority on religion, nor am I issuing a fatwa. Just pondering.

Can a woman serve as clergy or spiritual leader? Dr. Amina Wadud created a stir when she led men and women in Friday prayers in New York City in 2005. A photographer captured the image of Asim sitting in the front row, next to a young lady, their hands raised in prayer. Men and women side by side! He had taken time off from work to join the congregation and support a woman leading prayer. *Dear Asim. How he must have felt each time he saw his mother move to the back of the prayer rows. He was making a statement.* I was at a women's conference a few years ago where Imam Feisal was in attendance. As we assembled for prayer, Imam Feisal made an announcement. "This is a women's gathering. . . . It is only fitting that a woman lead the prayer." He then took his place in the back row, and one of the women led the prayer. Recently, at an interfaith book club meeting at my apartment, when it was prayer time, one of the Muslim women announced, "I will pray only if Sabeeha leads the prayer." Khalid smiled and waved his hand to usher me to the front.

Let's stick with women and look around: they now serve on the boards of mosques and head faith-based and religious organizations. Ingrid Mattson—a woman, as you would have gathered—served as the president of the Islamic Society of North America (ISNA), one of the largest Muslim organizations in the US. Daisy Khan, an imam's wife (who doesn't wear the head scarf, I might add), former executive director of ASMA, now heads WISE, Women's Islamic Initiative in Spirituality and Equality, and is a sought-after speaker on the media circuit.

My dream is for women to have equal right to space in a mosque. It bugs me to see women shepherded to a curtained-off balcony, or worse, relegated to a separate, tiny, cramped room with plasma screens. What troubles me more is that women accept that. I don't buy the argument put forth by men that women need privacy. Privacy to do what? It's outright male dominance, and as long as women go along and don't exert their rights, then they deserve what they get. *Phew! That was harsh!* We all choose the path of least resistance. Don't I just walk over to the back row instead of protesting? ISNA in 2015 launched its campaign for the inclusive, women-friendly *masjid*, stating that "women have a prayer space in the main *musalla* (prayer hall) which is behind the lines of men but not behind a full barrier that disconnects women from the main *musalla* and prevents them from seeing the imam." A promising start, but ladies, we have many rows to cross to the frontlines.

As long as we are on the subject of mosques, there is something else. In the seventies and eighties, first generation Muslim immigrants, driven by their need to preserve their cultural expression of Islam, established mosques along national lines: a Pakistani-Indian mosque, Egyptian mosque, Albanian mosque, etc. The Prophet Muhammad was praised in Urdu in the Pakistani-Indian mosque, in Arabic in the Egyptian mosque. Women wore *shalwar kameez* in the Pakistani-Indian mosque, *jalabiya* in Egyptian mosques, long skirts in Albanian mosques. At *iftar,* people broke their fast with biryani in the Pakistani-Indian mosque, *mezza* in the Egyptian mosque. You get the picture. Parents chatted in their native tongues, and children played in English. These children are now parents themselves—American parents, raising American children. They will establish mosques wherever their careers take them, and these will be American mosques—*iftar* with an American flavor. The lines of national identity will get blurred, and mosques will become less ethnic—just Muslim mosques—just as they were intended to be. Then there is the issue of sects. We have Sunni mosques and Shia mosques—*imambaras*. Will those congregations merge as well, into non-denominational, "just Muslim" mosques? That is what Daddy would have liked, and I am my father's daughter.

31.

An American Muslim in Pakistan

How do I feel each time I visit my country of birth? What is it like to juggle ambassadorial hats? Who do I speak for anyway? How does it feel to see the beautiful country of one's birth engulfed in terrorist attacks?

Pakistan before I Came to America
Ah! The Sixties
My generation came alive in that glorious era, when art and culture flourished, and we felt free and safe on the streets of Lahore. But it was not without its pain. In 1965, Pakistan went to war with India. Daddy was sent off to war, and I stood on the platform of the railway station in Quetta, trying not to cry, not wanting to wave, and trying not to lose Daddy's figure leaning out of the doorway, smiling and waving as the train pulled out. A telegram arrived. My uncle: killed on the battle-field of Kashmir, leaving behind a young widow and three little girls. A phone call: my cousin, killed in battle, single, with a lifetime ahead of him. At school—I was in high school—each time the principal stopped by our classroom, I'd hold my breath. She'd beckon to a student and escort her to her office, where a family member waited to give her the news: her father had fallen in battle.

I'd come home to a house full of women sitting in the drawing room on sheets spread on the rugs, furniture pushed back, praying over *tasbeeh* beads, praying for the safe return of our fathers and for the souls of the departed. Each time the phone rang, I'd freeze. Only the bravest would answer the phone, and as she nodded "All is well" to us, we'd exhale with a "Thank, you God." At night, when the sirens wailed, we would jump out of bed, rush outside, and crouch in the trenches in our backyard, shivering in the night until the all-clear siren sounded. At school, my friends (girls, of course) would gather in clusters in the courtyard during break, catching the sun in the cool days of autumn, and talk war politics. We were going to beat back those Indians; they would regret having attacked us. Spirits soared as the Pakistan air force and army pushed back. When the guns fell silent, we were elated at having won the war, and President Ayub Khan, the dashing field marshal, was our hero. Brimming in national pride, we reveled in making mean-spirited fun of the short-statured Indian prime minister Lal Bahadur Shastri. *Time* magazine was delivered to our homes on Saturday, and by Monday morning, we girls had devoured every page of it and were ready to share our take on world politics as soon as the bell rang for the break.

We'd lament over the long-widowed Jackie Kennedy and had our own conspiracy theory going—it had to be Johnson—and took pride in knowing that the riderless horse in the Kennedy funeral procession was the one given by President Ayub to Jackie when she visited Pakistan. One of the by-products of the war was music—national inspirational songs. When inspired by love of country, poets overnight composed songs, and the voices that pierced the skies and touched our hearts were those of Noor Jehan and Mehdi Hassan. At school, I would sing "*Aey watan ke sajeele jawano*" ("Oh, Our Nation's Young Warriors"), and at home I would immerse myself in the soft, velvety voice of Mehdi Hassan's *ghazals* as I prepared for finals. Mummy would wonder, "How can she concentrate on her studies with all this music?" but she also knew that music was my lifeline.

We took pride in being Pakistani, and the future felt bright, despite the pain of war.

Pakistan after Coming to America
The Heart-Wrenching Seventies

I returned home to a country in shock. It was my first visit back to Pakistan in 1973, with an eleven-month-old Saqib in my arms. Pakistan had lost half its country to a war with India, East Pakistan was now Bangla Desh, and nearly everyone I knew had a family member or a friend taken prisoner-of-war by India. Zulfiqar Ali Bhutto, a charismatic orator of socialist leanings, was prime minister, and those who revered him believed that only he could eradicate poverty, and those who hated his guts considered him a rogue. The nation was going through political convulsions. Morale was low, and people wondered if Pakistan would survive as a nation. Daddy, always believing that his little girl brought him good luck, said, "When you left, so did the nation's good fortunes."

My unmarried friends were beginning to wonder what was holding up Prince Charming. Much as I loved showing off baby Saqib, I felt a twinge of guilt sporting a handsome husband and a cute little toddler. My friends were in a holding pattern, waiting for the right marriage proposal to come. Starting a career was not an option, because if a good proposal came along, she would have to get married right away. "Your accent hasn't changed," one of them noticed. "Well, that's because I am working hard at keeping it." I didn't get to meet my married friends— they had lives of their own, and their schedules were no longer theirs. Some had moved away, making a home in far-off places. It would be another forty years before we'd meet again.

Saqib was the first to fall sick. A change of drinking water and one's intestinal flora is enough to cause diarrhea. Top that with family dinners, lunches, and breakfasts—not one-course meals, mind you. The two firstborns returning home for the first time as a couple, after two long years, with their firstborn is enough to be conferred with celebrity status, and my calendar got loaded with visits to family and the new in-laws of my in-laws. Turning down an invitation is disrespectful. Not taking second helpings is worse—doesn't matter that you just had a five-course luncheon. If I said, "No, thank you," it was taken as a sign of modesty, and food was poured onto my plate.

I loved all the love I couldn't handle. It was September, Multan was hot, and this spoiled young lady was missing her A/C and airy blouse. Each morning, I got dressed up in finery and jewelry, just in case a visitor dropped by, which they did. I'd be at a dinner, dressed up in an unmanageable, ornate sari, when a pungent whiff of diarrhea from baby

Saqib would send me scurrying to my hostess's immaculate bedroom, struggling to change the diaper with baby tugging at my dangling earrings, with my sari falling off my shoulder onto his face; then I'd be looking for a bathroom to rinse out his cotton diaper before dropping it in a plastic bag and tucking it inside the travel bag as he wailed to fend off all the attention he was getting. Everyone wanted to hold Saqib, and my baby, so used to being with Mummy all day, would shriek each time he saw those outstretched arms.

"What have you done to yourself? You look sick," was the greeting I received from almost everyone. "You have circles under your eyes. . . . Your face is so thin. . . . You used to be so pretty. . . ." *Used to.* Someone went so far as to ask in hushed tones, "Are you happy?" Translated: Is your husband treating you well? "Of course, I am happy." *It's OK. She means well.*

One afternoon, Mummy took me shopping in the Baara Bazaar of Rawalpindi. As our car left the wide streets of Murree Road, the lanes got narrower, and at the red light, a beggar approached, her hand outstretched, cupping her palm. "May Allah grant your children a long life. . . .", she said to Mummy in Urdu. Then she turned to me and said, "Hello, please . . ." in English. *How did she figure that I am to be addressed in English? I am wearing* shalwar kameez. *Does my bearing give it away?* I opened my purse, took out a five-rupee bill and handed it to her. Within seconds, the car was engulfed with beggars with pleading faces, pushing one another to get close. I quickly rolled up the window. I was embarrassed to look away. *Green light, hurry.* The street got narrower, with pedestrians crossing whenever they found an opening between cars. Mummy pulled over and stepped out. I slid my purse under my *dupatta* and tucked my diamond pendant inside my shirt. "This is not New York," Mummy said with a laugh, "look at all the women walking the streets laden with gold bangles and diamond rings." Mummy related the story to Daddy. "Do you know what Bia did in the bazaar? She has been gone only two years and already she has forgotten what a safe place Pakistan is."

I missed Khalid when he left. I stayed on for another two months. We wrote long letters, him telling me how much he missed me, and daily I waited for the postman. Who writes letters every day, but maybe I would be lucky, who knows? The excursion fare airline ticket was good for four months, so everyone was surprised when I told them that I was here for three months only. Why waste all that money, they would say. What's the rush, stay another month. I'd try to explain that Khalid misses me, and they would say, "Well, what about your parents, won't they miss you?" It came to a point that I dreaded being asked the question. Coming back was hard. I had carried only a dozen disposable diapers for airline travel—a major dent in our budget—and came home to an apartment where I had to start cooking again, cleaning, no one to serve me tea, no naps while someone watched baby, jet-lagged, in a quiet house, and no more chatter of family hovering over me.

Everyone cried when I left, Mummy most of all. She would start the countdown four weeks prior: "You will be gone in twenty-eight days . . . twenty-five days. . . . You were here for such a short time." After I left, she didn't have the heart to have the windows and furniture cleaned—baby Saqib's handprints were smudged all over. "When are you coming back?" She would repeat this over the next forty years, leaving me with a heart laden with guilt. I would live with that for as long as she lived, more so after she died.

Pakistan: Today

By the time I visited two years later, most of my friends had gotten married and left town. The few who remained were getting worried. After all, they were now in their late twenties. I lost touch with most of them, a consequence of distance and getting swept away by life. Globalization and the age of Internet had not yet dawned.

Each time I visited Pakistan, the uncles and aunties had more gray in their hair, the cousins were a little more mature and the children a little taller. Each time, I found the country to be less safe, less stable. One day, upon reading about a sectarian riot in Karachi, I called my parents from New York. "Everything is fine," Mummy said. "This is just propaganda by foreign countries." Mummy, like the rest of the country, was in denial.

What didn't change is the *khaloos*—the deep sincerity of family and friends. I'd see it in their eyes and feel it in their tight embrace. The welcoming feeling would warm me all over, make me teary-eyed, and I'd miss it each time I returned to the US. What didn't change is the Pakistani woman's love affair with style. She knows what defines elegance, and she looks ravishing. Always well groomed, hair styled in the latest fashion of the West, *shalwar kameez* in a new style on each visit, and with such impeccable taste. All custom-made, home designed. I have to groom myself each time I get onto the plane, lest I get a scolding for my beat-up looks. What didn't change is the *aaah!* I felt when I inhaled the smell of raindrops on dust, when I squeezed the ice-cold mango between my palms, sucking in the sweet nectar; when I heard the cry of the pushcart vendor on the street selling his plums, "*Aaloo bukhare lay lo.*" In moments like these, I felt as if I had never left.

On one visit in the early 1980s, sitting in Daddy's sunroom, I noticed the TV newscaster with a *dupatta* over her head. "Why is her hair covered?" I asked. "All women on TV now have to cover their hair," Neena answered. "President Zia's orders." Zia-ul-Haq, the dictator, was rapidly imposing a conservative brand of Islam. The movie industry was dying, movie theaters were closing, compensated by home VCR movies. Music programs on TV were replaced by religious sermons. People of means still had access to culture and arts, hosting private poetry recitals and *ghazal* singing sessions in their homes, but public places became devoid of art. The trajectory that Zia put the nation on would not be reversed, not by Benazir Bhutto, an Oxford and Harvard graduate, and not by General Pervez Musharraf. It was not for lack of trying. Oppression breeds activism, and women-led NGOs cropped up, fighting for women's rights through media, legislation, awareness, film, street theaters, and education—and won't stop pushing.

Women Leading

But there was a definite shift, despite the imposed conservatism. Women in the upper and middle classes were pursuing careers. No longer were the options limited to teaching and medicine. Banking, journalism, media, law, clerical work—it was across the spectrum. Walk into a bank, and the tellers and executives are women. Enter a shop, and a female cashier will check you out. Want your hair done? The beauty parlors are women-owned, women-operated businesses. Get on the Daewoo bus, and the woman conductor in a blue uniform will check you in. Turn on the TV, and watch the female reporter in the field and the female talk-show hosts. Open the daily newspaper, and read editorials penned by female journalists or read about female mountain climbers. Watch the parliament proceedings with female parliamentarians, one of them becoming speaker of the National Assembly. The human rights activist whom Asim worked with served as the president of the bar association of the Supreme Court. It didn't stop there. Women were entering the armed forces in roles of commandos and fighter pilots, with one of them graduating the military academy with the Sword of Honor. Why should arts be left behind? A woman journalist and filmmaker has won two Academy Awards for her documentaries. Three women have held the most coveted position in the Foreign Services: ambassador to the US. Top it with Benazir Bhutto being elected prime minister by the masses, illiterate voters from remote villages who voted with their thumb print—they had never learned to read or write—and exercised their choice by selecting the insignia of the candidate, voters who were so conservative in their leanings they never sent their daughters to school. They elected Benazir not once, but twice. When the 126-day sit-in took place on the streets of Islamabad in 2014 protesting the election results, women were there alongside the men, day after day, night after night. Today, it is the norm for a middle-class woman to be on a career path.

On a parallel track, there was the Hudud law imposed by President Zia, where women who claimed to have been raped but could not produce four witnesses were flogged for having sex outside marriage. In rural areas, there is forced marriage, honor killings, and acid burning. That both cultures are part of one fabric is a contradiction I am unable to reconcile.

Matchmaking?

And what about arranged marriages? In my family, I was probably the last to allow myself to be blindfolded into marriage. Within a couple of years, the culture started to change. Arranged marriages are less arranged, and the divorce rate is up. To what degree the boundaries of tradition have relaxed depends on whom you talk to. After forty years of cultural upheavals, Pakistan is still redefining its cultural identity. Today, there is no cultural norm for marriage. Each family or clan defines its own rules based on their family values.

On the one hand: on my visit to Pakistan in 2015, I met a family. The mother, a woman in her late forties, in a headscarf, was telling me about her son's recent engagement. "I had been looking for a suitable girl for my son, and my son had told me, 'I will *not* see the girl. This is your department. *You* pick the girl.'" I was not shocked. Was it trust in his mother's choice? Was it that he didn't want a girl to feel rejected in case he didn't approve? Or did he feel that it was inappropriate to be checking girls out? I didn't ask her that. I didn't want her to feel that I was being judgmental.

The center: we visited another family whose daughter had just gotten engaged to a young man in Khalid's family. The parents of the young man visited the family, had taken notice of their daughter, and decided to conditionally propose to the young lady's parents—the condition being that both children consent. Children! Getting a nod, the parents sent for their son, who was overseas, and the two intendeds met in the presence of both families in a chaperoned setting. He liked her, she liked him, and they got engaged. In another case, the two families— parents I mean—huddled, got the children to meet, and sent them out for dinner—an official date, with a "Get to know one another and let us know if it's a go." I can't say for sure if this practice falls in the middle of the bell curve, but maybe for middle-class families it does, with some variables tweaked here and there. I call them the quasi-arranged.

On the other hand: I asked a young lady, a married woman in her late twenties, to tell me about dating and marriage in college campuses in Pakistan. In government-sponsored universities, men and women cannot be seen walking together. The extremist presence is potent. In private universities, it's an open field—everything goes. You have women in headscarves, men who lower their gaze, and then you have men and women comingling, dating, and yes, some will, as they say, "go all the way." Women have gotten pregnant, and friends have pitched in for them to get an abortion—illegal but practiced. On occasion, you can sniff marijuana in the air and notice vodka camouflaged in water bottles—illegal but practiced. "Their parents know nothing about this, or are in denial," she told me. This time I was shocked.

Till Divorce Do Us Part

When I was growing up, divorce was unheard of, a taboo, and an outcome feared by married woman. To hear of a divorce was scandalous. Women, empowered by their careers, are now telling their husbands to take a walk. This is playing right into the hands of the ultraconservatives, validating their belief that girls should be kept out of school. See what happens, they say, when you educate the girls. It goes to their heads and they break up the family, destroying the lives of their children. Divorced women are remarrying, dispensing with the taboo that, once divorced, no man shall marry her. Divorced women with children are remarrying. That says something about men.

Facebook Did It

I had lost contact with most of my friends from Home-Ec. It took a visit from my college friend Fawzia from Atlanta to bring us all together. She and I were going through my college album, nostalgic over the black-and-white photos. "Where is Tallat?" she asked, pointing to the photo. I shot off an email to Tallat from my iPhone, and minutes later Tallat emailed us from Pakistan. Fawzia was ecstatic. Khalid, watching us from across the room, put down the newspaper, slid off his reading glasses, and tossed off one of his most enduring bright ideas: "Why don't you start a Home-Ec Facebook page?" Within days the page blossomed, and we found friends we thought we had lost forever. We were Skyping, WhatsApp-ing, Viber-ing, posting photos, our life stories. And a few months later, delirious with newfound old love, we flew down to Houston for a reunion. Not to be left behind, the ladies in Pakistan organized a reunion, and when I went back to visit in April 2015, there were reunions galore. We had found one another, and the years melted away. We squealed like schoolgirls and shrieked every time someone walked through the door. We were in love with each other, and I felt like we had never parted. It was the newfound time in our lives that brought us together: our children are on their own, many of us have retired, and we now have the luxury of filling our hours with friends. Many are now widowed; some are divorced, some remarried; and almost every one of them has made a career for herself. And this was a Home-Ec education, non-career-oriented. Neena is an attorney at the Supreme Court. One runs a nation-wide school system. Another is an event planner, an artist, a diplomat, an educator, a policy maker. There are business owners, farm owners, CEOs of NGOs, start-ups, and online companies, activists, and, of course, homemakers. These were the friends of my early years, liberal, outgoing, sophisticated—now grandmothers, bringing beauty into the lives of Pakistanis. Watching them, listening to them, I felt that they had accomplished so much more in circumstances with so many constraints than I had in the land of the free. In college days, my teachers would tell me that one day I would move mountains, but I had been rolling pebbles while these women had scaled icy peaks.

You Americans

I had put my evening outfit on the ironing board in Mummy's sunroom, when Mummy called out, "Razia can iron your clothes for you."

"It's alright. I can do it myself."

Over her protests to take it easy, I started ironing, taking in the sights of the flowers in the garden below. One side done, I placed the iron upright on the stand.

"You can put the iron face-down," she said. "It's asbestos."

I jumped back. "Asbestos!"

She explained that asbestos is fireproof. . . .

"I know it's fireproof, but it causes lung cancer!"

"Oh, you Americans! You are afraid of everything."

Whose War Is It?

In the 1980s, when Russia invaded Afghanistan and we enlisted Pakistan's support, Afghan refugees poured into Pakistan. "We are fighting America's war. . . . We have our hands full addressing our own poverty;

now we have to deal with poverty of the refugees. . . . It has brought drugs and a gun culture. . . . It's all America's doing," is what I heard.

Years later, sectarian feuds would erupt, and the port of Karachi would go up in flames. "America and India are behind it," I would hear.

After 9/11, we invaded Afghanistan. I would hear: "We cooperated with America. We allowed them to fight their war from our land, and they are saying that we are not doing enough. . . . More lives have been lost by Pakistanis fighting the war on terror than the number of lives lost in 9/11, and still they tell us that we are not doing enough."

A friend of my father came to visit, and when I asked him, "Uncle, how are you?" I was sorry I asked. "I will tell you how I am. My son lost his leg fighting the war on terror in Swat. He is now on crutches. A young man on crutches for the rest of his life. And your country tells us that we are not doing enough. That is how I am doing."

In 2014, when the Peshawar school bombing took place, for the first time Pakistanis across the nation were saying, "This is not America's war; this is our war." A friend told me, "I am afraid for my grandchildren. When I send them off to school, I pray and pray until they return home."

In the Dark

Amid the luxury of domestic workers is the scarcity of power and water. Load shedding would take place on designated hours. My parents dispensed with electric clocks. When power went out, no one was allowed to open the fridge, and you sat out on the lawn to make the most of the light. When power returned, we would run to iron our clothes, dry our hair, and run the dishwasher. We chased the electricity. In Lahore, when I was visiting Jedi Mamoon, the lights were one hour on, one hour off. We learned to dance to the lights. Want to read a book: charge your Kindle during "on" hours and then read the lighted screen during "off" hours. People of means installed UPS[19] to keep lights and fans running. It got worse when natural gas was restricted. There was

---

19 Uninterruptible Power Supply. An electrical device to provide backup power in the event of a power failure.

no work-around, not even for the wealthiest. Children went to school without a hot breakfast. People shivered in the cold, wrapping themselves in blankets. "Your Bush said that he would send us into the dark ages, and that is exactly what he has done," people said, waving their fingers at me, blaming America.

Water shortages compelled Mummy to collect rainwater for her plants and go into a permanent drought lifestyle.

Suicide bombings by Muslim militants started spreading, and once again I heard the familiar chant: "America is behind it. . . . India and Israel are behind it . . . because we have the nuclear bomb . . . because we are a Muslim country."

Robberies at gunpoint in broad daylight, kidnappings, and extortion fueled the problem. "Is this also America's fault?" I said. "Rather than shifting blame, leaders need to take responsibility for whatever it is that is causing the problem."

I wear two ambassadorial hats, actually three. In the US, it's: "That's not true, Islam is a peaceful religion. That's not true, Pakistan is a beautiful country." And in Pakistan: "That is not true. It is not America's fault."

Is It Safe?

I am asked this question every time I announce my plans to visit Pakistan. And it's not average Jane the hairdresser asking. It is my children, my daughters-in-law. Safe or not, I had to see my parents. So I'd place my trust in God and get on the plane. The year 2015 was different. My parents had passed on, and Khalid and I were going to visit the rest of the family. The Peshawar school incident was fresh in our minds. We took a look at our will, settled our affairs, handed over the keys and documents to our children, and with a *Bismillah* got onto the plane. Our life is in God's hands.

When I landed, I was almost embarrassed at even entertaining the thought of danger. It was business as usual. Hustle, bustle, all that energy on the streets, the festivities, celebrations, family reunions, women shopping, food vendors lining carts along the street, buses overloaded with people hanging out and perched on the roof, donkey carts blocking the roads, bicyclists ringing bells—in the rain, a motor-cycle carrying a family of four with mommy sidesaddle and baby in her lap—I mean, life goes on. The resilience of this nation amazes me.

At the Daewoo bus terminal, as announcements were being made in Urdu and English, a gentleman sitting next to us said, "Can you watch my bags? I will be right back," and strode off toward the men's room. *Should we run for our lives?* I visited my uncle in Lahore, and stationed outside his gate was an armed guard who escorted me in. Bombs went off in multiple churches, and life went on. In the neighborhood where my parents lived, the homeowners have pooled in to hire a security guard and installed a gate at the roadside. Walls outside government buildings and schools have gone up higher, topped with barbed wire, bolstered with roadblocks. Domestic help, a ubiquitous part of the culture, now seems to be an endangered phenomenon. A family member I visited told me that she no longer employs help because most of the robberies are an inside job.

Flash of Light

Years ago, Pakistanis were confused as to who the enemy was. For some, it was hard to accept the idea that a Muslim, or a group of Muslims, no matter what their tactics, could be the enemy. The establishment, with its deep-rooted corruption, had made life so difficult for the masses that they were ready to wish them away at any cost. To them it did not matter who rooted out the corruption—the army, the dictator, politi-cians, Pakistani Taliban—as long as they could have sufficient water, gas, and electricity and get the job done without having to bribe their way. The Peshawar school incident cleared the sandstorm that obscured their vision.

Religious scholars in academia are recognizing and addressing the issue. In one of my visits, a professor of Islamic studies at the Inter-national Islamic University, Islamabad, invited me to give a lecture on interfaith dialogue at the female campus. She explained that there is a large Christian minority in Pakistan, and she wants her students to learn from the interfaith model in the US, i.e. building harmony. In a packed hall, when the Q&A took off, I was struck by the open-mindedness of the young women and their yearning to make things right in their world. They had the courage to speak up, and I was floored when a young woman addressed me. I don't remember her precise words, but I do remember her punch line. She and a group of students were at an international conference in Europe and would break into group sessions. The people her team got along with the best and made the most headway with were the Jewish students. In these women, I see hope.

And there is one more phenomenon. Social media. The young generation is using Facebook and Twitter to mobilize opinion. They have infused energy into a nation in denial, have organized sit-ins, are reading, and taking action. I spent an evening with a visiting family—young girls in college—and my, did they have their pulse on anything that mattered! Even books. Each time I mentioned a book (and I am a reader), the girls had read it, and if not, they would whip out their smart phones and download it. They are connected across the oceans and deserts and are empowering one another to fuel change. They do not blame America, India, or Israel. They are looking inward. In them, I see hope.

Until then, I worry. I worry about whether Pakistan will survive the wave of extremism before the youth have had a chance to take charge. And what if the worst happens? Will my family be OK? We all know what happened in Europe. People who thought it wouldn't happen stayed, until one day it was too late. Will my family make it out on the last flight out, as I did in 1971?

32.

An American Muslim in New York

Let us dare to imagine: if the Prophet Muhammad were here in New York City today, what would he look like? Would he be wearing a long white thobe, a guthra head cover, or a hooded parka, pants, and snow boots? Would he be riding a camel or hailing a cab? Or would he be environmentally conscious and swipe his MetroCard to get onto the subway? Would he break his fast with dates and camel milk, or strawberries and apple juice? Would he order out for pizza? When he stood in line at the halal food vendor on the Avenue of the Americas, would he converse in Arabic or English? Would he say his prayers in a Sunni mosque, Shia mosque, Pakistani or Egyptian mosque, or any mosque? How would he shape the identity of an American Muslim?

I see the second generation of Pakistani immigrants peeling back the Pakistani culture and revealing a wholly American and wholly Muslim identity. Language: gone. Music and clothing: relegated for special occasions, and maybe lost in the third generation. Food: it will never be lost. There will be Christmas trees and interfaith couples. Our children will cut across national boundaries and embrace one another as Muslims, and not as Pakistanis or Egyptians. Religious freedom will allow a rebirth, a renaissance, in the land of the free. I see it in my children, who have embraced the best of both worlds. Much will be lost; much will be gained—for the better. America will be a safe place for Muslims, and more a home to Muslims than some Muslim countries are to Christians, Hindus, and Jews.

The second and third generation of Pakistani immigrants had a much different journey than my own. Our generation cleared the path and removed many a boulder. My transition from Pakistani Muslim to American Muslim compelled me to unravel the seams and reexamine the pattern of my expression of Islam, distinguish the colors of religion from culture, and thread the yarn of my prayer rug to bring out the flowering beauty of an American Islam. Along the way, I missed a stitch, or choose the wrong color. Sometimes I couldn't find the right thread, sometimes the colors of Islam would not blend with the American hue, and sometimes I pricked my finger. But gradually, the brilliant motifs took shape. For much of this journey, I lived within a space where I had to answer to sometimes conflicting expectations—parents, children, Muslim friends, and non-Muslim friends. I was faced with decisions my parents living in a Muslim country never encountered, all while defining a new set of norms my children would never need to consider. Being the link between two generations has been a tremendous responsibility. My ancestors: Pakistani. My descendants: American. I had the privilege of being both, of celebrating both cultures, and being the link between the two worlds. This privilege, however, came with its challenges. There were so many moments that insisted that I account for my identity and explain myself, when my allegiances were questioned, when my culture incited suspicion, when I felt compelled to explain my heritage, when I was expected to choose between my Muslim identity and my American one. At times I led a double life, answering to cultural demands of the Old Country and the new.

I may have two countries, two languages, and two sets of traditions, but I am one person, with one heart and one faith. My "double life" has wrestled with itself and tried to reconcile the two-sided me. This transition has been the hardest, and as I experienced the American side of me prevail, I felt it was my responsibility to make it easier for those who came after me. I wanted to create a space for dialogue and understanding. I wanted to be part of an American ummah, a community that transcends the "otherness." I wanted my fellow American Muslims and me to be in a place where we can be wholly Muslim and wholly American.

This urge compelled me to be part of community building in Staten Island and to take part in interfaith programs at the American Society for Muslim Advancement and the Cordoba Initiative. These and many other institutions are just some examples of Muslims giving back to the larger community, to share a space with Christians, Jews, and all faiths in a place of fellowship. It has compelled me to be part of civic activities, like the founding of the National Autism Association New York Metro Chapter, and to encourage civic consciousness in my children. This is not just a responsibility to Muslims in America; it is a Muslim responsibility to America. I already see that my grandchildren will be American Muslims in ways I don't know, but the faith and values haven't changed.

Immigrant Muslims like me have made the journey and transformation, diluting the cultural identity of the Old Country and threading the fabric of our attire in red, white, and blue. True to our faith, we pray to Allah, the God of Abraham, Moses, and Jesus. We pray like Muslims all over the world, facing Kaaba from all points of the globe, observing our standardized prayer ritual. We read the same Qur'an, identical in its original version in Arabic, not a syllable out of place. We fast during Ramadan, pay our poor due, and congregate once in a lifetime to make the pilgrimage to Mecca. Our values of honesty, dignity, human rights, social justice, patience in the face of adversity, compassion, and love of one's neighbor are embedded in the American values of life, liberty, and the pursuit of happiness. These pillars of faith remain intact and, God willing, will endure in my grandchildrens' generation and generations to come.

What has changed is our expression of faith, which is becoming American in culture. We have reshaped the architecture of mosques— narrow, slim buildings, squeezed in tight real estate, blending in with the skyline of New York City. I recall how awestruck I was when in Xi'an, China, expecting to see a mosque with domes and minarets. I saw a pagoda-style mosque, its wings arching into a curl. Small-statured old Chinese men, with thin long beards, in Chinese tunics, greeted us in Chinese. When vacationing in Rome, the four of us went for Friday prayers to a mosque, and I had a moment of disorientation when the imam started the sermon—in Italian. My stereotyped mind could not comprehend a Muslim sermon in Italian. Stepping out in the yard, we were greeted by Muslim Romeos, chatting in Italian.

What has changed is the face of Islam. Just walk into a mosque, take a seat at the back, and watch the people file in. An Arab, a Pakistani or maybe Indian, Indonesian, African American, African, White Anglo-Saxon, Turk, Albanian . . . men, women, and children, white, black, and brown, praying together and conversing in a potpourri of languages. This is the Muslim community, or ummah, of America—a marked contrast to countries like Pakistan, where the congregation is homogenous. There are only two places in the world where I have witnessed the diverse Muslim ummah: in New York and, at the time of hajj, in Mecca. Is New York becoming our Mecca? In terms of demographics, it is the most reflective of that holy place.

What has also changed is how we engage in public service, i.e. to represent America and to serve America's interests. On Election Day in 2008, watching the results on CNN, my not-quite-five-year-old grand-daughter Laila burst into tears. "He is losing!" she shrieked. "Who do you want to win?" Saadia asked. "Obama!" she wailed. The night before, Asim had been knocking on doors in Pennsylvania. The week before, Khalid and I had been making calls for MoveOn.org, getting the vote out for Obama. When hurricane Sandy devastated New York, Laila watched her dad with the relief workers at the mosque, packaging goods for the victims. Each year she waves goodbye to Saqib as he and his colleagues board a plane to Haiti to train paramedics in trauma management.

What has changed is how we celebrate the blessings God has bestowed on us, be it honoring Mom on Mother's Day (and Dad on Father's Day) or lining up by the East River to watch the Fourth of July fireworks. On Memorial Day, Khalid and I took little Laila to the ceremonies at Ulysses Grant Park. Sitting atop one of the guns, she watched the colorful march and listened to the speeches, and when it was all over, she said, "It wasn't a fun day, but it was an important day." Every November, we convene to give thanks, gathering around the table, each of us relating, "I am grateful for . . . ," a practice introduced by my daughter-in-law Brinda; and we wait for Khalid to say grace the

Muslim way—*shukr Alhamdulillah*, all thanks and praise to Allah—so they can dig into those steaming mashed potatoes. And that reminds me: please, keep the menu American. At least once a year, I can do without biryani, kebabs, and *kheer.* Give me turkey, yams, cranberry sauce, and pumpkin pie. Bridal red has given way to white, the *nikah* is no longer performed in a quiet ceremony in a room in the back but center stage for everyone to witness, and *ladoos* have been replaced by the wedding cake. Whereas once upon a time her mother, sisters, and girlfriends escorted the bride, now it's Dad on whose arm she walks down the aisle, as teary-eyed Mom watches from the sidelines. Feminists, are we going backward? Did Pakistani moms have it right?

What has changed is how women express their faith. Brides are retaining their maiden name in keeping with the Islamic tradition of calling oneself by the father's name. Watch Imam Feisal conduct a marriage ceremony and ask the bride to propose to the groom. Try Googling women Islamic scholars, and see what you find. Many are taking on the role of spiritual leaders, and now we have a women's mosque in Los Angeles. And yes, they are moving up the rows and taking the best seats in the mosque—some mosques.

What has changed is the hand that holds the mic. Imported imams from the Old Country, imposing alien cultural norms, are being replaced by homegrown imams from accredited seminaries in the US.

All all-American, all-Islamic.

In the land of freedom of religion, the opportunity to create one's own brand is astounding. We will be testing our skills in finding loopholes while mixing and matching line items from various schools of thought to suit our rationale, sensibility, and convenience. We will be offered a diverse range of mosques, Sunday schools, and associations. Want a Sunday school that forbids music—you got it. Want a musical one—you got that too. Want a moon-sighting mosque—got it. Want a scientific-calendar mosque—got it. Want a segregated or non-segregated mosque? How about a women-led mosque? Got that too. Interfaith marriages? Visit dial-an-imam and select from the drop-down menu: Muslim with Muslim only; Muslim man with Christian or Jewish woman; Muslim man or woman with Christian man or woman; Muslim with Hindu; Muslim with atheist. America will offer something for everyone.

I too have a dream. As America continues to learn and grow in the direction of pluralism, so will we. We will continue to build a country meant for all faiths, to create spaces that enhance the dialogue and champion fellowship. Together we will change the discourse, quell violence with knowledge, and banish phobias to the fringes as we work together in unity of the spirit. I dream that in the land of the free, Islam in all its spiritual manifestation, will find a home.

One nation under God.

ACKNOWLEDGMENTS

If it weren't for my husband, Khalid Rehman, my best friend and my soulmate, this book could not have been written. He pushed me year after year for more than twenty years, urging me to write it. When I finally found the nerve to pen my private thoughts, he was the happiest man. Every morning when I sat down to write, he would take away my phones, close the door, and give me the quiet I needed—and refresh my coffee.

I would also like to thank and acknowledge:

My dearest children, Saqib and Asim, who were the inspiration for my quest. Their earnest pursuit for answers put me on the path to finding the American expression of Islam. Khalid, Saqib, Asim, my daughters-in-law Saadia and Brinda, thank you for allowing me to share our intimate and sometimes awkward moments.

Calvert Barksdale, executive editor at Arcade Publishing, for his thorough editorial guidance, clarity in direction, and meticulous attention to detail. Having a responsive editor went a long way for giving me a comfort level with the pace and direction of the book; and Skyhorse Publishing, for placing their confidence in me and giving me the chance to tell you my story.

My teacher, Sidney Offit, who taught me the craft of memoir writing, and whose words of encouragement kept me moving.

Imam Feisal Abdul Rauf, whose spiritual counsel gave me the confidence to share my personal opinions on religious issues.

Alice Cody, Michele Duffy, Mary Burrell, and Marcia Osofsky—
my writers' group—for patiently listening to me read out my chapters,
month after month, critiquing, challenging, motivating, and being my
focus group from the prologue to the closing chapter.

My friend Kim Mack Rosenberg, who opened doors for me and
helped me navigate the world of publishing.

Zakawat Jah, Alan Segal, MD, Vincent Taylor, Aneela Arshed, Asim
Rehman, and Brinda Ganguly, for graciously agreeing to read the manuscript and give me critical feedback; Jan Goodwin for reading the early
draft of a chapter, providing her counsel, and mentoring me; Jenny
Golub, for reviewing the synopsis for the book and educating me in
the skill of writing; and in particular, Mary von Aue, for reviewing my
manuscript and helping me find my voice.

My friends who walked with me at every step, helping me cross
those milestones; and Kirstin Boncher, who lugged her photography
equipment to my apartment, set up a studio, even selected the Pakistani attire, and instructed me in the art of modeling (at my age), as she
snapped away with her camera.

My twenty-plus family members who humored me by entering into
a book-naming contest. The winners: Asim and my daughter-in-law
Brinda. I love the title!

And finally, my family, friends, colleagues, and acquaintances who
have shaped my life. Thank you for being part of my story and part of
my life.

GLOSSARY

Words and phrases translated from Urdu, the national language of Pakistan.

Aashian jal gaya, gulsitan lut gaya: the opening verse of a love song, which translates as, "The abode is extinguished, the garden vanquished"

Aba Jan: (honorific) dear Dad

Aba Jee: (honorific) similar to *aba Jan*, referring to one's maternal grandfather

acha: OK, yes, will do

acha jee: OK, yes, will do

alif: first letter of the Arabic and Urdu alphabet

Alhamdulillah: Praise be to God

Allah hafiz: God be with you (said in lieu of "good-bye")

ameen: amen; also a ceremony to commemorate a child's completing the recitation of the Qur'an

Ami Jan: (honorific) dear Mother, referring to one's maternal grandmother

Apa: honorific for elder sister or any woman older than oneself

arsi mushuf: ceremony of placing a mirror for the bride and groom to see one another for the first time

Assalam Alaikum: Peace on you; Muslim greetings

Baji Jan: (honorific) dear elder sister

baarat: the groom's wedding party

bhabi: sister-in-law; brother's wife

Bhai: honorific for brother, male family member

Bhaijan: (honorific) dear elder brother

bhangra: Pakistani folk dance

Bismillah: In the name of God; uttered as a blessing before starting anything

Chaand Raat: night of the new moon

chaat: salty and spicy salad of fruit or chickpeas and potatoes

charpoi: bed with a wooden frame and knitted jute rope for a mattress

chowaras: dried dates; distributed to guests to celebrate special occasions

Daadee Amma: (honorific) dear Grandmother, referring to one's paternal grandmother

Daada Jan: (honorific) dear Grandfather, referring to one's paternal grandfather

daal: lentil curry

daal tarka: sizzling sautéed onions poured over daal

dhobi: washerman; picks up soiled laundry from a house and cleans it

dholak: hand drum

diwan: armless couch to sit upon in lieu of a bed, with cylindrical pillows; divan

dua: supplication

dupatta: long scarf wide enough to drape over the head, shoulders, and bosom

Eid gah: location for Eid prayers, usually in a large open space

Eid mubarak: Eid greetings

fatwa: legal opinion issued by a Muslim jurist on a specific topic

gao takya: cylindrical, colorful pillows, used on a *diwan*

gharara: bridal outfit, with wide-legged flared pants, a short tunic, and a *dupatta*

ghazal: a song of love and longing; poetic lyrics

gori: white female; used to describe an American/European woman

gora: white male; used to describe an American/European man

gota: sparkling metallic thread used as trimming for *dupattas*; stitched on the edges

guthra: Arab head cover

hadith: sayings and deeds of Prophet Muhammad

halal: permissible

haram: forbidden

hijab: woman's head covering, usually a scarf or *dupatta*

iftar: breaking of the fast at sundown

imambara: congregation for Shia commemoration ceremonies

Insha'Allah: God willing

Isha: obligatory night prayer

Isra Meeraj: Prophet Muhammad's night journey to Jerusalem and to the heavens and a meeting with God

jalabeeya: Arab women's long dress

jelebi: candy in the form of orange pretzel-shaped spirals filled with syrup

jannah: paradise; heaven

jee: yes; OK

jeetey raho: may you live long

jeevay banra: may the groom live a happy life

jhumka: earrings with dangling hoops

jihad: to strive in God's way

joota chupai: literally, hiding the shoe; the tradition at weddings of removing the groom's shoe to hold for a symbolic "ransom"

jumma: Friday congregational prayers

keema: ground meat

keema matar: ground meat with peas

khair mubarak: greetings to you too

khaloos: sincerity

khattak dance: a group dance performed by men in the north of Pakistan

kheer: rice pudding, Pakistani style

Khuda hafiz: may God protect you; a Muslim good-bye greeting

khush raho: may you be happy; a prayer offered by an elder to the bride

kiran: sparkling metallic trim for *dupattas* that extends as a fringe

ladoo: yellow, meatball-sized traditional candy for celebrations

lehanga: bridal gown

luddi: folk dance, performed in a group, mostly by girls

mahr: monetary gift given by the groom to the bride

mamoon: mother's brother; maternal uncle

masha'Allah: by the grace of God; blessing offered when praising someone

masjid: mosque

master sahib: honorific for head tailor or teacher

maulvi: Muslim cleric; an imam

mayoon: tradition of keeping the bride-to-be at home

mehndi: henna-painting ceremony the night before the wedding

Milad-un-Nabi: Prophet Muhammad's birthday

milad: ceremony commemorating Prophet Muhammad's birthday

mithai: Pakistani candy

mubarak: congratulations; greetings

muezzin: the person who recites the call to prayer in a mosque

naan: flatbread

naat: poetry sung in praise of Prophet Muhammad

nazar: evil eye

nikah: Muslim marriage ceremony and contract signing

palak gosht: spinach and meat curry

paratha: fried and crispy flatbread

pullao: gourmet rice dish

qurbani: sacrifice; the term used for sacrificing the lamb

rihal: an X-shaped foldable bookrest for placing the Qur'an during recitation

rooh afza: sweet, rose-scented herbal and fruit drink

roop: glow; associated with a woman in love or pregnant woman

rukhsati: saying good-bye to the bride and giving her a send-off

sahib: (honorific) sir

salaam: peace

salaam alaikum: peace be upon you

salami: cash gift bestowed on the bride and groom by their in-laws, welcoming her or him into the family

salat: obligatory prayer, performed five times a day

sari: formal women's wear wrapped around the waist and draped over one shoulder

sehra: a headdress made of garlands of flowers worn by the groom, and draped over the face

shalwar kameez: tunic, with loose trousers; customary Pakistani outfit for men and women

shariah: Islamic legal system; the literal meaning is "the way to a watering hole"

sheer khorma: dessert made with vermicelli, milk, raisins, and nuts; served on Eid and other festive occasions.

sherwani: a long coat-like garment worn by men on formal occasions

shukr: thank you

surma: kohl powder eyeliner

suhagan: married woman

suhoor: breakfast before daybreak prior to starting one's fast

surah: chapter(s) in the Qur'an

tabla: set of two hand drums

tarana: national inspirational song

taraweeh: Ramadan congregational prayer, offered after the night *Isha* prayer

tasbeeh: string of beads for reciting names of Allah, similar to rosary beads

thobe: Arab ankle-length garment, usually white

tikka: bridal jewelry in the form of a pendant that rests on the forehead and is pinned in the hair

ubtan: body cream used by brides

ummah: community or nation of Muslims

Urdu: Pakistani national language

wa alaikum assalam: and peace upon you too; Muslim greeting said in response to "*salaam alaikum*"

walima: post-wedding reception given by the groom's family

warq: dessert garnish made with silver pounded into a fine, paper-thin layer

wudu: ablution; ritual cleansing performed before prayer

ya: a prefix to the name of the person one is addressing; a linguistic marker roughly like saying, "Oh you"

ye: last letter of the Urdu and Arabic alphabet

zakah: charity

zhikr: remembrance of God

ABOUT THE AUTHOR

Sabeeha Rehman was born and raised in Pakistan. She came to the United States in 1971 after a hurried arranged marriage to a Pakistani doctor in New York. With a bachelor's degree in Home Economics, she settled into the life of a homemaker. Once both her sons were enrolled full-time in school, she went back to college to get her masters in healthcare administration and began her twenty-five-year career as a hospital executive. Her career spanned hospitals in New York, New Jersey, and Saudi Arabia.

Raising children Muslim in the absence of a Muslim community was a daunting challenge. In the early 1980s, she and her husband began the work of establishing a Muslim community on Staten Island, New York, where they were living at the time. Their efforts culminated in the building of a mosque.

Ms. Rehman has spent the last several decades in engaging in inter-faith dialogue with faith communities. She served as the director of interfaith programs at the American Society for Muslim Advancement and as the chief operating officer at the Cordoba Initiative, a multifaith organization dedicated to building bridges between Muslims and the West. She is active on the interfaith circuit, raising awareness of Islam, and Muslims in America.

When her grandson was diagnosed with autism, she left her career and cofounded the New York Metro Chapter of the National Autism Association, and served as its first president.

Her memoir, *Threading My Prayer Rug*, received Honorable Mention in Spirituality in the San Francisco Book Festival Awards of 2017. It was listed as a Top 10 Religion and Spirituality Book of 2016 and a Top 10 Diverse Nonfiction Books of 2017 by *Booklist*. She has contributed op-eds to the *Wall Street Journal*, and she blogs on topics related to American Muslim and Pakistani immigrant experience at www.sabeeharehman.com.

She lives in New York City with her husband, Khalid, a retired hematologist/oncologist.